# Poverty in Scotland

## 2011

### Towards a more equal Scotland?

D0237838

**Edited by:**
**John H McKendrick, Gerry Mooney,**
**John Dickie and Peter Kelly**

CPAG • 94 White Lion Street • London N1 9PF

CPAG promotes action for the prevention and relief of poverty
among children and families with children. To achieve this, CPAG
aims to raise awareness of the causes, extent, nature and impact
of poverty, and strategies for its eradication and prevention; bring
about positive policy changes for families with children in poverty;
and enable those eligible for income maintenance to have access
to their full entitlement. If you are not already supporting us, please
consider making a donation, or ask for details of our membership
schemes, training courses and publications.

Published by Child Poverty Action Group, in association with
Glasgow Caledonian University, Open University and Poverty Alliance

94 White Lion Street
London N1 9PF
Tel: 020 7837 7979
staff@cpag.org.uk
www.cpag.org.uk

A CIP record for this book is available from the British Library

ISBN: 978 1 906076 59 7

Child Poverty Action Group is a charity registered in England
and Wales (registration number 294841) and in Scotland
(registration number SC039339), and is a company limited
by guarantee, registered in England (registration number 1993854).
VAT number: 690 808117

Cover design by Devious Designs
(based on an original design by John Gahagan)
Typeset by Boldface
Printed in the UK by Russell Press
Cover photos by Paul Box/Reportdigital;
Jess Hurd/Reportdigital

# About the contributors

**Bronwen Cohen** is Chief Executive of Children in Scotland.

**John Dickie** is Head of Child Poverty Action Group in Scotland.

**Keith Dryburgh** is Social Policy Officer for Citizens Advice Scotland.

**Tommy Gorman** is Senior Project Manager with Macmillan Cancer Support, responsible for the charity's financial advice services throughout Scotland.

**Richard Grant** is Policy Adviser with Shelter Scotland.

**Richard Holloway** is a writer and broadcaster. He was Bishop of Edinburgh and Primus (Archbishop) of the Scottish Episcopal Church until he stood down in 2000.

**Peter Kelly** is Director of the Poverty Alliance.

**Zoe McGuire** is Policy Assistant at Shelter Scotland.

**John H McKendrick** is Senior Lecturer in the Department of Social Sciences at Glasgow Caledonian University.

**Gerry Mooney** is Senior Lecturer in Social Policy, Faculty of Social Sciences at the Open University. He is also Visiting Professor at the University of Strathclyde.

**Eurig Scandrett** is Lecturer in Sociology at Queen Margaret University, Edinburgh and co-ordinator of programmes in Justice, Gender, Environmental and Social Justice.

**Kendra Strauss** is a feminist economic geographer and Research Associate in Urban Political Economy at the University of Oxford.

**Carol Tannahill** is Director of the Glasgow Centre for Population Health.

**Claire Telfer** is Policy and Advocacy Manager (Scotland) at Save the Children UK.

**Bruce Whyte** is Public Health Programme Manager at the Glasgow Centre for Population Health.

**Sharon Wright** is Lecturer in Social Policy and Deputy Head of Sociology, Social Policy and Criminology at the University of Stirling.

# About the organisations

**CPAG in Scotland** is part of CPAG. It promotes action for the prevention and relief of poverty among children and families with children. To achieve this, CPAG aims to raise awareness of the causes, extent, nature and impact of poverty, and strategies for its eradication and prevention; bring about positive policy changes for families with children in poverty; and enable those eligible for income maintenance to have access to their full entitlement. If you are not already supporting us, please consider making a donation, or ask for details of our membership schemes, training courses and publications. For further information, please visit www.cpag.org.uk/scotland.

With over 15,500 students across Scotland, **The Open University** is one of Scotland's leading providers of part-time higher education. We are committed to widening access to higher education and have an open admissions policy and, as a result, no previous qualifications are necessary to study at degree level. Many of our students are on a low income or unemployed; approximately half of all new students currently receive help towards the cost of their course fees. For further information contact The Open University in Scotland on 0131 226 3851, scotland@open.ac.uk, or visit www.open.ac.uk/scotland.

**The Poverty Alliance** is the national anti-poverty network in Scotland and was set up in 1992. It works with a range of community, voluntary and statutory organisations to find better solutions to the problems of poverty in Scotland. The Alliance attempts to influence anti-poverty policy by lobbying and campaigning, organising seminars and conferences, producing briefing papers and other information. A key goal for the Alliance is to have the voices of people experiencing poverty heard in policy processes. To do this we work with a number of partners across the UK and Europe and represent the UK Coalition Against Poverty and the European Anti-Poverty Network in Scotland. For further information on our work, please visit www.povertyalliance.org.

Emeritus Professor Gill Scott, then of the Scottish Poverty Information Unit (**Glasgow Caledonian University**) was the driving force behind the first four editions of *Poverty in Scotland*. Dr John McKendrick has ensured the continuity of this Glasgow Caledonian University connection, with his editorial and writing contributions to this and the previous edition. The study of poverty in Scotland remains a focus within Glasgow Caledonian University – including the work of the Scottish Poverty Information Unit, academic research on issues such as child poverty in Scotland and the role of the media in shaping public opinion, and expert academic support to practitioners through its association with the Community Regeneration and Tackling Poverty Learning Network. For further information contact: j.mckendrick@gcal.ac.uk.

# Contents

**Section Five: Issues and future challenges**

**Section Six: Conclusion**

# Acknowledgements

Many individuals assisted the authors with their individual chapters. Thanks are extended to: David Walsh (Chapter 11); Sarah Burton (Chapter 12); Dan Barlow, WWF Scotland, Colin Howden, Transform Scotland, Kathy Jenkins, Scottish Hazards Campaign, Morag Parnell, Women's Environmental Network, and Clare Symonds, Planning Democracy (Chapter 17); and Chris Carr, Alison Clark, Jeannie Holles and Emma Perring (Chapter 18).

Particular thanks are extended to Adrian Sinfield, Kathy Armstrong and Anne Ketley, and to CPAG staff for bringing the book to a tidy conclusion: Angela Toal, Jon Shaw, Mark Willis and Henri Krishna (for incisive reviewing and proof reading) and Alison Key (for patience, professionalism and more patience).

# Section One
## Introduction

# One

# Poverty and anti-poverty policy in Scotland: themes and issues

*Gerry Mooney*

This is the latest in a series of books that have been concerned to provide a detailed overview of poverty and anti-poverty policies in Scotland. Starting in the mid-1990s, the *Poverty in Scotland* series has aimed to provide an accessible account of the main themes and issues relating to poverty during the period in question. In addition, the books have also had an important role in providing a comprehensive, yet accessible, account of the evidence base of the state of poverty in Scotland, highlighting the main patterns and its impact on diverse groups and places across Scotland. Further, there has also been a concern to review existing anti-poverty policies, identifying strategies that have had a positive impact – as well as critiquing those that have either failed to ameliorate poverty or, more commonly, have worked to deepen the effects of poverty itself, or which have in different ways furthered the stigmatisation of people experiencing poverty.

One of the hallmarks of the *Poverty in Scotland* series, at least in its more recent forms, has been the inclusion of a series of thematic essays that focus on particular aspects of poverty, disadvantage and inequality in contemporary Scotland. This reflects a concern to provide a range of narratives and viewpoints, but in a way that also mirrors that this is the outcome of a genuine collaboration on the part of a number of practitioners, activists and academics who are working in this area.

This new edition, *Poverty in Scotland 2011: towards a more equal Scotland?*, follows a similar path, offering the most up-to-date data and evidence relating to poverty, examining different policies and strategies, and also providing an opportunity for a more detailed examination of particular topics or themes. In our previous issue, *Poverty in Scotland 2007*, we were able to locate our discussions within the context of Scottish devolution. Written largely in late 2006, *Poverty in Scotland 2007* looked forward to the May 2007 Scottish parliament elections, contributing to the debates that emerged, not only around the question of poverty in Scotland, but also around wider matters of social and economic inequality, public service provision, taxation and a range of other social issues relating to health, education and employability among others.

Similarly, such themes and issues feature prominently in this edition. Likewise, we are also looking forward to the next Scottish parliament elections scheduled for May 2011. It is our hope that, once again, we can both stimulate and contribute to a much needed debate on poverty in contemporary Scotland, and promote the development and implementation of new and more effective policies in addressing poverty. It is also an aim of this book to challenge many of the misconceptions that surround the discussion of poverty and of people who experience poverty, an issue to which we return below and elsewhere in this edition.

## Poverty in Scotland 2007–2011: continuity and change

There are, of course, strong continuities with the period in which we produced *Poverty in Scotland 2007*. As we highlight in Section Two, poverty remains a significant feature of Scottish society, affecting as it does a sizeable proportion of the Scottish population. As we explored in *Poverty in Scotland 2002* and again in *Poverty in Scotland 2007*, the policy approach to poverty is one that is strongly influenced and shaped by strategies that promote work activation, labour market participation and retraining, and which together share a view that paid employment is the best route out of poverty. While some of the language used and the way in which this is presented has changed to an extent, this remains the dominant discourse in political and policy-making arenas.

There are further continuities too in the view that poverty should not be reduced to a question of income alone, or material wellbeing, but is also a matter of wellbeing in other senses. In this respect, the idea of 'social exclusion' has generally been used in an attempt to capture these, the so-called 'wider' dimensions of poverty. Poverty is also, in this sense, 'about' poor health, poor education, housing, environment, social opportunities and so on. However, while the editors of this collection also share the perspective that poverty is 'about more than income', we are also conscious that income and material conditions remain the most fundamental determining dimensions of poverty, and that all too often an emphasis on non-income-related dimensions has been used to draw attention away from a concern with material wellbeing and issues of income.

Alongside the continuities, there have been major changes since 2006/07 and we highlight two developments as being of particular importance for our understanding of poverty in Scotland in 2011.

## The political and policy-making landscape

The political map of Scotland is very different in important respects from that of 2006/07. The 2007 Scottish elections saw the Scottish National Party (SNP) emerge as the new Scottish government, albeit a minority government with a one-seat advantage over its closest challenger, the Labour Party. This had not only Scottish, but wider UK (and indeed global), implications. For the first time since the devolution settlement in 1998, different political parties formed the governments in Edinburgh and in London. That the SNP was a minority government meant that its room for manoeuvre was somewhat limited, but this did not prevent it from introducing a series of policy measures which gained widespread support across Scotland.[1] Notable here were the abolition of prescription charges by 2011, a renewed emphasis on the construction of social housing and the promise of smaller class sizes, all of which are now threatened by the impact of large-scale budget cuts, announced by both the Scottish and UK governments in late 2010.

As we will see below, such policy making was couched in a language which spoke of 'fairness' and 'equality'. However, that the SNP has not been as radical as some would have expected, or hoped, in part reflects its minority government status, relying as it does on its rivals to secure support in the Holyrood parliament, as well as perhaps an unresolved tension over the relative priority it gives to its 'solidarity' and economic growth ambitions.

There is a second dimension to the changed UK political landscape. This book is being produced in late 2010, with the May 2010 UK elections still fresh in the memory. This has had significant implications for politics across the UK – not least in Scotland. In brief, following 13 years of New Labour rule at Westminster, the May 2010 elections saw the Conservatives emerge as the single largest political party in terms of seats and votes – but with no clear overall majority. For the first time in a generation, a coalition has been created in the shape of the Conservatives and the Liberal Democrats who now form the UK government. Not for the first time, however, the political landscape of Scotland following the 2010 UK elections was markedly different from the rest of the UK, with Labour and the SNP emerging as the two largest parties in terms of votes (and Labour the overwhelmingly largest in terms of votes and seats), with the Conservatives managing only to hold onto the one single seat that they held prior to May 2010.

For us, the significance of the 2010 UK general election is that we now have in power (albeit thanks to a coalition) a party that has promised a different approach to poverty from that of New Labour (following the 2010 Labour Party conference at which Ed Miliband was elected leader, New Labour is now rebranded as Labour). We return to consider the approach of the Conservatives shortly.

However, there has been another major development which has also impacted on government policy, both in Edinburgh and in London.

## The economic crisis

The UK, as much of the rest of the Western world, is currently experiencing the deepest financial crisis since the Wall Street crash and great depression of the inter-war period. The crisis of 2008 is of considerable importance, given its far-reaching impact on the world economy, bringing with it repeated pronouncements of a prolonged economic slump. The financial crisis, and the reactions to it by different governments and transnational organisations, has major implications for our understanding of social welfare today, and the future shape and direction of social welfare and anti-poverty policy in Scotland and across the UK.

With a Conservative/Liberal Democrat UK government committed to major cuts in public services and jobs, and with the promise of a renewed attack on 'welfarism' in an attempt to reduce the vast national debt, the immediate future for social welfare in the UK looks bleak, with much talk of the deepest cuts amid the most significant recession since the Second World War.

In what is now being widely referred to as the 'new age of austerity',[2] long-cherished forms of state-provided social welfare are already under sustained attack from the new government. In his emergency Budget on 22 June 2010, Chancellor George Osborne promised a Budget that would be 'tough but fair' as he announced an increase in VAT from 17.5 per cent to 20 per cent, a two-year pay freeze for public sector workers, a three-year freeze on child benefit, a tightening of housing benefit entitlements and on eligibility for child tax credit among other austerity measures. In the Comprehensive Spending Review announced on 20 October 2010, an additional £7 billion was cut from welfare spending (in addition to the £11 billion cut announced in June). Elsewhere, some £46 billion was cut from other government department spending.[3] We return to the impact of this in the concluding chapter, but the immediate future is one of cuts, the running down of welfare and public services, rising unemployment as almost 500,000 public sector jobs are slashed, and a harsher regime for benefit claimants.

As many critics have highlighted,[4] the June 2010 Budget (and October Spending Review) has been one of the most regressive in living memory and, despite UK government claims that 'we are all in it together' and that government cuts are 'fair' with all sections of UK society affected, it is all too evident that the impact will fall disproportionately on the poorest and most vulnerable groups, and on those who deliver the services on which those groups so depend. There has been widespread condemnation from campaigning and third-sector organisations that the Budget and austerity measures will further increase poverty and inequality.

In the decade of devolution, the level of poverty in Scotland, especially child poverty, has for the most part fallen, although poverty remains widespread and deep.[5] The interaction of devolved powers and reserved powers (that is, legislative powers controlled by the Westminster government), in a context of relative economic growth, played a major part in this – but this is now threatened by the onset of economic crisis.

Once again, poverty, and social welfare more generally, are at the heart of 'contentious politics' across the UK – at the centre of debates about the future direction of government policy and of the kind of society to which we aspire.

## The SNP government 2007–2011: a new approach to poverty?

'Making poverty history in Scotland will be central to everything we do.' Thus commented Deputy First Minister Nicola Sturgeon, launching the government's consultation process on a new approach to addressing poverty.[6] As part of this new approach, a new language was introduced with terms such as 'social justice' and 'closing the opportunity gap' being replaced by an emphasis on 'solidarity' and 'social cohesion' – changed terminology but continuing ambiguity over meanings and outcomes. There was some expectation that the arrival of an SNP government would lead to a very different kind of approach to social policy making in Scotland , in particular in relation to the issue of poverty. However, the fact that the SNP was a minority government and a party with no history in government (and arguably little history in terms of a clear and committed ideology around social welfare) resulted in an approach to poverty that shared many of the underlying assumptions of the previous two Labour/ Liberal Democrat coalition administrations.

In particular, as with its predecessors, the SNP administration attached considerable importance to 'sustainable' economic growth and employment as part of a social inclusion agenda. Published in November 2007, *The Government Economic Strategy*,[7] followed in 2008 by *Taking Forward the Government Economic Strategy*[8] and *Achieving Our Potential*,[9] outlined the key aspects of the SNP's approach by emphasising the importance of work as a way out of poverty.

The government's approach was couched in a relatively new narrative, around which a set of 'golden rules' would govern its economic and social policy making. The 'solidarity' rule aims to increase the proportion of income and overall income of the bottom 30 per cent of the population by 2017. The 'cohesion' rule aims to narrow the gap in participation between the best and worst performing regions in Scotland, again by 2017. In turn, these are supported by a range of 'purpose targets' and 'national outcomes'.

The approach recognises the importance of tackling the underlying income inequality that drives poverty by setting a specific income inequality 'solidarity' target, something the government at UK level has failed to do. There are also indications of a new approach, in terms of the emphasis on consultation and partnership working, not least with Scotland's councils. In the context of deepening fiscal constraints and cuts, such partnerships are already experiencing considerable tension, however, and there is a question about how much is significantly new in the overall approach.

## Inequalities and equalities

While it has long been acknowledged and understood that poverty and inequality are distinct, at the same time it is important to grasp that they are interconnected and entangled in many different ways. We live in a period of deep-seated poverty and inequality on a global scale. Across the planet, as is well and increasingly documented, there is widespread poverty, hunger, malnutrition, discrimination and oppression.[10] It is also, however, a world in which the inequalities between rich and poor have reached an unparalleled level. One illustration of this from the UK serves to underline the fact that our world is an unequal world: on 25 April 2010 the *Sunday Times* published the latest in its annual series of 'rich lists'. The *Rich List* for 2010 makes for jaw-dropping reading: the top 1,000 multi-millionaires in the UK saw their collective wealth increase by 29.9 per cent on 2009 levels – a whopping £77.25 billion. With a wealth stash of some £335.5 billion, this is almost twice the UK's well-publicised and historically largest national debt.[11] In the 22 years of the *Rich List*, this is the largest percentage increase on a year-by-year basis. And let us remind ourselves that this increase has happened as the UK (and much of the rest of the global economy) goes through its deepest economic crisis since the great depression of the 1920s and 1930s.

Such wealth inequality is, of course, repeated on a global scale. Not only does it indicate the huge gulf in incomes and economic security between (super) rich and poor, as has been forcefully argued, but such inequalities also have devastating consequences for all aspects of human (and planet and animal) life. As Wilkinson and Pickett have demonstrated, the more unequal a society, the greater the range and depth of 'social problems', from deteriorating community and social life, through mental health issues, high obesity, morbidity and mortality levels through to higher rates of incarceration and punishment, violence, teenage pregnancy and lower rates of social mobility.[12] Further, as Dorling has also shown, the five social evils (want, idleness, ignorance, squalor and disease), identified by Beveridge at the dawn of the British welfare state in the early 1940s, have been replaced by what he terms the five new tenets of injustice: elitism is efficient; exclusion is necessary; greed is good; prejudice is natural and despair is inevitable.[13]

Such injustices raise important questions about the winners and losers in society – and immediately draw attention to the unequal and socially divided nature of contemporary Scotland. Poverty and wider issues of social welfare are entangled with social inequality and social differentiation: class, gender, race/ethnicity, sexuality, age and disability. The subtitle of this book, *towards a more equal Scotland?*, places the question of in/equality at centre stage. Throughout the volume we have worked to embed the issue of 'equalities' as a core aspect of the understanding of poverty in Scotland today. Arguably, an equalities approach was reflected in the anti-poverty approach of the first devolved Scottish administration in 1999. In *Social Justice: a Scotland where everyone matters*,[14] for instance, there was some recognition of the need to extend equality to a range of different social groups across Scotland, going beyond the issue of income inequality alone.[15] However, in the period since then, this has been diluted to some extent. The establishment in November 2007 of a new 'concordat' between the Scottish government and councils, whereby both would work together, along with the private and voluntary sectors, towards improvements in the quality of opportunities and life chances for people across Scotland, was accompanied by the development of single-outcome agreements for all of Scotland's 32 local authorities. With community planning partnerships a key part of this, the view adopted here was that single outcome agreements would be developed more in tune with local circumstances and priorities, thereby more effectively addressing local needs.[16] However, the concordat and single-outcome agreements also mean the effective ending of any consistent national approach to poverty and equality, arguably making progress more difficult to achieve. This is an issue we pick up again in the concluding chapter.

## Promoting equality: challenging the disrespect and misrecognition of poverty and poor people

A central theme running through this book is that we must challenge the view that people experiencing poverty are in some way 'deviant'. The distinction between a 'deserving' and 'undeserving' poor has a long history. Echoing nineteenth-century poor laws and policies towards people in poverty, these continue to permeate and influence the representations of poor populations today, and are also evident at times in policy outcomes.

Disadvantaged populations have long been seen as distinctive from 'the rest of society'. In this way, we can talk of 'the poor' being 'other'. 'Othering' refers to the construction and categorisation of 'the poor' and other populations (eg, some migrant groups and single parents) as 'undeserving', as 'a problem' and as lacking or deficient in some way or another.[17] Othering works to stigmatise and to stereotype such groups as distinct, as distant from normal society/'us' and underpins how some among the non-poor and, in particular, politicians, policy makers and the media think, talk and act towards 'the poor'. As Ruth Lister has argued, such processes help to make it easier for poor people to be blamed for both their own and society's problems, while also acting as a 'warning' to others.[18]

That such humiliations are sharpest when inequality is rising betrays the unequal social relations that underpin and permeate processes of 'othering'. Poor people may be demonised, constructed as a problem, but they are also feared, feared for who they are (or are thought to be) and resented for representing a state of existence into which others fear to fall. There is a double stigmatisation of people experiencing poverty and other disadvantaged populations at work here: the stigma of poverty and a lack of respect.

The misrecognition and disrespect experienced by people experiencing poverty works to reproduce inequality. It means infringing human and citizenship rights, a lack of freedom to act and an erosion of personal respect as it denies voice and agency to those who are treated as such. We return to consider this in more detail in Chapter 9.

## The structure of *Poverty in Scotland 2011*

Following the previous editions in the series, *Poverty in Scotland 2011* seeks to provide a comprehensive summary of the state of poverty as it affects Scottish society today. **Section Two: The nature of poverty in Scotland** begins by exploring the issue of how poverty is to be best defined and measured. As is well known, this is a long-standing and controversial issue, reflecting as it does the many different viewpoints and approaches to poverty. Of similar importance, and again also of controversy, is the question of the causes of poverty. In Chapter 4, the main causes of poverty in Scotland are considered.

In **Section Three: Poverty in Scotland: the evidence**, the contributors highlight some of the key quantitative and qualitative aspects of living in poverty. The extent of poverty and inequality is considered here, with particular emphasis on the degree to which these are increasing or falling (Chapters 5 and 6). In Chapter 7 there is a particular focus on the groups affected by poverty in Scotland today, followed in Chapter 8 by a discussion of the real, daily lived experiences of a considerable proportion of the population of Scotland.

In **Section Four: Scotland in focus, 2007–2011**, Chapter 9 considers some of the ways in which poverty is being presented and represented in Scotland today. Continuing with the structure and format of *Poverty in Scotland 2007*, **Section Five: Issues and future challenges** provides a range of thematic essays which focus on particular dimensions of poverty. Chapter 10 introduces the essays, drawing out the main themes and issues, particularly in relation to the policy, practice and provision of services. As in previous issues, it has not been possible to provide a coverage and review of each and every aspect of poverty and disadvantage. Instead, we have chosen to focus on particular areas which are both central to the discussion of poverty, and offer a place for consideration of other aspects which are sometimes overlooked, such as the connections between environmental issues and poverty as well as the question of cultural representation. In a departure from the previous issues, here we have not included thematic essays which highlight the complex entanglements and inter-relationships between different aspects of social differentiation and division, such as class, gender and ethnicity and poverty. Instead, we see these as key threads that run through and across the entire collection.

**Section Six: Conclusion** draws together the discussions across the collection and, in particular, considers the subtitle of the book – *towards a more equal Scotland?* What has to be done to make Scotland a more equal society, and how can we more effectively tackle poverty in Scotland as we look beyond the next Scottish parliamentary elections?

Finally, and again in keeping with the format of the previous edition, the **Appendix** provides a policy diary, which highlights many of the most important anti-poverty policies and legislation since 2007, with a particular focus on the policies of the Scottish government.

## Notes

1   S Maxwell, 'Principles and Absences: a critique of the Scottish Government's approach to combating Scotland's problem of poverty and inequality', *Scottish Affairs*, 67, 2009, pp57–69; G Mooney, G Scott and G Mulvey, 'The 'Celtic Lion' and Social Policy: some thoughts on the SNP and social welfare', *Critical Social Policy*, Vol 28, issue 3, 2008, pp378–94; G Scott and G Mooney, 'Poverty and Social Justice in the Devolved Scotland: neo-liberalism meets social democracy?' *Social Policy and Society*, Vol 8, issue 3, 2009, pp379–89; G Mooney and S Wright, 'Wealthier and Fairer? Reflecting on SNP proposals for tackling poverty, inequality and deprivation in Scotland', *Scottish Affairs*, 67, 2009, pp49–56

2   D Summers, 'David Cameron warns of new age of austerity', *The Guardian*, 26 April 2009

3   HM Treasury, *Spending Review 2010*, Cm 7942, HM Treasury, 2010

4   J Browne and P Levell, *The Distributional Effect of Tax and Benefit Reforms to be Introduced between June 2010 and April 2014: a revised assessment,*

Briefing Note BN108, Institute for Fiscal Studies, 2010; Institute for Fiscal Studies, *New IFS Research Challenges Chancellor's 'Progressive Budget' Claim*, Institute for Fiscal Studies, 2010

5　Joseph Rowntree Foundation, *Devolution's Impact on Low-income People and Places*, Joseph Rowntree Foundation, 2010

6　Scottish Government, 'Targets to tackle poverty', Press Release, 31 January 2008

7　Scottish Government, *The Government Economic Strategy*, 2007

8　Scottish Government, *Taking Forward the Government Economic Strategy: a discussion paper on tackling poverty, inequality and deprivation*, 2008

9　Scottish Government, *Achieving Our Potential: a framework to tackle poverty and income inequality in Scotland*, 2008, available at www.scotland.gov.uk/publications/2008/11/20103815/0

10　B Milanovic, *Worlds Apart: measuring international and global inequality*, Princeton University Press, 2005

11　*Sunday Times*, 25 April 2010

12　R Wilkinson and K Pickett, *The Spirit Level: why equality is better for everyone*, Penguin, 2010

13　D Dorling, *Injustice: why social inequality persists*, The Policy Press, 2010

14　Scottish Executive, *Social Justice: a Scotland where everyone matters*, 1999

15　A Jarvis and P Gardner, *Poverty and Inequality in Scotland: report of expert seminars and stakeholder feedback on the relationship between equality and poverty*, Equality and Human Rights Commission, 2009

16　Scottish Government, *Concordat Between the Scottish Government and Local Government*, 2007

17　R Lister, *Poverty*, Polity Press, 2004, pp100–01; J Young, *The Vertigo of Late Modernity*, Sage, 2007, pp5–7

18　R Lister, *Poverty*, Polity Press, 2004

# Section Two
## The nature of poverty in Scotland

Two
# What is poverty?

*John H McKendrick*

## Summary

- Poverty is about not having enough. Typically, 'poverty' refers to not having enough resources. Income is the primary resource lacking for people living in poverty in Scotland. However, poverty is sometimes the word that is used to describe when people have 'capability deprivation' (a lack of freedoms that collectively we value).
- Most experts would agree that a lack of resources (in particular, insufficient income) has a central role to play in creating or sustaining capability deprivation. 'Income poverty' has also been of central importance in anti-poverty activity, debate and policy in Scotland.
- Thus, for practical purposes in Scotland, 'not having enough' is understood to be a point below which people do not have sufficient disposable income to purchase the goods and services, and participate in the activities, that it is expected the majority of the UK population should be able to afford.
- In Scotland (and the UK), income poverty tends to be understood in one of four main ways – absolute poverty, relative poverty, persistent poverty and severe poverty. The interpretation that is used most is relative poverty. Indeed, persistent poverty and severe poverty are merely different ways of defining relative poverty.
- Poverty is not the same as income inequality, social exclusion, social justice, multiple deprivation and material deprivation. However, poverty is closely related to each of these issues.

## Poverty: a deceptively simple idea

The heart of the matter is that poverty is about 'not having enough'. However, what starts out as a straightforward idea is quickly complicated as attempts to define and measure poverty more precisely invariably become overly technical and theoretical, written by academics and statisticians for 'people like them'. This can be off-putting. However, the way in which we understand and define poverty has far-reaching implications on anti-poverty activity, debate and policy. It determines the number of people who are counted as living in poverty; and it can have a major influence on the policy solutions that are developed to address 'the problem'. Therefore, we must all be concerned about how poverty is defined and measured. Of course, definition and measurement are inextricably linked; how we measure poverty depends on how it is defined. Yet, definition is essentially about ideas and measurement inevitably becomes a technical challenge. Hence, in this chapter we consider how poverty in Scotland is defined. In the following chapter, we consider how poverty in Scotland is measured.

There is little doubt that ideas about poverty are complex, often contradictory and influenced by factors such as personal experiences, value judgements and belief systems. Consequently, definitions of poverty are also contested. There is no single, universally accepted, definition of poverty. In this opening section, we explain what we mean by poverty, and we describe how poverty is related to ideas of income inequality, material deprivation, multiple deprivation, social exclusion and social justice.

## Poverty as not having enough

It is not sufficient to state that poverty is about 'not having enough'. It begs the question, 'enough of what?' Broadly speaking, poverty might be understood as being either a lack of resources (such as income or material possessions) or a lack of functional capabilities (the means to achieve a good life).

Furthermore, in each case, it is possible to consider poverty *as a whole*, or to consider one particular dimension of poverty. For example, rather than defining poverty as a lack of resources in aggregate (using an input measure such as household income, or an output measure such as material deprivation), it is possible to measure aspects of lacking resources, such as 'food poverty', 'fuel poverty' or 'housing poverty'. Campaigning organisations often adopt a narrower focus on a particular dimension of poverty. For example, Shelter Scotland is concerned with poor housing conditions in Scotland and has used Scottish government statistics to report that 292,000 homes in Scotland are affected by dampness and condensation, and 43,000 children (4 per cent) are living in overcrowded conditions.[1] Similarly, a narrower approach to poverty, as having a lack of functional capabilities, might mean a focus on 'political participation', which, in turn, might focus on the poverty of people's political association, free speech, right to vote and the like.

The idea of poverty as capability deprivation is most closely associated with the work of Amartya Sen and has been used to promote the understanding that development is about more than economic output (poverty is more than income deprivation).[2] It continues to gather support and is increasingly being applied in high-income economy contexts. It has intuitive appeal as it focuses on the root causes of the problem. Living life on a low income might be one of the reasons why people are deprived of capabilities. For example, 'bodily health' is one capability that is associated with Sen's theory. It is widely accepted that poverty, at least in part, has a negative impact on people's health – eg, having insufficient income to heat a home adequately may lead to dampness going unchecked, which in turn might exacerbate respiratory conditions.[3] Although work is progressing to develop capability indicators,[4] at present anti-poverty activity tends to focus around the headline of 'lack of resources' rather than 'lack of functional capabilities'.

It is also pertinent to note that striving for fulfilment might be viewed ultimately as a worthier cause than seeking an adequate level of resource. The UK coalition government, for example, gave notice in autumn 2010 that it intended to work toward establishing a measure of national wellbeing ('happiness') for the UK.[5] At present, progressive social policy focuses around 'lack of resources' rather than 'lack of personal fulfilment'. However, the UK government work may open up the opportunity for a policy-driven approach to improve 'happiness' in the future. However, measuring poverty or measuring happiness should not be viewed as two options over which a choice must be made. They are linked, but they are essentially different ideas. On one hand, living life on a low income is argued by many to be a contributory factor toward not achieving happiness.[6] On the other hand, there is undoubtedly the need to accord importance to psychological wellbeing in understanding poverty.[7]

Thus, lack of resources (and lack of income in particular) has a role to play in creating or sustaining problems in Sen's alternative interpretation of poverty, and in the quest to increase happiness. Pragmatically, measures of income poverty may be easier to digest and utilise than measures of capability deprivation (or happiness). However, there is a more significant reason for an income poverty focus in *Poverty in Scotland 2011*. It is a fundamental right that people should have adequate resources to enable them to participate in society. In a consumer economy, adequate resources means adequate income. In addition to the substantive importance of having adequate resources, it must also be acknowledged that 'income poverty' has been the pre-eminent focus of anti-poverty activity, debate and policy in Scotland and the UK. Hence, in the first two sections of this book, 'income poverty' is the point of entry to this wider poverty debate.

## Money, money, money

For clarification, in the context of poverty as a lack of resources, 'not having enough' income does not refer to the likes of a billionaire's insatiable thirst for Dom Perignon champagne. Rather, it refers to the realities of life for almost one million people in Scotland who have insufficient income to be able to afford what the majority of people in Scotland would agree is what the majority of people in Scotland should be able to afford.

The approach adopted in the first two sections of the book is also to focus on poverty *as a whole*. Just as the decision to focus on lack of income as opposed to capabilities or fulfilment does not imply dismissal of their significance, so the focus in the early sections in this book on poverty *as a whole* should not be taken to imply that particular dimensions of poverty are unimportant.

After all, most would agree that all of these problems are, to a significant extent, inter-related. More particularly, in a market society like ours, income poverty is both cause and effect of particular dimensions of poverty. For example, while the Organisation for Economic Co-operation and Development (OECD) has reported on how income poverty leads to poor educational outcomes among school children in Scotland (income poverty as a cause of poor education),[8] Scottish government statistics highlight that poor educational outcomes lead to poor post-school prospects (poor education as a cause of income poverty).[9]

*Poverty in Scotland 2011* embraces different approaches to understanding poverty in Scotland. In Chapters 1 to 10, it focuses on poverty as a whole, whereas in Chapters 11 to 22 there is a focus on particular dimensions of poverty. Differences of emphasis are best accounted for by the particular concerns of authors and their preferred point of entry to the wider debate on the good society that is hoped will result from tackling poverty. Taken together, these overarching and particular insights achieve the aims of the editors of *Poverty in Scotland 2011* – ie, to understand better the evidence and issues pertaining to the way in which anti-poverty activity, debate and policy is currently framed in Scotland and the UK.

## Understanding poverty

### Absolute poverty

Absolute poverty refers to the level of resources needed to sustain physical survival. People are poor if they cannot feed, clothe or house themselves and their dependants. This is a definition of poverty that is only about subsistence, the amount needed to keep body and soul together. As Ruth Lister points out, absolute definitions of poverty are closely linked to nutrition, whereby a person or family can be considered to be poor if they do not have sufficient resources to feed themselves.[10] This conception of poverty is one that is often viewed as a 'common sense' approach to defining poverty. Its use in relation to Scotland or the UK is often made in comparison to other parts of the world ('there is real poverty in Malawi, but not here') or in relation to other times ('we used to have poverty in Scotland, but not any more'). This absolute definition of poverty shows that income is central to the way we conceptualise poverty, as poverty is not having enough income to buy life's necessities. However, the definition of 'necessity' must be based on some assessment of need, and our understanding of what is an essential need varies over time and across place. For this reason, few serious analysts and none of the major political parties would use an absolute measure alone to understand poverty in Scotland in the twenty-first century.

However, it is important to note that the term 'absolute' is used in the official UK and Scottish poverty statistics in a very different sense. This will be explained in the following chapter.

## Relative poverty

Relative poverty is defined in relation to the standards of living in a society at a particular time. People live in poverty when they are denied an income sufficient for their material needs, and when these circumstances exclude them from taking part in activities that are an accepted part of daily life in that society. It is argued that one problem with this approach is that in an affluent society it could become difficult to distinguish between those who are poor and those who are just less well off.

Despite the perceived shortcomings, in this book we primarily use the relative measure of poverty, believing that poverty should be defined by the standards of society as it is today. By using a relative measure we arrive at a better understanding of poverty in the twenty-first century:[11]

> ... an understanding based on a measure that has the lack of income at its heart, but which acknowledges that poverty is about what that lack of income implies – the inability to obtain the types of diet, participate in the activities and have the living conditions and amenities which are customary... in the societies to which they [the poor] belong.

Two further ways of describing income poverty – persistent poverty and severe poverty – are also grounded in this relative definition.

## Persistent poverty

More recently, the limitations have been acknowledged of only using moment-in-time measures of poverty, as the population experiencing poverty is not static. Recent poverty dynamics research has shown that poverty can be transient (a condition experienced only for a short period of time) or recurrent (a condition into which households repeatedly enter and leave at different points in time).[12] Although it would be wrong to dismiss the importance of transient poverty or recurrent poverty, especially as their impact over time can push people into prolonged poverty, it would be remiss not to pay particular attention to those whose experience of poverty is persistent.

Persistent poverty is defined over time. In the UK, it is used to describe the situation when relative income poverty is experienced in three of the preceding four years. Persistent low income, relative low income and absolute low income are all used to estimate the level of child poverty in Scotland and the UK. The fourth measure used to measure progress against child poverty targets in the UK combines material deprivation and low income, an approach that is also used by Save the Children to estimate 'severe child poverty'.

## Severe poverty

There is no official measure of 'severe poverty' in Scotland. Indeed, the very idea of 'severe poverty' might be viewed as politically problematic, as one unintended consequence of promoting this idea could be that it undermines the significance of the problem of poverty that is experienced by those whose poverty is not defined as being 'severe'.

Save the Children has promoted the idea of 'severe child poverty' and use a combined measure of income poverty and material deprivation to define the number and proportion of children living in households with 'severe child poverty'.[13] In effect, it uses a more stringent definition than that used by the UK government in one of its four measures of 'child poverty' to ascertain whether children are living in 'severe poverty'. The same approach could be used to estimate 'severe poverty' among adults.

## Poverty and related ideas

### Poverty and income inequality

Interest in income inequality has grown in recent years. First, here in Scotland, the Scottish National Party Scottish government has set itself apart from earlier Scottish governments and the current UK government by introducing a new focus on income inequality, while retaining a strong focus on income poverty. Through the solidarity purpose target, the Scottish government aims to 'increase overall income and the proportion of income earned by the three lowest income deciles as a group by 2017'. More generally, growing interest in income inequality in the UK has followed the publication of *The Spirit Level* by Kate Pickett and Richard Wilkinson, in which they use international evidence to demonstrate that societies with higher levels of income inequality have excessively high negative social outcomes – ie, inequality *per se* contributes directly to social problems.[14] Finally, in light of the international banking crisis, subsequent global economic slowdown and austerity cuts, growing levels of discontent have been expressed at what are increasingly deemed to be excessive levels of pay (and non-waged income) that are enjoyed by bankers, business elites and high-ranking officers in public service.

There is a close relationship between income inequality and income poverty and all too often the terms appear to be used interchangeably, in particular when relative poverty is discussed. The confusion is understandable, although it should be avoided. Income inequality is not a measure of income inadequacy; rather, it is a measure of the way in which income is distributed across a population. In contrast, income poverty specifies a level below which income is deemed to be inadequate. Of course, it is highly likely that where there is income inequality, there will be income poverty and that the eradication of poverty will require action to tackle income inequality. However, income inequality does not provide us with an estimate of how many people exist on an inadequate income. Although we consider the question of income inequality in Chapter 6, in this book we are primarily focused on the character and experiences of those who do not have sufficient income (income poverty).

## Deprivation

Deprivation is used to describe the lack of access to, or possession of, particular aspects of life. Deprivation is not entirely dependent on income. Thus, a rich woman and a poor man would both be judged to be 'housing deprived' if they did not have access to adequate housing conditions (the former perhaps as a result of the difficulties involved in maintaining an older heirloom property to an adequate standard, the latter perhaps as a result of not earning or receiving an adequate income). Housing, education and employment are among the issues for which deprivation is most commonly measured.

## Material deprivation

The OECD offers a helpful definition of material deprivation when it describes it as 'the inability of individuals or households to afford consumption goods and activities that are typical in the society of which they are part'.[15] Material deprivation might be described as an 'output' measure of poverty, in that it describes whether an adequate standard of living has been achieved (through direct public service provision and independent purchases using disposable income). In contrast, income poverty might be described as an 'input' measure of poverty, in that it is based on the financial resources that are available to secure an adequate standard of living.

Clearly, it would be expected that there is a close association between income poverty and material deprivation; those with fewer financial resources will be less able to provide for their material needs. However, intervening factors mean that it cannot be assumed that people living with income poverty will be materially deprived. For example, people who are 'income poor' may receive support in kind from members of their wider family, which prevents them from experiencing material deprivation, or they may have recently lost a well-paid job and have an income below the poverty line but have many material possessions bought on their previous higher income. On the other hand, people who have recently escaped income poverty may find themselves materially deprived for some time thereafter, particularly if their increased level of disposable income is to be used to service debts that accumulated when they were living in poverty.

## Multiple deprivation

As the name suggests, multiple deprivation is used to describe the situation when individuals, households or collections of people in small geographical areas are deprived of a range of conditions at the same time – eg, they are deprived of adequate housing, education and employment. In Scotland, multiple deprivation is most closely associated with small geographical areas through the Scottish Index of Multiple Deprivation. Areas of multiple deprivation in Scotland are currently identified using 38 indicators spread across seven domains (see Chapter 3). Multiply deprived areas are defined relatively; most typically, 15 per cent is used as the threshold for defining a multiply deprived area – ie, of the 6,505 data zones in Scotland, those whose deprivation score is ranked 1 to 975 (the bottom 15 per cent) are described as 'multiply deprived' areas.

While multiple deprivation in Scotland is an area measure, not all people residing in multiply deprived areas will live in poverty. Similarly, many people living in poverty will not be residing in multiply deprived areas. However, intuitively we would expect that people living with income poverty would be more likely to live in the most deprived areas. However, not too much should be made of this relationship for the Scottish Index of Multiple Deprivation, as 'income deprivation' (the proportion of people living in an area who are without an adequate income) is one of seven domains that comprise the deprivation index. Thus, income poverty is one of the factors that contributes to area multiple deprivation in Scotland.

## Social inclusion and social exclusion

The idea of social exclusion – and social inclusion, the variant preferred in Scotland – had been prominent in the anti-poverty work associated with New Labour in both Scotland and the UK as a whole. Changes in the political landscape at Holyrood and Westminster have heralded a less prominent position for social exclusion/inclusion in recent years, although in Scotland, social inclusion is still presented as a topic theme.[16] Similarly, the UK may still have to report to the European Commission on efforts to address social exclusion as part of the new Europe 2020 strategy.[17] As part of this commitment to date, the UK government has prepared and maintained a National Strategy for Social Protection and Social Inclusion.[18]

Definitions of social exclusion usually describe how and why it occurs, as well as its implications. The European Union notes that social exclusion occurs when people cannot fully participate or contribute to society because of '… the denial of civil, political, social, economic and cultural rights'.[19] This is very similar to the thinking behind relative poverty in that relative poverty is based on the understanding that low income is significant as it prevents participation in wider society at a level all would be expected to enjoy. Thus, social exclusion can result from 'income poverty'. The idea of social exclusion remains important in understanding poverty in Scotland, even if it is given less prominence than before.

Of course, it must be clarified that social exclusion is viewed as resulting from combinations of linked problems, only one of which may be low income – eg, other causes of social exclusion include discrimination, unemployment, poor skills, poor housing, bad health and changing family and household composition. Social exclusion and income poverty are related – one may result from the other – but they can also exist independently of each other (people living in poverty may not be socially excluded, and the non-poor may be socially excluded) and should not be used interchangeably.

## Social justice

As with social exclusion, the prominence of the use of the description 'social justice' in public circles has fluctuated through time. It was particularly prominent in the early years of the Scottish executive when its anti-poverty strategy was focused around social justice milestones. This encapsulated the early thinking of New Labour, following from the work of the Commission on Social Justice. Set up in 1992 by the late John Smith, the leader of the Labour Party (in opposition) at that time, this carried out an independent enquiry into economic and social reform and noted: '... our view of social justice consists of four key ideas.' These were: equal worth of all citizens; citizens' entitlement to be able to meet their basic needs; the widest possible spread of opportunities; and the reduction or elimination of unjust inequalities.[20]

When social justice milestones were replaced with the *Closing the Opportunity Gap* approach,[21] social justice became less prominent. However, social justice is a broad and contested term and definitions vary across the political spectrum. They include ideas of distributive justice, utilitarianism, equality and libertarian ideas of 'governance'. Fundamentally, social justice is to pursue the belief:[22]

> ... that society can be reshaped – its major social and political institutions changed – so that each person gets a fair share of the benefits, and carries a fair share of the responsibilities, of living together in a community.

Ideas of social justice are returning to prominence in Conservative Party circles through the work of the Centre for Social Justice[23] in London (formed in 2004) and the re-launch in 2010 of Social Justice Scotland as the Social Justice Foundation – a right-of-centre think-tank – to explore new ways of finding solutions to the critical issues facing Scotland (and the UK).[24] This may herald the return of ideas of 'social justice' to the fore in debates on tackling poverty in Scotland.

## Conclusion

Poverty in Scotland can best be understood in terms of Peter Townsend's definition that:[25]

Individuals, families and groups in the population can be said to be in poverty when they lack the resources to obtain the types of diet, participate in the activities and have the living conditions and amenities which are customary, or are at least widely encouraged and approved, in the societies in which they belong.

Three key issues should be drawn from Townsend's ideas. First, resources can accrue through both incomes and services. However, the marketised nature of Scottish society means that income must be central to discussions about poverty. Second, poverty is relative to the needs and wants of the wider society. This means that poverty in Scotland is qualitatively different to that experienced in the global South. Third, poverty in the twenty-first century is not only about survival and minimum subsistence in order to avoid starvation; it is about a standard of living that allows adequate participation within society.

## Notes

1  Shelter Scotland, *National Housing Statistics*, 2010, available online at: http://scotland.shelter.org.uk/housing_issues/research_and_statistics/key_statistics

2  A Sen, *Commodities and Capabilities*, Oxford University Press, 1985

3  C McCormack, *The Wee Yellow Butterfly*, Argyll, 2008

4  P Anand, G Hunter, I Carter, K Dowding and M van Hees, 'The Development of Capability Indicators', *Journal of Human Development and Capabilities*, 2009, Vol 10, pp125–52

5  See www.ons.gov.uk/about/consultations/measuring-national-well-being

6  D Walsh, M Taulbut and P Hanlon, *The Aftershock of Deindustrialisation: trends in mortality in Scotland and other parts of post-industrial Europe*, Glasgow Centre for Population Health, 2008

7  C Craig, 'Ringing the Bell' in *The Tears That Made the Clyde: well-being in Glasgow*, Argyll Publishing, 2010, pp356–78

8  Organisation for Economic Co-operation and Development, *Quality and Equity of Schooling in Scotland*, 2007

9  Scottish Government, *Destinations of Leavers from Scottish Schools 2008/09*, 2010. Save the Children Scotland, in arguing for a pupil premium to provide additional money to support the schooling of children experiencing poverty in Scotland, teases out the complexity of the relationship between poor education and income poverty: C Telfer, *Better Odds At School: targeted investment to help close the educational achievement gap*, Save the Children Scotland, 2010

10 R Lister, *Poverty*, Polity Press, 2004

11 P Townsend, *Poverty in the United Kingdom*, Penguin, 1979

12 N Smith and S Middleton, *Poverty Dynamics Research in the UK*, Joseph Rowntree Foundation, 2007

13 C Telfer, *Measuring Severe Child Poverty in Scotland*, Save the Children, 2010

14 R Wilkinson and K Pickett, *The Spirit Level: why more equal societies almost always do better*, Penguin, 2009

15 OECD, 2007, available at http://stats.oecd.org/glossary/detail.asp?id=7326

16 See www.scotland.gov.uk/topics/people/social-inclusion

17 At the time of writing, the reporting requirements for member states under the new Europe 2020 strategy had not been clarified. However, it is likely that some form of reporting to the Commission will still be required.

18 J H McKendrick and P Kelly, *Poverty: the European dimension. A briefing paper for community regeneration practitioners in Scotland*, Community Regeneration and Tackling Poverty Learning Network, 2011

19 C Oppenheim and L Harker, *Poverty: the facts*, Child Poverty Action Group, 1996

20 The Commission on Social Justice, *The Justice Gap*, Institute for Public Policy Research, 1993

21 N Smith, N Branosky, J H McKendrick and G Scott, *Closing the Opportunity Gap: scoping work for design of impact assessment*, Scottish Executive Social Research, 2007

22 D Miller, 'What is Social Justice?' in N Pearce and W Paxton (eds), *Social Justice: building a fairer Britain*, Politicos, 2005

23 See www.centreforsocialjustice.org.uk

24 See www.socialjusticefoundation.org.uk

25 See note 11, p31

# Three

# How do we measure poverty?

*John H McKendrick*

## Summary

- In Scotland, the UK and across Europe household income is the key factor used to estimate poverty – those with low household income are considered to be living in poverty.
- A consensus has emerged that poverty is present when a household's income is below 60 per cent of the median national income (adjusted for household size and composition).
- The government's official measure of poverty tracks progress *before* housing costs. This is how poverty is measured in Europe and measuring poverty in this way facilitates international comparisons. CPAG and many poverty experts argue that poverty should be estimated *after* housing costs as this gives a better indication of disposable income, which is a clearer indication of the lived experience of poverty.
- The challenge of measuring poverty should not be underestimated. Difficulties are faced in getting accurate income data in the first instance and then there are a series of technical issues that must be addressed by experts. Even when these obstacles are surmounted, it must be recognised that household income alone does not precisely reflect the income resources that are available to everyone, and that the same level of household income may not offer similar households the same purchasing power.
- In recent years, new estimates of local poverty in Scotland based on household income have been introduced.
- The minimum income standard is gaining support as another means to estimate the threshold below which people might be deemed to be living in poverty. It is a measure of the minimum income the British public believe is needed to live a socially acceptable quality of life.

## A measurement consensus... of sorts

There is a broad consensus that household income can be used to estimate poverty (when poverty is defined as a lack of resources). Having a
very low income indicates poverty. Typically, this approach involves asking
people for information about their household's income and household
composition, and then using this data to find out if that household's
income is below a threshold income value that defines the point below
which that household should be considered to be living in poverty. The
threshold value that is most commonly used is 60 per cent of the median
income (adjusted for household size and composition). In monetary terms,
in 2008/09 this was equivalent to a weekly income, after housing costs
were deducted, of less than £333 for a couple with two children aged five
and 14.[1] The use of a 60 per cent threshold value is the main way in which
poverty is measured in Scotland (the UK and Europe).

Box 3.1:
**Measuring poverty *before* housing costs or *after* housing costs?**

Many poverty analysts argue that it is more accurate to measure poverty *after* housing costs
have been deducted, as this better reflects the actual disposable incomes of low-income
households (housing being a fixed cost over which people living in poverty have little control).
In contrast, the UK government target for tackling poverty uses a *before housing costs*
estimate. The difference this makes is explained fully in this chapter. For clarification, the *after
housing costs* approach is used throughout this book, unless specific reference in made to
the UK government targets.

However, for a variety of reasons, measuring poverty is far from straightforward. This chapter's review of how poverty is measured in Scotland first
explains how the 'measurement consensus' was reached. Although there
is agreement on the key point that income should be used to measure
poverty, there are technical issues to consider (some of which divide
expert opinion), other challenges to overcome and limitations that must be
acknowledged. Box 3.1 flags up one of these issues. However, all are
considered in more detail below, before turning attention to how poverty
is measured for local areas within Scotland. Some alternatives to using
household income to measure poverty are considered at the end of the
chapter.

## How the consensus was reached and the dissenting voice that threatens to undermine it

No measurement carries the status of the single official government measure of poverty for Scotland (and the UK). Even so, incremental steps taken over the last decade have brought us to the point of consensus, in effect a *de facto* national measure of income poverty for Scotland and the UK.

First published in 1988, *Households Below Average Income* (HBAI) is an annual review of the UK income distribution compiled by the Department for Work and Pensions (DWP) (previously the Department of Social Security) using data collected in the *Family Resources Survey*. It is a major source of information on people living on low incomes and provides '... an explicitly relative measure which looks at how people at the bottom of the income distribution have fared in relation to the average'.[2] HBAI provides official figures on low income, although no official status is accorded to any measure.

In 1998, the Statistical Programme Committee of the European Union decided that 60 per cent of *median* income should be used as the measure of income poverty when making international comparisons.[3] As noted above, this is now the favoured measure of the UK government. The emergence of the 'Lisbon strategy' to tackle social exclusion and poverty throughout the nation states of Europe gave further impetus to the use of the 60 per cent income threshold as the pre-eminent measure of income poverty.[4]

However, the New Labour UK government's desire to tackle child poverty was the primary driver of the rise to prominence of the 60 per cent income threshold measure in Scotland and the UK. In 1999, the UK government committed itself to eradicating child poverty within a generation, a vision that is shared by the Scottish government and which was reaffirmed in 2010 with the passing of the Child Poverty Act.[5] Following a user consultation between 2002 and 2003, the DWP, in conjunction with HM Treasury, initially devised a three-tier measure of child poverty, which consisted of measures of absolute low income, relative low income, and material deprivation and low income combined (Table 3.1).[6] A fourth tier – persistent low income – was added as part of the Child Poverty Act 2010. Where poverty is to be measured by low income alone, the threshold of 60 per cent median income is used.

Table 3.1:

**UK government's four-tier measure of child poverty**

**Tier 1: Absolute low income**

Number and proportion of children in households whose equivalised net income before housing costs is below 60 per cent of inflation-adjusted UK median income in 2010/11. This is a measure of whether the poorest families are seeing their incomes rise in real terms.

**Tier 2: Relative low income**

Number and proportion of children in households whose equivalised net income before housing costs is below 60 per cent of UK median income in the same year. This is a measure of whether the poorest families are keeping pace with the growth of incomes in the economy as a whole.

**Tier 3: Material deprivation and low income combined**

Number and proportion of children who are both materially deprived and are in households whose equivalised net income before housing costs is less than 70 per cent of the UK median in the current year. This is to provide a wider measure of children's living standards.

**Tier 4: Persistent low income**

Number and proportion of children in households whose equivalised net income before housing costs is below 60 per cent of UK median income in the same year for three of the previous four years. This is a measure of whether or not families are consistently living in relative low income poverty.

Note: Until 2010, the base year against absolute low income was 1998/99. The change to 2010/11 was introduced with the passing of the Child Poverty Act 2010.

Although child poverty has been the driver of the measurement consensus in the UK, annual updates on 'income poverty' are also presented for adults of working age and pensioners. Data on 'income poverty' in Scotland is routinely published as part of the HBAI annual report (Scotland can be compared to other UK nations and regions in England in all tables comparing government office regions). Furthermore, the Scottish government publishes a shorter annual report on income inequality and income poverty that focuses exclusively on Scotland as a whole.[7]

Although the UK government gave notice in June 2010 of a Review on Poverty and Life Chances, which would 'examine the case for reform to poverty measures, in particular for the inclusion of non-financial elements', it is highly probable that income poverty and its 60 per cent threshold will remain central to how child poverty is estimated; after all, the Child Poverty Act 2010 formalised targets to reduce child poverty by 2020 using these measures. Furthermore, income poverty (and the 60 per cent income threshold) is central to how poverty is measured in the European Union and the UK is party to the new Europe 2020 target to reduce by 20 million the number of people living in poverty in the European Union.

However, the European Union also recommends that other thresholds (eg, 40, 50 and 70 per cent of the median) should also be used when considering poverty, in order to obtain the fullest picture. Some of these alternative thresholds are used in the UK. For example, below 70 per cent median income is used as an element in the UK combined child poverty measure of material deprivation and low income, and Save the Children uses the below 50 per cent median income threshold as an element in its measure of severe child poverty. Indeed, not only does the European Union recommend the use of different thresholds for the low-income measure, it has developed a comprehensive suite of 18 different indicators to enable it to reach a comprehensive understanding of poverty across the European Union.[8]

## Using household income to estimate poverty

The pre-eminence of the below 60 per cent of typical income threshold should not be taken to imply that measuring poverty by household income is without problems. On the contrary, there are four broad types of challenge to overcome, each of which presents more than one particular problem.

### Technical challenges when interpreting household income data

Using household income to measure 'income poverty' is far from straightforward and problems are encountered at many levels. The technical challenge of using household income to measure poverty has meant that collecting 'income poverty' data tends to be undertaken by research experts.

First, although it would be easier, it is not sensible to identify a single monetary value that defines the level below which all households in Scotland would be deemed to be living in poverty; a whole range of monetary values must be used as threshold levels of 'income poverty' in order to compare household income across different household types. For example, a couple with four children will require a higher level of income to maintain the same standard of living as one adult living alone and there-fore the 'poverty threshold' will be higher for the larger household.

Table 3.2 describes the key values for 2008/09 for four common household types. In addition to describing the mean and median weekly household income for each household type, the final two columns of this table specify the 'income poverty thresholds'.

Table 3.2:

**Weekly income (after housing costs) and income-based poverty lines (before and after housing costs), including self-employed, for different family household types, UK, 2008/09**

| | Weekly income (after housing costs) | | Weekly income-based poverty lines (60% median) | |
| | £ | £ | £ | £ |
| Family household type | Mean | Median | Before housing costs | After housing costs |
| --- | --- | --- | --- | --- |
| Single with no children | 251 | 199 | 164 | 119 |
| Couple with no children | 433 | 343 | 244 | 206 |
| Single with two children (aged 5 and 14) | 519 | 411 | 293 | 247 |
| Couple with two children (aged 5 and 14) | 701 | 555 | 374 | 333 |

Source: Department for Work and Pensions, *Households Below Average Income: an analysis of the income distribution 1994/95–2008/09*, Corporate Document Services, 2010, Table 2.4

Note: Poverty would be defined at an income below the figures listed in columns 4 and 5 of this table.

This adjustment of household income to account for household composi-tion is known as equivalisation. From 2005/06, the HBAI series has used the modified Organisation for Economic Co-operation and Development (OECD) equivalisation scale. The Scottish government has published a tech-nical note to provide guidance on understanding how equivalisation works.[9]

Second, a much more controversial issue among poverty analysts is whether poverty should be measured 'before housing costs' or 'after housing costs' have been deducted (Box 3.1). Although this seems a mundane and technical issue, its impact is highly significant. The number of people considered to be living in poverty in Scotland is much higher using an after housing costs measure – 970,000 in Scotland in 2008/09, compared with 860,000 using a before housing costs measure.[10]

Furthermore, the risk rate of poverty changes dramatically for different groups. Poverty rates are lower for those groups whose direct housing costs are lower (such as those owning their homes outright, but living on a low income) if an after housing costs measure is used. The impact this difference makes is most marked by comparing children and pensioners. Using a before housing costs measure suggests that the number of children living in poverty in Scotland is lower (210,000, compared with 260,000 with an after housing costs measure), whereas the level of poverty among pensioners is higher with a before housing costs measure (150,000, compared with 110,000 with an after housing costs measure).[11]

Many poverty analysts would argue that the after housing costs measure should be used, as housing costs represent a fixed budget item over which low-income families have little choice. This is particularly important when comparing across government office regions and national regions, as it smooths out the distorting effect of the marked variations in housing costs across the UK. It is argued that discounting housing costs from calculations of low income ensures that we are better able to compare what low-income families across different regions have at their disposal to spend. However, in line with practice in Europe, official government measures for tracking progress on poverty tend to be based on measuring poverty before housing costs, as do the definitions used for the targets set by the Child Poverty Act 2010. HBAI and the annual Scottish report on poverty and income inequality provide poverty estimates using both the before housing costs and after housing costs approaches. For the reasons outlined in Box 3.1, Section Three of this book tends to present data using an after housing costs measure. This avoids the risk of underestimating the number of children living in poverty in Scotland that comes with using a before housing costs measure.

Third, far more consensus has been reached about the technical challenge of whether household income should be calculated using the mean or median. Mean and median refer to different ways of measuring the average. Although the mean is most commonly used as the way of measuring an average, the favoured way of measuring poverty and low income is to use the median. Mean income is found by adding all the incomes of households and dividing the total by the number of households. Mean income can be easily distorted by very low or very high income. The *median* refers to the mid-point of a given set of figures. The median measure of average income is less susceptible to distortions, in particular from those on high incomes, and hence is a more appropriate measure of what constitutes a typical income.

A fourth and final technical challenge is whether 'income poverty' should be considered as 'absolute low income' or 'relative low income'. Until this year, absolute low income in relation to the HBAI figures referred to those households with less than 60 per cent of 1998/99 UK median income before housing costs were deducted.[12] This threshold was adjusted by inflation for each subsequent year. According to the DWP, absolute low income '... is important to measure whether the poorest families are seeing their incomes rise in real terms'.[13] Relative low income in relation to the HBAI figures refers to the number and proportion of households with below 60 per cent of UK median income before housing costs were deducted for each year. The threshold is, therefore, recalculated every year to account for increases in median incomes, rather than simply being fixed for one year then adjusted to account for inflation. This measure allows us to consider whether those on low incomes are keeping up with the rest of society.

As the 'absolute' and 'relative' figures for low income are measured in different ways, it is necessary to be clear about what these figures may mean. It could be argued that the figures for 'absolute' low income have been of less use when attempting to understand what has happened with low incomes over the last decade. As incomes have steadily risen over this time, even for those on low incomes, we would expect the proportion of people with incomes below a fixed figure to fall. This has been the case overall since 1996/97.[14] 'Relative' low income figures can be a better way of assessing whether government policies are specifically ensuring that those at the bottom of the income distribution are seeing their incomes improve, rather than if their incomes are simply rising with inflation.

There are good reasons to use both types of low income measure (and see Table 3.1), but it is important to be aware of the advantages and disadvantages associated with each. HBAI and the annual Scottish report on poverty and income inequality provide poverty estimates using both the 'absolute' and 'relative' measures. Something that neither measure is able to do is to tell us anything about the standard of living that anyone living below the threshold experiences.

## Getting accurate household income data in the first instance

Income is a sensitive issue and questions on household income are often not included in social surveys in the UK. Experience has shown that, having been asked to provide details on household income, survey respondents have expressed concern at the detail that is required to generate accurate data, the personal nature of income data, and the perceived uses to which the data would be put.[15] The *Family Resources Survey* is exceptional in that it asks very detailed questions on household income.

The *Family Resources Survey* is subject to robust data quality checks to increase the reliability of its data. These checks are not always feasible in smaller scale social surveys and, consequently, the reliability of household income data from smaller scale social surveys should not always be assumed. There are many reasons for regarding cautiously any unofficial poverty estimate based on household income – eg, the complex earning patterns of those with irregular sources of income; the challenge of collating household income data when several members of the household contribute to the total and when income is not pooled for the household; and the likelihood that those who do not return an accurate tax return or submit an accurate benefits claim will also be unlikely to state an accurate household income in a social survey. The robust data quality procedures used by the *Family Resources Survey* means that we can have greater confidence in *Family Resources Survey* income data, which carries the National Statistics stamp of approval.

## Limitations of household analysis

Poverty based on household income is, by definition, a measure of poverty for private households. Thus, the main measure of poverty in Scotland does not claim to measure whether those living in communal establishments are living in poverty. For example, over 1,500 looked-after children in Scotland live in 'residential establishments'[16] and the average prison population in Scotland is almost 8,000 adults;[17] national poverty statistics do not relate to such groups.

Furthermore, a household income does not necessarily imply that all members of that household will have equal access to this resource. Gender-sensitive analysis has demonstrated that women in Scotland, in particular, are prone to foregoing their household share at the 'expense' of other household members.[18] On the other hand, due to the dependency of their parents, children of substance abusers, for example, may not have access to the level of resource that household income suggests.[19]

It is unreasonable to expect that a national estimate of household poverty should account for poverty in institutions or intra-household poverty, but it is important to acknowledge that a fuller understanding of poverty in the UK would require data or studies that are complementary to HBAI data.

## Limitations of disposable household income as a measure of poverty

All things being equal, disposable household income – gross income, net of tax and national insurance and housing costs – should provide a measure of how much income households have available to meet their living needs. If that level of income falls below a benchmark, the household is considered to be living in poverty. However, disposable household income is not always an accurate indicator of the extent to which households are able to meet their daily living needs.

For example, disposable household income does not adequately reflect the income that is actually available to meet daily living needs for all households. Specifically, households with individuals who have a high level of debt to service may have less income to use (and therefore a lower standard of living) than others who earn less, but have no debts. These debt problems may be compounded for those on the lowest incomes by the greater likelihood that they will be using financial service providers who charge a relatively higher fee for their service.

Even if disposable net income adequately reflects the income that is available to meet daily living needs, it may not adequately reflect what some groups are able to purchase with it – ie, some groups face higher costs of living. For example, there has been longstanding concern that the additional social security payments which supplement the income of families with disabled people are insufficient to meet the additional costs of living with disability.[20] Similarly, costs of living vary across place. The Joseph Rowntree Foundation acknowledges this and has used research-based evidence to adapt its minimum income calculator to account for the higher cost of rural living, which it estimates at between 10 per cent and 20 per cent more than in urban areas.[21]

## Information sources

Very different answers must be given to the question, 'does Scotland have adequate household income data in order to measure poverty?' depending on whether we want to estimate poverty for Scotland as a whole, or for local areas within Scotland.

## Scotland

There are five main sources of household income data that can be used to estimate poverty for Scotland as a whole. Two sources have been referred to earlier in this chapter, each of which is based on an analysis of the HBAI dataset from the *Family Resources Survey* – ie, the annual report for the UK as a whole (through which Scotland can be compared with other government office regions in the UK) and the annual report of Scottish government (which focuses exclusively on Scotland).

From 2005, the Scottish government-funded 'Growing up in Scotland' study has been able to use aggregate household income data to estimate poverty for very young children in Scotland.[22] As this has a longitudinal design, it is now at the stage where it can measure the persistence of poverty among young children in Scotland.[23] Funding has been extended through until 2013 and 'Growing up in Scotland' will be able to monitor changes in the annual level of poverty and short-term trends in persistent poverty for very young children in Scotland in the years ahead.

Since 1999, the *Scottish Household Survey* has been collecting and publishing information on household income in Scotland.[24] With caution, data on household income can be used to understand the significance of living life on a low income. However, for the reasons outlined earlier in this chapter, it is far more helpful if household income is converted into a measure of household poverty. In 2010, for the first time, the Scottish government published a paper that provided estimates of poverty in Scotland using *Scottish Household Survey* data.[25] This should be used cautiously as it currently has the status of 'data being developed'.

'Understanding Society' is a new development that will incorporate and enhance the coverage of the British Household Panel Survey in Scotland to provide an even stronger information base to measure poverty trends in Scotland, including the possibility of estimating persistent poverty for Scotland as a whole.[26] This is set to be an important source for understanding Scottish poverty in the years ahead.

## Local

Scotland is not yet well served with household income-based measures of poverty for local areas. HBAI is not designed, and does not have a sufficient sample size, to estimate directly poverty for areas within Scotland. However, emerging developments mean that there should be optimism over the future prospects for local estimates of poverty in Scotland based on household income. First, as noted above, the Scottish government has produced an estimate of poverty using the *Scottish Household Survey*. Although only using a before housing costs approach, this provides estimates for Scotland's 32 local authorities, as well as the national estimate for Scotland as a whole. Second, the population characteristics that the HBAI analysis has shown to be associated with poverty could be used in conjunction with *Scottish Household Survey* household population data to model estimates of poverty for local authorities in Scotland. Less robust models could be constructed for smaller areas such as data zones, neighbourhoods or localities if these models were constructed using the more limited population data that is available for these geographical areas. Finally, small areas in England have been well served in recent years with a highly localised estimate of child poverty based on UK government analysis of data drawn securely from HM Revenue and Customs and the Department for Work and Pensions.[27] National Indicator 116 estimates the proportion of children living in poverty as being the proportion of all children living in the area who are either (i) living in families in receipt of out-of-work benefits, or (ii) living in families receiving tax credits whose reported income is less than 60 per cent of the median income before housing costs have been deducted. However, as yet, this data is only published for England. Given that this is UK-wide data, there is no compelling technical reason why it should not be published for small areas within Scotland in future years.

## Measuring poverty without household income

## Benefits

Given that welfare aims to provide claimants and their dependants with social protection, there is some merit in using information on benefit claimants to estimate poverty. As discussed above for National Indicator 116, benefits data can be particularly effective at providing local estimates of child poverty, if this is used in conjunction with income-based tax credit data. However, data of this quality is not yet available for Scotland. Yet welfare statistics are accessible, updated regularly and are available for the smallest geographical areas (data zones in Scotland).

However, limitations must be acknowledged in using welfare statistics to estimate poverty. First, benefit and tax credit levels are very often inadequate in protecting households from poverty – eg, out-of-work benefits for a couple with one child amount to only 66 per cent of the relative income poverty threshold discussed above.[28] Second, using out-of-work benefit statistics alone will dramatically underestimate the extent of poverty as, by definition, they will not provide estimates of in-work poverty.

Tax credit data is published by HM Revenue and Customs and could be used to estimate the level of in-work poverty for children. Helpfully, HM Revenue and Customs publishes this data alongside counts of out-of-work claimants. Together, this provides a more complete poverty count for children (counting in-work low-income and out-of-work families).[29] However, this is not a panacea for local poverty estimation, as eligibility for tax credits extends beyond people living in poverty. Hence, this data tends to overestimate the numbers of children and adults of working age who are living in poverty. Nevertheless, in the absence of National Indicator 116, this data can be used to estimate local area poverty in Scotland. The Scottish government recommends using the 'number of children living in households that are dependent on out-of-work benefits or child tax credit more than the family element... as one of the best child poverty proxy indicators available at a local authority level'. However, it makes clear 'it is important to note that this is not the same as being 'in poverty' according to official measures'.[30]

The proportion of those eligible for local welfare benefits – such as free school meals, school clothing grants or educational maintenance allowance – could also be useful as proxies for local poverty. Clearly, consideration has to be given to conditions of eligibility, administration and service uptake in appraising their utility as a proxy measure for local poverty.

## Material deprivation

As mentioned earlier in the chapter, data on material deprivation is used alongside household income in one of the four government measures of child poverty (also Table 3.1, Tier 3). Material deprivation is a good measure of the impact of poverty, or more accurately, the extent to which poverty impacts on a population. The possibility of in-kind support from the wider family (eg, a grandparent buying a winter coat) or from the wider community (eg, a local sports club subsidising the costs of participation) means that material deprivation indicators alone may fail to capture the extent of poverty among a population.

## Areas of multiple deprivation

Since its launch in 2004, the *Scottish Index of Multiple Deprivation* has provided a useful comparison of relative deprivation at small area level across Scotland. With 6,505 data zones in Scotland, this micro-geography has enabled the identification of pockets of deprivation that may have been missed in previous analyses using larger geographical areas as the basis of comparison – eg, electoral wards. In particular, residing within one of the 15 per cent 'most deprived areas' has become established as a key marker of deprivation in Scotland.

Multiple deprivation is a broader concept than poverty (see Chapter 2). There may be more merit in using the 'income deprivation' domain (one of the deprivations that count toward the multiple deprivation) as a more accurate proxy for poverty. However, both the multiple deprivation measure and the narrower income deprivation measure are of more limited value in estimating rural poverty (and rural deprivation). As is noted in Chapter 18, poverty in rural Scotland is spatially dispersed and area-based measures of deprivation tend to underestimate the scale of the problem.

## Minimum income standards

The minimum income standard project was launched in 2008, is uprated every year, updated every two years, and is funded by the Joseph Rowntree Foundation until 2014. The minimum income standard is the budget required by households to cover the cost of goods and services that are considered to be essential to meet a minimum socially acceptable standard of living in the UK. In this respect, it can essentially be seen as another household income-based approach to measuring poverty. It specifies an income level below which people are considered to be unable to have a socially acceptable standard of living.

The minimum income standard approach differs from the HBAI approach to poverty measurement in two key respects. First, the minimum income standard is based on robust focus group research and expert consultation to define what the people of the UK consider is required to achieve this minimum living standard, rather than a notional figure of 60 per cent below median income. Second, it factors in a multiplier to account for the higher costs of living in rural areas. Minimum income standard research suggests that the 60 per cent median income level that is used to measure poverty, whether measured before or after housing costs, is actually far below what is required as a minimum income by many household types in the UK.

## Conclusion

Considerable progress has been made, and continues to be made, in how we measure poverty in Scotland. Every edition of *Poverty in Scotland* has reported on new developments and better data. Although data is by no means perfect, Scotland is now fairly well served with information to inform anti-poverty activity. Future priorities for improving how poverty is measured in Scotland should focus on enriching the tools that are available to measure local poverty for data zones, neighbourhoods and local authority areas.

### Notes

1   Department for Work and Pensions, *Households Below Average Income: an analysis of the income distribution 1994/95–2008/09*, Corporate Document Services, 2010, Table 2.4

2   C Oppenheim and L Harker, *Poverty: the facts*, Child Poverty Action Group, 1996

3   Eurostat Task Force, 'Recommendations on Social Exclusion and Poverty Statistics', Paper presented to the 26–27 November Meeting of the EU Statistical Programme Committee, 1998

4   J H McKendrick and P Kelly, *Poverty: the European Dimension. A briefing paper for community regeneration practitioners in Scotland*, Community Regeneration and Tackling Poverty Learning Network, 2011

5   Child Poverty Act 2010

6   Department for Work and Pensions, *Opportunity for All: eighth annual report*, DWP, 2006

7  Scottish Government, *Poverty and Income Inequality in Scotland, 2008/09*, 2010

8  See note 4

9  J Chanfreau and T Burchardt, *Equivalence Scales: rationales, uses and assumptions,* Scottish Government, 2008, available at: www.scotland.gov.uk/Resource/Doc/933/0079961.pdf

10 See note 7, Table A1

11 See note 7, Table A1

12 With the passing of the Child Poverty Act, absolute low-income poverty has been recalibrated and is now to be measured against a new base year (financial year starting 1 April 2010). For details, see www.legislation.gov.uk/ukpga/2010/9/section/5

13 Department for Work and Pensions, *Measuring Child Poverty*, DWP, 2003, available at www.dwp.gov.uk/docs/finalconclusions.pdf

14 The possibility of incomes falling in real terms over the coming years would lend a different complexion to recent trend data on 'absolute low-income poverty'.

15 A Teague, *Income Data for Small Areas: summary of response to consultation*, Titchfield: Census Advisory and Working Groups, National Statistics, 1999; J Collins, D Elliot, S Walker, J Watson and M dos Santos, *2007 Census Test: the effects of including questions on income and implications for the 2011 Census*, Office for National Statistics, 2008

16 Scottish Government, *Children Looked-After Statistics 2008/09*, Statistical Publication Health and Care Series, 2010, Table 1.8

17 Scottish Government, 'Prison population', *Prison Statistics Scotland 2009–10*, 2010, available at www.scotland.gov.uk/topics/statistics/browse/crime-justice/trendpris

18 J H McKendrick, S Cunningham-Burley and K Backett-Milburn, *Life in Low-income Families in Scotland*, Scottish Executive, 2003

19 M Barnard and N McKeganey, 'The impact of parental problem drug use on children: what is the problem and what can be done to help?', *Addiction*, Vol 99.5, pp552–59, 2004

20 N Smith, S Middleton, K Ashton-Brooks, L Cox, B Dobson and L Reith, *Disabled People's Costs of Living*, Joseph Rowntree Foundation, 2004

21 N Smith, A Davis and D Hirsch, *A Minimum Income Standard for Rural Households*, Commission for Rural Areas and the Joseph Rowntree Foundation, 2010

22 See www.growingupinscotland.org.uk

23 M Barnes, J Chanfreau and W Tomaszewski, *The Circumstances of Persistently Poor Children*, GUS Topic Findings 2010/11, Scottish Government, 2010

24 See www.scotland.gov.uk/topics/statistics/16002/surveyoverview

25 Scottish Government, *Relative Poverty Across Scottish Local Authorities*, 2010

26 See www.understandingsociety.org.uk

27 See www.hmrc.gov.uk/stats/personal-tax-credits/child_poverty.htm

28 See www.poverty.org.uk/12/index.shtml

29 For child tax credit and working tax credit geographical statistics (including a count of out-of-work benefits), see www.hmrc.gov.uk/stats/personal-tax-credits/cwtc-geog-stats.htm

30 See www.scotland.gov.uk/resource/doc/933/0088607.xls

# Four

# What causes poverty?

*John H McKendrick*

## Summary

- Government at every level – local, national and UK – has a key role to play in tackling poverty in Scotland.
- Both the UK and Scottish governments have made firm commitments to tackle child poverty and policy interventions have helped reduce, but not yet eradicate, child poverty in Scotland.
- The reasons for poverty are complex and multi-faceted. The primary poverty-generating mechanisms are social, economic and political. Tackling poverty requires a sustained and long-term comprehensive strategy, rather than a quick-fix single-issue intervention.
- The way in which poverty-inducing factors take effect is complicated. It is overly simplistic to both reduce poverty to a single cause and to ignore the intervening factors that policy solutions need to take into account.
- Until recently, a growing economy had contributed to reductions in the level of absolute (low-income) poverty in Scotland. However, a much more ambitious and focused anti-poverty strategy is needed if poverty in Scotland is to be reduced on all key measures in the years ahead.

## Introduction

This chapter accounts for the causes of poverty in Scotland. This is by no means a straightforward task.

First, there are several possible reasons for why people experience poverty. Poverty is sometimes attributed to the **behaviour of individuals**.

Here, consideration is given to how personal knowledge of the 'feckless poor', grounded in everyday social theorising based on stereotypes, is used to support the viewpoint that poverty results from the failings of individuals. It is argued that this type of explanation is of limited value in accounting for poverty in Scotland. Poverty can be attributed to **social factors**, that is, characteristics that define groups of people and which place additional demands on their resources and/or make them more vulnerable to other poverty-inducing factors. Here, reference is made to the social factors that induce poverty among the groups identified as being vulnerable to poverty. Poverty in Scotland can also be attributed to **political factors**, that is, the extent to which government is prepared to intervene to tackle poverty and the effectiveness of these interventions. The specific ways in which government has tackled poverty in Scotland is considered in detail in Chapter 10 (and across Section Five). Here, the focus is on the options that are available to government. Finally, poverty can also be attributed to **economic factors** – eg, the strength of the macro-economy.

Second, the poverty experienced by individuals tends to result from more than one of these poverty-inducing factors. For example, the susceptibility to poverty of single adults without children, migrating to work in remote rural Scotland from Eastern Europe, might be attributed to: language barriers limiting their ability to move beyond the low-paid employment which brought them to Scotland to work in jobs that are populated with other migrants who share their cultural background (social factor); limited opportunity in the wider local labour market to earn a decent living wage (economic factor); and a lack of state intervention, as rural poverty is not deemed to be a pressing priority for policy intervention (political factor). Progress in some factors may not be sufficient to counteract other persistent poverty-inducing circumstances.

Third, the factors which cause people to experience poverty are inter-related. For example, the susceptibility to poverty of lone parents might be attributed to restricted labour market options given lone parents' need to combine work with parental responsibilities (social factor), resulting in difficulties in accessing employment that pays a decent living wage (economic and political factor). Here, the social situation influences the economic possibilities, both of which contribute to the poverty experienced by the individual.

Finally, the ways in which poverty-inducing factors influence individuals can be complex, hidden and indirect. For example, Scotland has a small domestic market and, like other small European nations, it is very dependent on exports and inward investment. It is, therefore, vulnerable to changes in both the global economy and the UK national economy. However, the extent to which these macro-economic forces result in poverty is dependent on a host of intervening factors such as the economic strategies of transnational corporations, inducements and support from inward investment agencies, national social protection and pay policies, and the ability of the local economy to absorb job losses or supply workers with the skills demanded in growth sectors.

## Individual factors

Many of us have anecdotal knowledge of an individual who seems to do little to arrest the poverty that s/he experiences. We may also be aware of others who would be classified as 'poor' using official data sources, but who supplement their income through the informal economy. More generally, many do not understand why people can be poor given apparent anti-poverty mechanisms such as: state support through social security payments (eg, employment and support allowance); safeguards against low income (eg, the national minimum wage); opportunities provided in communities and by the state to support people in poverty (eg, the Flexible New Deal programmes); and local interventions to reduce the costs associated with living on a low income – eg, local food co-operatives sourcing quality food and selling it more cheaply than local retailers. Furthermore, public debate on poverty in Scotland often draws on deeply entrenched stereotypes, which rationalise people's life trajectory on the basis of where they live or on their social profile. For example, 'she'll be poor because she lives in Onthank in Kilmarnock', is likely to be the thought process following the screening of *The Scheme* (see Chapter 9). In short, individuals are sometimes deemed to be the primary cause of their poverty and official measures of poverty are perceived to overstate the problem. Such arguments carry some intuitive appeal and are reinforced by sensationalist or superficial media coverage.

There are five key points that critique the line of thinking that attributes poverty to the action or inaction of individuals. First, poverty experienced by children has little to do with children's own actions; the 260,000 children experiencing poverty in Scotland (Table 5.1) do so exclusively on account of chance, that is, the accident of birth, which determined the families into which they were born. Clearly, not all people experiencing poverty can be held responsible for this condition. Second, reducing explanations for poverty simply and singularly to the actions of individuals does not allow the possibility of poverty being influenced by other factors, and takes no account of the large-scale structural (social, political and economic) forces that shape people's lives. As was argued in Chapter 1, the causes of poverty are multi-faceted. Third, on closer analysis, what appear to be 'individual-level' factors often reflect underlying social and economic processes. For example, the understanding that poverty is transmitted down through generations of the same family is often perceived to be a problem of the individual, when more correctly it should be viewed as a social and economic factor. And as James McCormick argued so persuasively many years ago in an earlier CPAG publication, poor places keep people poor.[1] Fourth, focusing on individual behaviour as a cause of poverty risks distracting attention from the social, economic and political factors over which it is possible for policy makers to exert influence and which, therefore, hold most potential for successful policy intervention to tackle poverty. Finally, there is a numerical challenge to those who argue that poverty is the fault of individuals. According to Scottish government figures (and using CPAG's preferred definition), 970,000 people experience poverty in Scotland (Table 5.2). There can be no credibility in the argument that almost one-sixth of the population in Scotland experience poverty on account of their own personal failings.

## Social factors

As Chapter 7 demonstrates, the distribution of poverty in Scotland is uneven across social groups and place. This must not, however, lead to an explanation for Scotland's poverty that is based on describing the changing composition of Scotland's population. Thus, for example, the changing composition of families in Scotland since the early 1970s – including the rise in lone parenthood – should not, *per se*, be used to explain the corresponding growth in poverty at that time. It is more accurate to explain that the rise of poverty was down to the high risk of poverty faced by a group growing in size and the failure of policies to intervene to reduce this risk. There is clearly an association between these trends (and between the extent of poverty and other social trends), but this offers no insight into the root causes of poverty. Most problematically, this approach encourages scapegoating and a culture of blame – eg, lone parenthood causes poverty.

However, there are common shared characteristics among social groups that make some more susceptible to poverty, and make the escape route from poverty more difficult than otherwise would be the case. Table 4.1 summarises some of the social factors that are experienced by some of the groups identified in Chapter 7 as being particularly susceptible to poverty.

Of course, Table 4.1 is only a summary overview of some of the main social factors which may cause or exacerbate the poverty experienced by groups of people in Scotland. Although space does not permit presentation of evidence that would justify the assertions made in Table 4.1, further comment is provided for two of the group-specific poverty-inducing factors.

First, suggesting that the national minimum wage is a contributory factor for young people's poverty seems counter-intuitive. After all, the introduction of the minimum wage has sought to safeguard pay rates for younger people since it was introduced in April 1999. In particular, the specification of a 'development rate' for workers aged 18–21 at the outset in 1999; the extension of wage protection to workers aged between 16 and 17 years old in 2004; the introduction of an apprentice minimum wage in 2010; the extension of the adult rate to 21-year-olds from 2010; and the annual uprating of the minimum wage since 1999, have each sought to protect young workers from low wages. However, on closer analysis, it could be argued that the national minimum wage could be a more effective aid in tackling poverty among young people. In effect, it justifies relatively lower wages for young people: the main rate for workers aged 21 and over increased to £5.93 an hour on 1 October 2010, which is higher than the 'development' rate set for young adults between 18 and 20 years (£4.92 an hour), 16/17-year-olds (£3.64 an hour) and apprentices (£2.50 an hour).[2] Thus, while the minimum wage has tackled some of the worst excesses, low pay among young people remains a major problem and the minimum wage gives credibility to lower rates of pay for younger workers.

Second, the existence of gender pay gaps is at odds with long-standing government legislation and recent steps to promote equal pay among local authorities in Scotland through single-status pay agreements. The right of women to equal pay has been enshrined in UK legislation since the Equal Pay Act in 1970 (which came into force in 1975) and has since been strengthened by amendments, such as that in 1984 to ensure equal pay for equivalent work. More recently, in 1999 single-status agreements were reached between the trade unions and local government in Scotland to ensure verifiable pay equality between men and women.

Table 4.1:

## Social factors as a cause of poverty

| Group | Factors (examples) |
| --- | --- |
| **Lifecycle** | |
| Children | • Limited ability to earn money to lift themselves out of poverty.<br>• Poverty status is dependent on their parents or guardians. |
| Youth | • Lower wages for this age group, with a lower rate of the national minimum wage.<br>• Benefit rates are lower for this age group.<br>• Lack of opportunity to accumulate wealth that could be used to ameliorate the effects of short-term bouts of poverty.<br>• Poverty may be a transitional state associated with periods of education and training. |
| Working-age adults | • Welfare system is oriented toward providing for young and old. |
| Pensioners | • Many have not provided for private pensions, having been brought up believing that the state pension would provide for their needs in old age. Thus, pensioner poverty reflects the circumstances of their working lives. If they were unemployed for long periods, worked in low-paid jobs, had insecure or interrupted work histories, were ill for long periods, or involved in unpaid work, they are more likely to experience poverty in old age.<br>• State pension complexity results in low take-up.<br>• Higher heating and fuel costs. |
| **Families and households** | |
| Lone parents | • Cost of childcare.<br>• Availability of childcare (barrier to participation in the labour market).<br>• Work-life balance – eg, mismatch between school hours and working hours. |
| Partnered parents | • Unequal distribution of income among householders.<br>• Unequal expenditure responsibilities among householders – eg, women spending on all family members. |
| Childless adults | • Welfare system is oriented toward providing for young, old and families with children.<br>• Inadequate welfare payments for single adults. |
| **Social** | |
| Work status | • Low pay.<br>• Costs associated with a 'flexible' workforce.<br>• Under-employment. |
| Gender | • Costs associated with being primary carers of children (interrupted work histories and have to work in lower paid jobs).<br>• Gender segregation in the labour market (over-concentration in lower paid jobs).<br>• Gender gap in pay. |

| | |
|---|---|
| | • Intra-household distribution of income. |
| Ethnicity | • Pensioner poverty among immigrants (having not built up pension entitlement on account of being engaged in low-paid work and beginning to contribute in the middle of their working lives). |
| | • Language barriers during transitional phase for immigrants. |
| | • Racist harassment and victimisation; stereotyping. |
| | • Tendency to work in sectors of the economy in which wages are low (especially Pakistani and Bangladeshi). |
| Disability/illness | • Extra costs associated with managing particular disability or illness, such as medicine, housing adaptation or transport costs (the majority of disabled people do not receive additional costs). |
| | • Higher cost of living associated with shopping locally (difficulty in accessing more distant, but cheaper, supermarkets). |
| | • Costs of caring. |
| | • Discrimination based on stereotyping. |
| | • Disabling environments, hampering access. |
| **Place** | |
| Local authorities | • (Under) strength of local economy. |
| Rural areas | • Lack of public transport in rural areas (restricting access). |
| | • Additional cost of transport in rural areas – eg, the necessity of running a car. |
| | • Fewer public services. |
| | • Low pay. |
| | • Higher cost of living. |
| | • More restricted employment/career opportunities. |
| Local area | • By definition, these will vary across place. |

However, by 2006, these agreements had not been implemented and the unions were concerned that single status was being implemented by imposing pay cuts and by driving down wages through job evaluation.[3] The employment status of women in Scotland is similar to that which applies in the rest of the UK; fewer women are economically active (58 per cent, compared with 69 per cent of men in August–October 2010),[4] the concentration across occupational type is highly gendered and women tend to be under-represented in the higher paying sectors and over-represented in the lower paying sectors (81 per cent of workers in personal service occupations are women, compared with 9 per cent in skilled trades),[5] and while equivalent numbers of men and women are employed (1,266,000 men and 1,198,000 women in Scotland in 2010), men are 1.4 times more likely than women to be working full time, while women are more than three times as likely as men to be employed part time.[6] While these gender patterns in work would explain why men earn more than

women, as explained in Chapter 6 (Table 6.1), what is particularly disconcerting is that the pay gap between men and women is evident across all
occupation types – for full-time work ranging from as low as 67 per cent
of male earnings in skilled trades to 90 per cent in sales and customer
services. Across occupations, women on average earn only 81 per cent
of their male counterparts.

However, the gendered character of poverty should not be accepted as inevitable in the world in which we live. For example, implementation of single status should have made inroads to reduce the gender pay
gap in Scotland, as should the UK-wide gender equality duty (from April
2007). Indeed, there has been very little progress in closing the gender
pay gap since the last edition of *Poverty in Scotland*, when it was reported that women working full time earned 80 per cent of what men earned
in 2004.[7] The gap remains substantial. Clearly, more and more wide-ranging work needs to be done to close the gender pay gap in Scotland.

## Political factors

Government action – or inaction – is one of the key factors which could
determine the extent and level of poverty in Scotland. To their credit, in
2010, both the UK and Scottish governments reaffirmed their commitment to eradicate child poverty within a generation. However, poverty is
also experienced in households without children and our governments
have been less specific about setting targets to eradicate poverty for people within these households. Furthermore, the effectiveness of the strategies used by government to tackle child poverty must also be appraised.
The questions that must be answered are, 'are our governments doing
enough?' and 'how effective are our government interventions?' In this
book, the specificities of these questions are answered more fully in
Chapter 10. In this chapter, the array of tools that are available for use by
the UK, Scottish and local governments to tackle poverty in Scotland are
appraised.

## UK government

The UK government retained responsibility following devolution for the
main levers of control over poverty in Scotland – the welfare system and
taxation.

## Welfare system

Social security protects the vulnerable from the worst excesses of poverty. However, although it is undoubtedly a tool for poverty amelioration, social security is not necessarily designed to provide an income that removes households without work from poverty. Indeed, there is an ideological train of thought that welfare payments must be kept at poverty levels to act as a disincentive to individuals who are disinclined to work. Proponents of this approach would argue that the welfare system could eradicate poverty by ensuring that only poverty-level incomes were available to claimants, effectively, encouraging or co-ercing claimants to find work and escape poverty.

The UK coalition government elected in 2010 has given notice of wide-ranging welfare reforms that aim to reduce the total cost of welfare arguably premised on the ideological position outlined above.[8] Although the proposed welfare reforms point toward a more austere future for benefit claimants, the ideological position is merely an extension of that held by the previous government. Welfare in the UK is not currently designed to remove people from poverty; rather it seeks to protect people from the worst excesses of abject poverty.

There are limitations to the way in which successive UK governments have used social security as a poverty-reduction strategy. First, the level of benefits has been tied to prices which, although ensuring that the spending power of benefit recipients is maintained year on year, also implies that the relative value of benefits declines year on year in periods of economic growth with low inflation (when growth in prices is lower than increases in average incomes). Relatively speaking, benefit recipients become poorer compared with wage earners. With the likelihood that the years ahead will be characterised by higher prices and lower wages, there would be the possibility that benefit recipients would, relatively speaking, become less poor compared with wage earners. However, the coalition UK government has intimated that claimants must take their 'share of the pain' in the austerity cuts and the value of benefits is actually projected to decrease. Thus, both in times of economic growth and decline, the welfare system has operated to make claimants relatively poorer.

Second, successive UK governments have subscribed to a welfare-to-work strategy through which they seek to 'make work pay'. Although there is evidence that this approach has been successful in assisting people to escape poverty, this is an ineffective anti-poverty strategy for those who cannot work, for those for whom work is not available and for those who undertake unpaid work. The 'work not welfare' mantra has been strongly championed by the UK coalition government and is set to feature more prominently and explicitly in the coming years.

Third, although UK government policies have had some beneficial effect in reducing the level and intensity of child and pensioner poverty (eg, the value of child benefit has increased in real terms), the use of social security to tackle child and pensioner poverty falls short of being a universal approach to overcome poverty, as social security is deployed in a more limited fashion to tackle the poverty of working-age claimants without children. It might be more accurate to assert that, until recently, the UK government has used social security as a *child* poverty reduction strategy. Even here, the progressive interventions of social security as a poverty alleviation strategy for households with children is set to diminish with coalition government plans – eg, to freeze and restrict entitlement to child benefit.

Finally, the UK government has not been averse to using the social security system to effect behavioural change in a way that overrides its poverty-reduction credentials. Thus, the previous administration saw fit to withdraw some benefits from those who did not comply with its New Deal programmes. Although there are differences of opinion over the moral legitimacy of using such punitive measures, they clearly demonstrate that the poverty-reducing value of social security can be overridden by other goals. The coalition government has given notice of its intent to introduce much tougher sanctions and more requirements for those benefit claimants who are judged to be able to work.

## Taxation

Higher earners pay more tax than lower earners in absolute terms, although not, as we shall see, as a proportion of their income. For example, in 2008/09, the average annual amount paid by the richest fifth of non-retired households in the UK was £20,538 in direct taxation and £7,589 in indirect taxation. In contrast, the average amount paid by the poorest fifth of non-retired households in the UK was £1,561 in direct taxation and £3,496 in indirect taxation.[9]

It must be recognised that taxation, *per se*, does not lead to a reduction in income inequality or a reduction in poverty. Rather, both direct and indirect taxation are elements of a broader government strategy through which cash benefits (welfare support) are added to original income (eg, wages and investments) to give gross income (stage one). Gross income is then subject to direct taxation to give disposable income (stage two). In 'disposing of this income', we are liable to indirect taxation. At this point, two calculations can be made to help us understand the impact of government intervention on income. First, the sum of the indirect taxes can be deducted from the disposable income to give us a measure of post-tax income (stage three – ie, [original income + cash benefits] – [direct taxation + indirect taxation]). Finally, we can take account of the benefits in kind (eg, education, health and social services) to give us a measure of final income. Taxation is the means through which government can redistribute earnings through cash benefits and benefits in kind.

Two criticisms can be made against the effectiveness of current taxation policy as a means to tackle income poverty. First, taxation reduces the incomes of those on already low incomes: the poorest fifth of households in the UK have £5,057 deducted in taxation from a gross income of £13,784 (36.7 per cent of gross income is deducted in taxation).[10] In fairness, it could be argued that, to some extent, this is an administrative necessity as it would otherwise be too complex to refrain from taxing low-income groups, particularly at the point of consumption for indirect taxes. Second, although higher earners pay more in absolute sums, the lowest earning fifth of households in the UK pay a greater share of their gross income in taxation – eg, the 'tax burden' of the lowest earning fifth at 36.8 per cent is higher than that of the highest earning households (33.8 per cent of the gross income of the highest earning fifth of households is deducted in tax).[11] Indirect taxes and the direct council tax are particularly regressive. For example, the poorest fifth pay three times the proportion of their gross income on council tax (4.8 per cent, compared with 1.8 per cent of the highest earning fifth) and twice the proportion of their income on indirect taxes (25.4 per cent, compared with 9.1 per cent).[12] It should come as no surprise, as reported in Chapter 6, that there has been little change in income inequality in Scotland in recent years.

## Scottish government and local government

As noted above, an appraisal of the anti-poverty interventions of the Scottish government is provided in Chapter 10 (and throughout the contributions in Section Five). Although not able to dictate who receives cash benefits, the Scottish government can influence the extent and level of poverty in Scotland: through using its tax-varying powers;[13] by wholesale area regeneration; by creating the conditions necessary to facilitate the labour market participation of those without work; by early intervention and improved early years provision to tackle inter-generational poverty; by effective service delivery and intervention in the fields of education, training and health; by promoting take-up of benefits and tax credits; by ensuring people have access to advice and information on maximising their incomes; and by intervening to provide benefits in kind. Local government is responsible for the direct provision of key services and supports people experiencing poverty (and others living on a low income) by providing an array of benefits in kind.

*Achieving Our Potential* articulates the Scottish government's approach to tackling poverty in Scotland, at the heart of which is a concordat with local government through which it has responsibility for determining and addressing local anti-poverty priorities. In addition to this devolution of responsibility to local government, the Scottish government is funding a more limited range of anti-poverty interventions at the national level, including funding income maximisation work (including through CPAG) and advice helplines (for lone parents, through One Parent Families Scotland). A detailed summary and review of the work being pursued under *Achieving Our Potential* was published in May 2010.[14] This review describes what has been undertaken to address key commitments for the five broad goals of: (i) tackling income inequality; (ii) long-term measures to tackle poverty and the drivers of low income; (iii) supporting those experiencing poverty; (iv) making the benefits and tax credits system work better for Scotland; and (v) supporting partners and engaging wider society.

The work of the Scottish government is also supported by the Tackling Poverty Board to oversee and drive forward policy to tackle poverty in Scotland.[15] A Community Regeneration and Tackling Poverty Learning Network also exists as a community of practice for anti-poverty practitioners.[16] The Scottish government also acknowledged that 2010 was European Year for Combating Poverty and, at the time of writing, was consulting on a child poverty strategy for Scotland.[17]

## Economic factors

The performance of the macro-economy is one possible reason for the existence of poverty in Scotland. The logic is that there is an inverse relationship between the economy and the extent and level of poverty – ie, the stronger the economy, the lower the intensity and extent of poverty.

Scottish government statistics show that the Scottish economy continued its pattern of sustained and steady growth until mid-2007, after which it changed direction and the economy began to contract. There is much evidence that can be cited to support this point.

Gross domestic product (GDP) is a measure of the value of the goods and products being produced in a nation state in any one year, and is widely accepted as a robust measure of economic growth.[18] Scotland's economy has grown steadily for many years, with peaks in the rate of growth in 2004 and 2007.[19] Poverty remained stubbornly high throughout this period. However, from 2007 until the start of 2010, Scotland's economic growth first slowed down, before entering a period of economic decline from the end of 2008 to the start of 2010. A recovery in the GDP trend was evident at the start of 2010, although initially the 'positive' trend was that the economy started to decline less markedly than it had in 2009.

Employment peaked at an all-time high of almost 75 per cent of the working-age population in 2007 (April–June), only to fall steadily to 70 per cent at the start of 2010.[20] Indeed, for three years (2006–2009) employment rates in Scotland were the highest of all national regions in the UK, before returning at the start of 2010 to the more typical position of being higher than Wales and Northern Ireland, but lower than in England. The downward trend in employment rates was checked in the second quarter in 2010, with a modest increase.

The number and proportion of Scotland's population claiming benefits has been on a downward trend since the start of the millennium. In the middle of 1999, almost one in five adults of working age were claiming some form of benefit (615,680 or 19.6 per cent).[21] Although the numbers fluctuated, the trend was clearly downward until the end of 2007, by which time the number of claimants had fallen to one in six (519,500 or 16.1 per cent). Since this time, a quarterly rise, then fall, has been followed by a steady increase in the number of claimants and, by the start of 2010, the 583,270 figure (17.9 per cent) of adult claimants of working age was greater than at any time since the start of 2004.

In contrast to these economic trends, there has been a steady increase in Scotland's real gross disposable household income throughout this period. This sum of all household income in Scotland suggests (using 2008 prices) a steady year-on-year rise in household income in Scotland from £58 billion in 1998 to £74 billion in 2008.[22] The economy may have entered a period of decline, employment rates may be falling and the number drawing on welfare may be rising, but overall household income continues to rise. Although it would be foolish to overstate the point (as the economic vitality of Scotland will clearly impact on household poverty), taken together, these economic trends suggest that household income is not solely determined by the economy alone. Poverty cannot be reduced to economy; economy is not the only factor explaining why people are living in poverty in Scotland.

Although not irreducible to poverty, the broader economic context sets the parameters within which distributional mechanisms will create, ameliorate or eradicate household poverty – that is, the economy determines the size of the cake that is to be shared. In times of economic growth, there is less resistance to progressive distribution. The widely anticipated job losses in Scotland in 2011, and the period of economic and public sector adjustment that is foreseen (which may include pay restrictions and the loss of more highly paid staff), may lead to a reduction in the overall income that is shared among the people of Scotland. In such conditions, people experiencing poverty are particularly vulnerable, as those living beyond poverty seek to protect their share of overall income resource in Scotland.

## Conclusion

We have identified four broad multi-faceted factors, which account for the prevalence of poverty in Scotland. Although *some* individuals may contribute to their own poverty, structural explanations are of far greater significance in explaining the extent of Scotland's poverty. Until recently, the strength of the Scottish economy, notwithstanding geographical variation and inequalities in the distribution of reward, was such that explaining poverty could not be reduced to economics alone. Thus, political intervention and social factors must be considered. Both the UK and Scottish governments have made commitments to tackle poverty, and have devised strategies and made policy interventions that have had an important impact, particularly in relation to child and pensioner poverty. However, the persistence of poverty for many social groups and the halting of the progress in reducing the level of child poverty in Scotland lead to the conclusion that our governments are not doing enough, quickly enough.

### Notes

1   C Philo and J McCormick, 'Poor Places and Beyond: summary findings and policy implications' in C Philo (ed), *Off the Map: the social geography of poverty in the UK*, CPAG, 1993, pp175–88

2   See www.lowpay.gov.uk

3   UNISON, 'Single Status and Equal Pay in Local Government', *MSP Briefing 124*, available at www.unison-scotland.org.uk/briefings/singlestatmsp.html

4   Office for National Statistics, *Regional Labour Market Summary: seasonally adjusted*, 2010, Webtable 18sa-1.xls; available at www.statistics.gov.uk/statbase

5   *Annual Survey of Hours and Earnings*, 2010, Table 3.1a, available at www.statistics.gov.uk/downloads/theme_labour/ashe-2010/2010-gor.pdf

6   See note 5

7   J H McKendrick and J Dickie, 'Factors Leading to Poverty' in *Poverty in Scotland 2007*, CPAG, 2007, p43, Table 3.2

8   See www.dwp.gov.uk/consultations/2010

9   A Barnard, 'The Effects of Taxes and Benefits on Household Income 2008/09', *Economic and Labour Market Review*, Vol 4, Part 7, 2010, p44, Table 6

10  See note 9

11  See note 9, p45, Table 8

12  See note 9

13  Although the ability to utilise these tax-varying powers has been allowed to lapse. For key details, see www.bbc.co.uk/ news/uk-scotland-11825229. On the other hand, a UK government White Paper passing through Westminster at the time of writing, incorporates the recommendation of the Calman Commission that Scotland assumes a degree of responsibility for raising its own income tax. For an overview, see www.timesonline.co.uk/tol/news/uk/scotland/article6932051.ece

14  Scottish Government, *Achieving Our Potential, Monitoring Table*, May 2010, available at www.scotland.gov.uk/topics/people/tackling-poverty/initiatives/tacklingpovertyboard

15  See www.scotland.gov.uk/topics/people/tackling-poverty/Initiatives/tacklingpovertyboard

16  See www.scotland.gov.uk/topics/built-environment/regeneration/pir/learning networks/cr

17  Scottish Government, *Tackling Child Poverty in Scotland: a discussion paper*, 2010

18  One of Scotland's purpose targets is to raise Scotland's GDP growth rate to match that of the UK and small independent countries of the European Union.

19  Drawn from the economic purpose target web pages. See www.scotland.gov.uk/about/scotperforms/purposes/economicgrowth

20  Scottish Government, *High Level Summary of Economic Trends Datasheet – Labour Market*, 2010

21  All data drawn from the Department for Work and Pensions data tabulation tool at http://research.dwp.gov.uk/asd/index.php?page=tabtool

22  Drawn from the solidarity purpose target web pages at www.scotland.gov.uk/About/scotPerforms/purposes/solidarity

# Section Three
## Poverty in Scotland: the evidence

# Five

# Is poverty falling?

*John H McKendrick*

## Summary

- Poverty is no longer falling in Scotland. Since 2004/05, on the whole, there has been no reduction in either relative poverty or absolute poverty in Scotland.
- In the decade leading up to 2004/05, Scotland experienced significant reductions in the number of children living in poverty. The number of children living in poverty in Scotland has not reduced since 2004/05.
- The latest data, for 2008/09, shows that after housing costs are taken into account, more than one in four of Scotland's children live in poverty (26 per cent). One in six children in Scotland live with income poverty/material deprivation combined (16 per cent), while, using the government's preferred before housing costs measure, more than one in five children in Scotland live in relative poverty (21 per cent).
- Reduction in absolute poverty in Scotland over the last decade is much more marked than reduction in relative poverty. Although this suggests that standards of living may be rising for people experiencing poverty, the lower marked progress with relative poverty suggests that many people still have an income that would not allow them to enjoy what is considered to be necessary to participate without undue restriction in Scottish society.
- European comparisons suggest that the poverty risk in Scotland is marginally higher than that in Europe as a whole. Scotland fares less favourably when compared with those European nations (Scandinavian and other small European nations) against which it often seeks to compare national performance.

## Introduction

Chapter 3 described the pre-eminence of household income as a means of measuring poverty in Scotland. In this chapter, the Scottish analysis of the *Households Below Average Income* (HBAI) data is used to estimate the number of people living in poverty in Scotland and to assess whether poverty is falling, remains static or is increasing.[1] Here, the focus is on the total number of people living in poverty, first for children and then for the population as a whole. Estimates of the number of people living in poverty from sub-groups of the population (eg, by family type or by local authority area) are considered in Chapter 7.

## Child poverty

There was a steady growth in child poverty in Scotland and across the UK over the last few decades of the twentieth century. By 2000, it was well established that children were over-represented at the bottom of the income distribution and under-represented at the top: according to the annual HBAI report at this time, 'Children are now the group most likely to be in low-income households, and most likely to remain in low-income households for a long period of time.'[2]

The UK government's historic commitment in 1999 to reduce child poverty within a generation gave impetus to a trend that started in 1996/97. From 360,000 children living in relative poverty in 1996/97, child poverty fell in five of the following eight years to reach 250,000 in Scotland in 2004/05 and 2005/06 (after housing costs are taken to account) (Table 5.1).[3] This was equivalent to a fall in the rate of child poverty from 33 per cent in 1996/97 to 24 per cent in 2005/06, but still left child poverty far higher than in the late 1970s and early 1980s.

According to current Scottish government figures, 260,000 children living in Scotland are part of households whose income is so much lower than the median income for households in Scotland that they are considered to be living in poverty (below 60 per cent of median equivalised income, after housing costs are considered). Similarly, 150,000 children in Scotland are living in households that have not experienced a sufficient real rise in income levels to lift them out of absolute (low income) poverty. In terms of proportions, and using the same Scottish government figures, more than one in four children in Scotland (26 per cent) live in relative

Figure 5.1:

**Proportion of children living in absolute poverty and relative poverty (after housing costs), Scotland, 1994/95 to 2008/09**

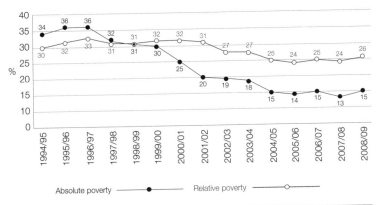

Source: Scottish Government, *Poverty and Income Inequality in Scotland, 2008/09*, 2010, Tables A1 and A2

Note: Figures are derived from the *Family Resources Survey*. The modified OECD equivalisation scales have been used in the calculations and the figures refer to income after housing costs have been deducted. See Table 2.1 for definitions of absolute poverty (low income) and relative poverty (low income).

Table 5.1

**Number of children living in absolute poverty and relative poverty (after housing costs), Scotland, 1994/95 to 2004/05**

Thousands

| | 1994/95 | 1995/96 | 1996/97 | 1997/98 | 1998/99 | 1999/00 | 2000/01 | 2001/02 | 2002/03 | 2003/04 | 2004/05 | 2005/06 | 2006/07 | 2007/08 | 2008/09 |
|---|---|---|---|---|---|---|---|---|---|---|---|---|---|---|---|
| Absolute poverty | 380 | 400 | 400 | 350 | 330 | 320 | 270 | 210 | 200 | 180 | 160 | 140 | 150 | 130 | 150 |
| Relative poverty | 330 | 360 | 360 | 330 | 330 | 350 | 340 | 330 | 280 | 280 | 250 | 250 | 250 | 240 | 260 |

Source: Scottish Government, *Poverty and Income Inequality in Scotland, 2008/09*, 2010, Tables A1 and A2

Note: Figures are derived from the *Family Resources Survey*. The modified OECD equivalisation scales have been used in the calculations and the figures refer to income after housing costs have been deducted. See Table 2.1 for definitions of absolute poverty (low income) and relative poverty (low income).

poverty and almost one in six children in Scotland (15 per cent) live in absolute poverty. Even using the before housing costs measure that is used by the government when measuring progress against child poverty

Figure 5.2:

**Children living in low-income households with below 60 per cent UK median income (after housing costs), including self-employed, Scotland and other parts of the UK, 2008/09**

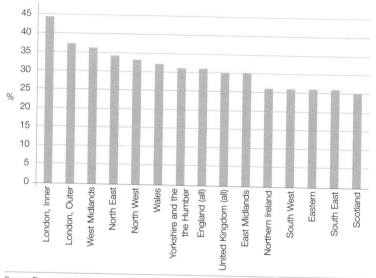

Source: Department for Work and Pensions, *Households Below Average Income 2008/09*, Corporate Document Services, 2010, Table 4.6

Note: Using modified OECD equivalised scale.

targets, for reasons highlighted in Chapter 4, one in five children in Scotland (210,000) are still living in poverty.

As the figures above show, child poverty persists at a disturbingly high level in Scotland. Furthermore, since 2004/05, the level of child poverty in Scotland has stabilised and UK and Scottish government interventions to date have not reduced the numbers of children experiencing relative poverty below 240,000 (after housing costs) in any year.

Figure 5.2 compares the percentage of children living in households with incomes of below 60 per cent median earnings (relative poverty) in Scotland, using the after housing costs measure, with those from other government office regions and national regions in UK for 2008/09 (using three-year running averages).

What is clear from Figure 5.2 is that a lower proportion of children live in poverty in Scotland than in any of the other national regions in the UK (Wales, Northern Ireland and England as a whole) and in any of the other government office regions in the UK – eg, North West England, South East England.

Figure 5.3 compares the percentage of children living in households with incomes of below 60 per cent median earnings in their own nation (relative poverty) across the European Union for 2008, using the before housing costs measure that is favoured by the European Union.

A slightly higher proportion of children live in poverty in Scotland than in the European Union as a whole. Children in Scotland also fare considerably worse than those growing up in Norway and Denmark. Indeed, children in Scotland are more than twice as likely to experience poverty than in these nations. In terms of the risk of child poverty, Scotland shares more in common with Poland, Lithuania, Malta and Portugal than it does with the Scandinavian countries and those of northern and central Europe.

The Scottish HBAI has now generated sufficient time series data on the 'Tier 3' measure of child poverty (Table 3.1 in Chapter 3) to comment on recent trends in child poverty, as measured by a combination of low household income and material deprivation. Not surprisingly, this measure of child poverty reinforces the findings of the absolute low-income and relative low-income measures. There has been virtually no overall change in the extent of low-income poverty/material deprivation among children in Scotland in recent years. For 2008/09, using a before housing costs measure in the income component, it is estimated that 160,000 children in Scotland were living in income poverty/material deprivation combined (16 per cent of children).

Whichever government measure is used, it is clear that recent trends in child poverty in Scotland are no longer the basis of a 'good news' story.

## Overall poverty in Scotland

Although children and pensioners have been the primary focus of the UK and Scottish governments' anti-poverty activity, a fuller understanding of poverty in the UK requires a more broadly based analysis of poverty among the population as a whole.

Mirroring the presentation of evidence for child poverty, Table 5.2 shows the number of individuals in Scotland who are living in poverty and Figure 5.4 shows the changes to the proportion of individuals living in poverty in Scotland from 1994/95.

Figure 5.3:

## Children living in low-income households with below 60 per cent national median income (before housing costs), including self-employed, Europe, 2008

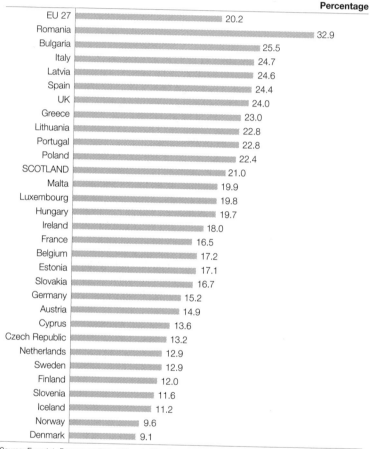

Percentage

| | |
|---|---|
| EU 27 | 20.2 |
| Romania | 32.9 |
| Bulgaria | 25.5 |
| Italy | 24.7 |
| Latvia | 24.6 |
| Spain | 24.4 |
| UK | 24.0 |
| Greece | 23.0 |
| Lithuania | 22.8 |
| Portugal | 22.8 |
| Poland | 22.4 |
| SCOTLAND | 21.0 |
| Malta | 19.9 |
| Luxembourg | 19.8 |
| Hungary | 19.7 |
| Ireland | 18.0 |
| France | 16.5 |
| Belgium | 17.2 |
| Estonia | 17.1 |
| Slovakia | 16.7 |
| Germany | 15.2 |
| Austria | 14.9 |
| Cyprus | 13.6 |
| Czech Republic | 13.2 |
| Netherlands | 12.9 |
| Sweden | 12.9 |
| Finland | 12.0 |
| Slovenia | 11.6 |
| Iceland | 11.2 |
| Norway | 9.6 |
| Denmark | 9.1 |

Source: Eurostat, *Persons at Risk of Poverty After Social Transfers*, 2010

Notes:

1. Using modified OECD equivalised scale.
2. Data from 2008 is used as 2009 data was missing for five European nations at the time of writing.
3. Data for Scotland is measured in the same way as data for EU nations, but is drawn from a different source (HBAI for Scotland, rather than EU-SILC). EU-SILC does not permit disaggregation of data to areas smaller than EU nation states. Therefore, this data comparing Scotland and EU risk rates must be used with caution.
4. Data for France is provisional.

Figure 5.4:

**Proportion of individuals living in absolute poverty and relative poverty (after housing costs), Scotland, 1994/95 to 2008/09**

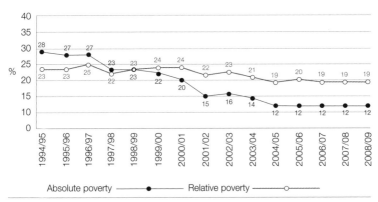

Absolute poverty ————●———— Relative poverty ————○————

Source: Scottish Government, *Poverty and Income Inequality in Scotland, 2008/09*, 2010, Tables A1 and A2

Note: Figures are derived from the *Family Resources Survey*. The modified OECD equivalisation scales have been used in the calculations and the figures refer to income after housing costs have been deducted. See Table 2.1 for definitions of absolute poverty (low income) and relative poverty (low income).

According to these figures, 630,000 individuals are in households regarded as experiencing 'absolute poverty' (60 per cent below inflation-adjusted equivalised household income in 1998/99). 970,000 individuals in Scotland are living in households regarded as experiencing 'relative poverty' (60 per cent below median equivalised household income at current levels, after housing costs have been deducted). In terms of proportions, almost one in four individuals in Scotland (19 per cent) live in relative poverty and more than one in ten individuals in Scotland (12 per cent) live in absolute poverty.

These figures show that it is not only child poverty that is a problem in Scotland. The late 1990s and early 2000s were not characterised by the same scale of progress in reducing poverty for the population as a whole in Scotland. The late 2000s have been characterised by the same overall stagnation in the level of poverty. Furthermore, although the rates remain fairly static, the number of individuals living in relative poverty in Scotland increased between 2006/07 and 2007/08.

Nevertheless, over the medium term, it is important to acknowledge

Table 5.2:

**Number of individuals living in absolute poverty and relative poverty (after housing costs), Scotland, 1994/95 to 2008/09**

**Thousands**

| | 1994/95 | 1995/96 | 1996/97 | 1997/98 | 1998/99 | 1999/00 | 2000/01 | 2001/02 | 2002/03 | 2003/04 | 2004/05 | 2005/06 | 2006/07 | 2007/08 | 2008/09 |
|---|---|---|---|---|---|---|---|---|---|---|---|---|---|---|---|
| Absolute poverty | 1,380 | 1,340 | 1,360 | 1,170 | 1,130 | 1,120 | 990 | 740 | 770 | 670 | 620 | 600 | 600 | 590 | 630 |
| Relative poverty | 1,140 | 1,160 | 1,230 | 1,120 | 1,130 | 1,200 | 1,220 | 1,110 | 1,120 | 1,020 | 960 | 990 | 950 | 970 | 970 |

Source: Scottish Government, *Poverty and Income Inequality in Scotland, 2008/09*, 2010, Tables A1 and A2

Note: Figures are derived from the *Family Resources Survey*. The modified OECD equivalisation scales have been used in the calculations and the figures refer to income after housing costs have been deducted. See Box 3.1 for definitions of absolute poverty (low income) and relative poverty (low income).

that some progress had been made in reducing whole-population poverty in Scotland. Between 1994/95 and 2007/08, the number of individuals living in absolute poverty in Scotland fell from 1,380,000 (28 per cent) to 590,000 (12 per cent). Similarly, a fall in relative poverty can be observed – from 1,230,000 (25 per cent) in 1996/97 to 970,000 (19 per cent) in 2007/08. Thus, these figures suggest that, following a decade of fluctuations around the one million mark, the number of individuals living in relative poverty in Scotland has remained consistently below one million people for the last five years (Table 5.2).

Figure 5.5 compares the percentage of individuals living in households with incomes below 60 per cent of the median in Scotland, after housing costs have been deducted (relative poverty), with those from other government office regions and national regions in UK.

As for children (Figure 5.2), there is evidence to suggest that the level of poverty in Scotland compares favourably with that in other parts of the UK. Poverty in Scotland, on the whole, is lower than in Wales, England and Northern Ireland and in all English regions, except for the South East (with which it shares the same level of poverty).

Once again though, although UK comparative data casts Scotland in a positive light, this should not be allowed to obscure the fact that many thousands of people in Scotland are currently living in poverty – 630,000 people if the more stringent measure of absolute poverty is used and just 30,000 short of one million if we adopt the relative measure of poverty

Figure 5.5:

**Individuals living on a low income with household income below 60 per cent of UK median (after housing costs), including self-employed, Scotland and other parts of the UK, three-year average to 2008/09**

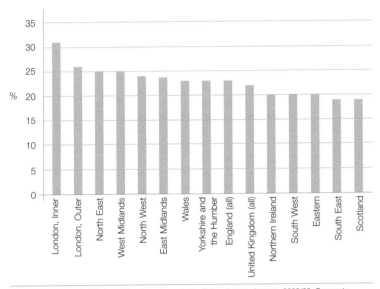

Source: Department for Work and Pensions, *Households Below Average Income, 2008/09*, Corporate Document Services, 2010, Table 3.6

Note: Using Modified OECD equivalised scales.

(Table 5.2).

Figure 5.6 compares whole-population poverty across Europe using the same approach (and with the same caveats) as Figure 5.3 did for children. The proportion of people living in poverty in Scotland is marginally higher than that of the European Union as a whole. This means that Scotland fares relatively poorly in some nation-on-nation comparisons. For example, people in Scotland are almost twice as likely to be living in relative poverty, compared with those living in the Czech Republic. In terms of the overall risk of poverty, Scotland shares more in common with Poland and Portugal than it does with the Scandinavian countries and other small European nations such as Iceland.

Figure 5.6:

**Individuals living in low-income households with household income below 60 per cent national median (before housing costs), including self-employed, Europe, 2008**

Percentage

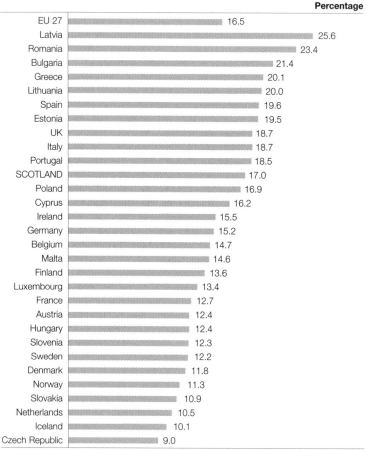

| | |
|---|---|
| EU 27 | 16.5 |
| Latvia | 25.6 |
| Romania | 23.4 |
| Bulgaria | 21.4 |
| Greece | 20.1 |
| Lithuania | 20.0 |
| Spain | 19.6 |
| Estonia | 19.5 |
| UK | 18.7 |
| Italy | 18.7 |
| Portugal | 18.5 |
| SCOTLAND | 17.0 |
| Poland | 16.9 |
| Cyprus | 16.2 |
| Ireland | 15.5 |
| Germany | 15.2 |
| Belgium | 14.7 |
| Malta | 14.6 |
| Finland | 13.6 |
| Luxembourg | 13.4 |
| France | 12.7 |
| Austria | 12.4 |
| Hungary | 12.4 |
| Slovenia | 12.3 |
| Sweden | 12.2 |
| Denmark | 11.8 |
| Norway | 11.3 |
| Slovakia | 10.9 |
| Netherlands | 10.5 |
| Iceland | 10.1 |
| Czech Republic | 9.0 |

Source: Eurostat, *Persons at Risk of Poverty after Social Transfers*, 2010

Notes:
1. Using modified OECD equivalised scale.
2. Data from 2008 is used as 2009 data was missing for five European nations at the time of writing.
3. Data for Scotland is measured in the same way as data for EU nations, but is drawn from a different source (HBAI for Scotland, rather than EU-SILC). EU-SILC does not permit disaggregation of data to areas smaller than EU nation states. Therefore, this data comparing Scotland and EU risk rates must be used with caution.
4. Data for France is provisional.

## Conclusion

The figures in this chapter have outlined the broad trends in poverty using the key measure of household income. All the data shows that income poverty is a significant problem in Scotland, and that the emerging problem of the late noughties is that poverty is persisting in Scotland, rather than reducing as it was in the early noughties. There is clearly a need to reappraise how poverty is tackled in Scotland if the government aim – as stated – is to reduce the numbers living in poverty. However, as will be shown in Chapter 7, some groups in Scottish society are at even greater risk of poverty than these aggregate figures suggest.

### Notes

1 Scottish Government, *Poverty and Income Inequality in Scotland, 2008/09*, 2010

2 Department for Work and Pensions, *Households Below Average Income 2000/01*, Corporate Document Services, 2001, available at http://statistics. dwp.gov.uk/asd/index.php?page=hbai

## Six

# Is income inequality reducing?

*John H McKendrick*

### Summary

- The Scottish government aims to reduce income inequality by 2017.
- Income inequality has not reduced in Scotland over the last decade. Indeed, if anything, the income share of Scotland's poorest households has decreased in recent years.
- Recent and projected trends for the key drivers of change in income inequality do not suggest that Scotland is moving in the right direction to tackle income inequality.
- It is unlikely that, without substantial policy changes, income inequality in Scotland will reduce dramatically by 2017.

### Introduction: income inequality comes centre stage

The Scottish government has set itself the target of reducing income inequality in Scotland. As discussed in Chapter 2, the high-level solidarity purpose target commits Scotland 'to increase overall income and the proportion of income earned by the three lowest income deciles as a group by 2017'. The Scottish government commitment to reduce income inequality (the distribution of income) is set within a commitment to increase overall income. For the overall income component of this measure, the Scottish government uses Office for National Statistics estimates of gross disposable income to conclude that overall income in Scotland has risen consistently year on year over the last decade from £58 billion in 1998 to £74 billion in 2008.[1]

However, the central focus of this target is the measurement of the

Figure 6.1:

**Share of total income by income groups (deciles), Scotland, 2006/07 to 2008/09**

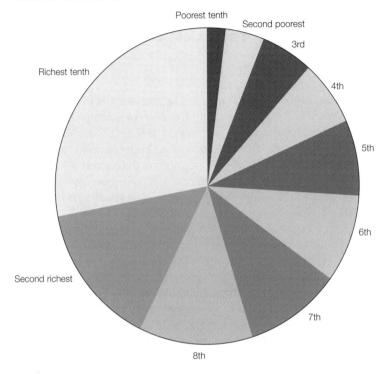

Source: The Poverty Site, based on analysis of Department for Work and Pensions, *Households Below Average Income* dataset, August 2010. Reproduced with kind permission from Guy Palmer, The Poverty Site, www. poverty.org.uk

distribution of household income. As important as the current evidence of income inequality is 'direction of change' evidence for the key drivers of income inequality. According to the Scottish government,[2] income inequality will be tackled by: (i) the accessibility of employment opportunities, especially for those on lower incomes; (ii) opportunities for the lower paid to improve their skills; (iii) changes in the income differential between the lowest and highest paid occupations; and (iv) entitlement to, and take-up of, benefits. This chapter presents evidence on the current state of income inequality in Scotland and the key drivers that may shape it toward 2017.

## Income inequality: a persistent problem in Scotland

### The big, bad picture

Income inequality in Scotland is stark. The 'poorest'[3] tenth of Scotland's households share only 2 per cent of Scotland's income. The second 'poorest' tenth fare little better, with an income share of 4 per cent (Figure 6.1). These figures stand in sharp contrast to Scotland's richest tenth, who receive 29 per cent of Scotland's income and the second richest tenth who receive 15 per cent. Indeed, the income of the richest tenth of households in Scotland is greater than the income of all households on 'below average incomes'.

Although grossly unequal, this pattern of income distribution is not atypical in the UK. Indeed, it could be argued that Scotland is less unequal than the UK as a whole in terms of income inequality. The gap between the richest tenth and poorest tenth in overall income share is 27 percentage points in Scotland (the richest tenth received 29 per cent of all income in 2008/09, while the share of the poorest tenth was 2 per cent), compared with 29.8 percentage points for the UK as a whole (31 per cent and 1.2 per cent in 2008/09). While laudable, the size of the gap is hardly something to celebrate and it would be misleading (albeit statistically accurate) to describe Scotland as having less income inequality than the UK as a whole; better to acknowledge that Scotland is marginally less unequal in its distribution of income.

Indeed, in the broader European context, income inequality in both Scotland and the UK is among the worst in Europe (Figure 6.2). Using the Gini co-efficient estimate (a widely used measure of income inequality for nations) the level of income inequality is only greater in Latvia, Romania, Bulgaria and Portugal (and in other national regions of the UK).[4]

### Increasing income, increasing inequality

Income trends in Scotland show both progressive and regressive tendencies. Positively, over the last decade, the growth in income for all but those

Figure 6.2:

## Income inequality in European nations, as measured by the Gini Co-efficient, 2008

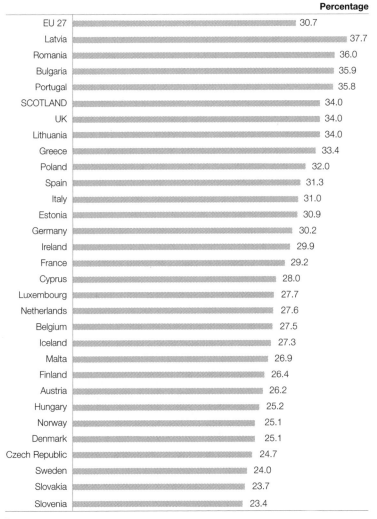

Percentage

| Country | Percentage |
|---|---|
| EU 27 | 30.7 |
| Latvia | 37.7 |
| Romania | 36.0 |
| Bulgaria | 35.9 |
| Portugal | 35.8 |
| SCOTLAND | 34.0 |
| UK | 34.0 |
| Lithuania | 34.0 |
| Greece | 33.4 |
| Poland | 32.0 |
| Spain | 31.3 |
| Italy | 31.0 |
| Estonia | 30.9 |
| Germany | 30.2 |
| Ireland | 29.9 |
| France | 29.2 |
| Cyprus | 28.0 |
| Luxembourg | 27.7 |
| Netherlands | 27.6 |
| Belgium | 27.5 |
| Iceland | 27.3 |
| Malta | 26.9 |
| Finland | 26.4 |
| Austria | 26.2 |
| Hungary | 25.2 |
| Norway | 25.1 |
| Denmark | 25.1 |
| Czech Republic | 24.7 |
| Sweden | 24.0 |
| Slovakia | 23.7 |
| Slovenia | 23.4 |

Source:
1. EU data: European Union Statistics on Income and Living Conditions (EU-SILC). Drawn from the Eurostat Data Explorer Tool. Data table with the income distribution, 2010
2. Scottish data: drawn from Scottish government analysis of the *Households Below Average Income* dataset

Notes:
1. Higher numbers represent higher levels of income inequality.
2. Data from 2008 is used as 2009 data was missing for six European nations at the time of writing.
3. The European data is drawn from EU-SILC data.
4. Data for Scotland is drawn from the Scottish government's own analysis of *Households Below Average Income* data. In this analysis the GB Gini co-efficient was described as 36.0. The EU-SILC estimate for the UK is lower than this GB estimate. Although this may reflect GB/UK differences, this may also suggest that the Scottish Gini co-efficient would be slightly lower if data were available through the EU-SILC.
5. Data for France is provisional.

with the very lowest and very highest incomes has been broadly progressive – ie, on the whole (and particularly from the 'third poorest tenth' to the 'third richest tenth' of Scotland's households), 'poorer' households have experienced a higher rate of income growth (Figure 6.3). By itself, this would herald a move toward lower income inequality.

However, this progressive trend is more than countered by regressive tendencies at the extremes of the income distribution spectrum – ie,

Figure 6.3:

**Growth in income by income groups (deciles) in Scotland, 1998/99 to 2008/09**

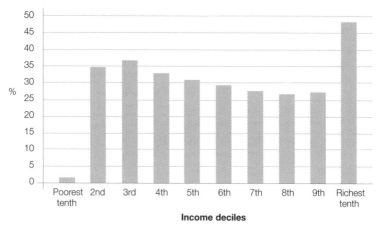

Source: The Poverty Site, based on analysis of Department for Work and Pensions, *Households Below Average Income* dataset, August 2010. Reproduced with kind permission from Guy Palmer, the Poverty Site, www.poverty.org.uk

Note: For each income group, average percentage change in real net household incomes between 1998/99 and 2008/09, after deducting housing costs.

the poorest tenth of Scotland's households experienced almost inconse-
quential income growth over the last decade (2 per cent), while the richest
tenth enjoyed the highest level of income growth (48 per cent). The adage
that 'the rich get richer and the poor get (relatively) poorer' would appear
an apt description for Scotland's most and least affluent households.

Other ways of measuring income inequality reinforce the regressive
trends of late. The Scottish government estimate of our Gini co-efficient
suggests that Scotland's distribution of income has become more unequal
each year since 2004/05.[5] Scotland's Gini co-efficient has worsened by
one point per annum from an index value of 30 in 2004/05 to 34 for
2008/09.

However, strictly speaking, according to the Scottish government
criterion, income inequality has neither reduced nor increased in Scotland
in recent years. According to the solidarity target, income inequality is
increasing if the income share of the poorest 30 per cent falls by one percentage point or more (or if total income falls). Income inequality is improv-

Figure 6.4:

**Profile of bottom two income deciles and bottom third decile
households in Scotland, 2008/09**

Percentage of households

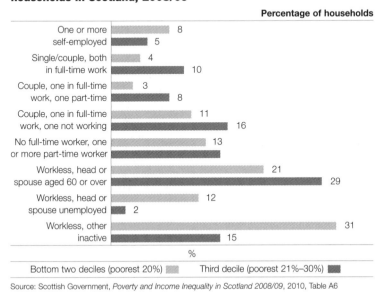

Source: Scottish Government, *Poverty and Income Inequality in Scotland 2008/09*, 2010, Table A6

ing if the same group increases its share of income by one percentage point (and total income does not fall). These targets are set against a baseline for 2006/07, when the poorest 30 per cent of individuals in Scotland shared only 14 per cent of income. Although the income share of this group has fallen since 2006/07, it has not fallen below 13 per cent and thus income inequality is not considered to have increased according to the definition set for the solidarity target.

It is also significant that the solidarity target focuses on the poorest 30 per cent in Scotland. This includes individuals who would not be defined as living in income poverty (17 per cent of all individuals using the

Table 6.1:

**Gender gap in median weekly gross earnings of full-time and part-time employees by occupational group, Scotland, 2009**

|  | Full time | | | Part time | | |
|---|---|---|---|---|---|---|
|  | Men £ | Women £ | Women as a % of men | Men £ | Women £ | Women as a % of men |
| Managers and senior officials | 753.10 | 574.90 | 76% | n/a | 264.60 | n/a |
| Professional occupations | 723.90 | 640.70 | 89% | 240.50 | 326.00 | 136 |
| Associate professional and technical | 555.90 | 508.30 | 91% | 163.50 | 256.40 | 157 |
| Administrative and secretarial | 394.80 | 349.50 | 89% | 154.20 | 179.20 | 116 |
| Skilled trade | 458.30 | 300.60 | 66% | 186.70 | 129.40 | 69 |
| Personal service | 384.80 | 335.80 | 87% | 171.00 | 180.10 | 105 |
| Sales and customer service | 304.90 | 276.20 | 91% | 115.80 | 120.80 | 104 |
| Process, plant and machine operatives | 421.70 | 321.60 | 76% | 159.60 | 155.20 | 97 |
| Elementary | 346.10 | 258.70 | 75% | 115.90 | 111.20 | 96 |
| All occupations | 509.90 | 420.30 | 82% | 143.30 | 164.20 | 115 |

Source: *Annual Survey of Hours and Earnings*, 2010, Table 3.1a, available at www.statistics.gov.uk/downloads/theme_labour/ASHE-2009/2009_gor.pdf

Note: Employees on adult rates whose pay was not affected by absence for the survey period.

before housing costs relative income poverty measure). Figure 6.4 compares the family work status profile of the poorest 20 per cent and the profile of those in the third bottom decile of the income distribution that is the additional focus of the solidarity target – ie, those between the 21 per cent and 30 per cent poorest individuals in Scotland.

In contrast to the focus on the poorest 20 per cent, the Scottish government's approach to 'income inequality' (with its focus on the poorest 30 per cent) significantly alters the target groups. More attention is paid to low-paid and older (retired and non-working) households and potentially less attention is paid to workless households, although workless households remain the largest populations to be targeted by the solidarity target.

## Gender pay gap

Income inequality is measured for households, as a whole. However, income inequality in Scotland comes in different guises. Most significant of the income inequalities that exist among the population in Scotland is the gender pay gap. Regrettably, the gender pay gap has been an ever-present feature in earlier editions of *Poverty in Scotland*.

Table 6.1 shows that women working in full-time paid employment earn just over £4 for every £5 that men earn (83 per cent of men's earnings). Expressed differently, at present levels of pay, women would need to work almost a 50-hour week to earn the same amount as men working a 40-hour week in Scotland. A significant gender pay gap for full-time workers is evident for all occupational groups, with women's pay falling to two-thirds of that of men's for skilled trades.[6] The gender pay gap is more complex for part-time workers, with inequity being less marked and some examples of women in some occupations appearing to be paid more than men.[7]

The Scottish government notes the complexities of gender pay gaps, and acknowledges that this gap is narrowing, while remaining marked – down from 12.4 per cent in 2009 to 11.9 per cent in 2010 for full-time work.[8] Through its *Gender Equality Scheme, 2008–2011*, the Scottish government has detailed a programme of action to tackle gender income inequality through equal pay and occupational desegregation.[9]

## Key drivers of change for income inequality in Scotland

### Employment opportunities

It is widely anticipated that the years ahead will be a period of flux and adjustment in the Scottish labour market with the loss of public sector jobs and a consequent structural shift away from public sector employment. In terms of greater employment opportunities challenging income inequality, all that can be said with certainty is that it is not at all clear whether the changing landscape of employment opportunities will reduce, maintain or exacerbate income inequality in the medium term.

However, at the current time and in the short term, there can be little doubt that employment opportunities will not be a major force in tackling income inequality. Seasonally adjusted unemployment in Scotland rose over the two-year period from 2008 to 2010 from 4.7 per cent to 8.7 per cent (both June–August).[10] Although there were signs that unemployment peaked for men in late 2010 (having risen from 5.1 per cent in 2008 to 10 per cent for March–May 2010, it then fell to 9.7 per cent for June–August), it continued to increase steadily for women, from 4.3 per cent in 2008 to 7.7 per cent in 2010.

### Skill development

Enhancing the skills of those traditionally at greater risk of lower income is recognised by the Scottish government as one means of tackling income inequality. In an advanced economy, one key means to achieve this is through participation in further education and higher education.

Almost 375,000 students were undertaking courses at one of Scotland's 43 colleges in 2008/09, with the vast majority of these students enrolled on programmes which led to a formally recognised qualification (94 per cent of activity).[11] More directly, there is evidence of steps being taken by the Scottish government to provide opportunities for those at greater risk of finding lower paid work to participate in further education (and hence enhance their skills). Over 4,000 extra further education places were created in 2010/11, specifically for students from Scotland's most deprived areas, by £15.3 million of joint investment from the Scottish Funding Council and European Structural Fund.[12] On the other hand, the Scottish Budget in autumn 2010 reduced funding to the Scottish Funding Council.[13]

Recent participation trends are also progressive (Table 6.2). Indeed, those from the (20 per cent) most deprived areas in Scotland are now more likely than those outside these areas to be participating in further/higher education combined. If the number 100 was given to represent the proportionate share of young people from Scotland's most deprived areas going to university or college, then the number 103 represents their actual share – ie, young people from deprived areas are slightly over-represented in post-school education in Scotland. Indeed, for further education alone, if the same number 100 was given to represent the proportionate share of young people from Scotland's most deprived areas going to college, then the number 143 represents their actual share – ie, young people from deprived areas are significantly over-represented in Scotland's colleges. The increase in participation of teenage students from the (20 per cent) most deprived areas has been marked in recent years.[14]

However, although trends are 'progressive', these are unlikely to impact on income inequality by 2017 to any significant degree. First and foremost, participation rates of students from Scotland's (20 per cent) most deprived areas remain much lower in higher education, rising to only 64 students per 100 students from non-deprived areas in 2008/09 from 60 students in 2004/05. Indeed, given that graduating from higher education is likely to bring greater lifetime financial rewards than graduating from further education, current participation levels may merely serve to perpetuate existing patterns of income inequality.

Second, there are significant variations across Scotland, some of which are reported in Table 6.2 for 2008/09. For example, while in Angus 86 students from the district's (20 per cent) most deprived areas participate in higher education for every 100 students that should have attended if children from deprived areas were represented in equal proportion, in Stirling there are only 38 students from the district's (20 per cent) most deprived areas for every 100 students that would have been expected to attend if children from deprived areas were represented in equal proportion.

Third, a comparison of headcount and full-time equivalent data suggest that students from the (20 per cent) most deprived areas tend to spend more time in further education studies and less time in higher education studies.

Fourth, trends for higher education are only 'relatively' progressive – ie, participation in higher education peaked at 37.5 students per 1,000 population in Scotland's (20 per cent) most deprived areas in 2005/06

Table 6.2:

## Participation in further and higher education in Scotland, by deprived area status, 2004/05 to 2008/09

| | Ratio of most to least deprived | | | | |
| --- | --- | --- | --- | --- | --- |
| | 2004/05 | 2005/06 | 2006/07 | 2007/08 | 2008/09 |
| **Participation in further and high education** | | | | | |
| Scotland, FTE | - | 0.87 | 0.89 | 0.92 | 0.96 |
| Scotland, headcount | 0.92 | 0.93 | 0.97 | 1.01 | 1.03 |
| Scottish Borders, headcount | - | - | - | - | 1.18 |
| Angus, headcount | - | - | - | - | 1.33 |
| Aberdeenshire, headcount | - | - | - | - | 1.17 |
| Stirling, headcount | - | - | - | - | 0.81 |
| East Renfrewshire, headcount | - | - | - | - | 0.80 |
| **Participation in further education** | | | | | |
| Scotland, FTE | - | 1.60 | 1.62 | 1.68 | 1.75 |
| Scotland, headcount | 1.24 | 1.27 | 1.32 | 1.38 | 1.43 |
| Edinburgh, headcount | - | - | - | - | 1.83 |
| Scottish Borders, headcount | - | - | - | - | 1.82 |
| Aberdeen City, headcount | - | - | - | - | 1.79 |
| West Dunbartonshire, headcount | - | - | - | - | 1.12 |
| Clackmannanshire, headcount | - | - | - | - | 1.10 |
| North Lanarkshire, headcount | - | - | - | - | 1.08 |
| **Participation in higher education** | | | | | |
| Scotland, headcount | 0.60 | 0.61 | 0.61 | 0.63 | 0.64 |
| Angus, headcount | - | - | - | - | 0.86 |
| Perth and Kinross, headcount | - | - | - | - | 0.79 |
| Renfrewshire, headcount | - | - | - | - | 0.75 |
| East Dunbartonshire, headcount | - | - | - | - | 0.51 |
| Glasgow, headcount | - | - | - | - | 0.50 |
| Stirling, headcount | - | - | - | - | 0.38 |

Source: Scottish Funding Council, *Scottish Participation in Further and Higher Education, 2004/05 to 2008/09*, 2010, Tables 2.4.1, 2.4.2, 2.4.3, 3.6.1, 3.6.2, 3.6.3, 4.6.1 and 4.6.2

Notes:
Headcount = the number of students.
FTE = full-time equivalent students.
Both measures are important and necessary as not all students attend on a full-time basis.

(estimates for 2008/09 were 37.2 students per 1,000 population). The trend is 'progressive' only as a result of participation of students from Scotland's least deprived areas falling at a greater rate in recent years (from 62.5 per 1,000 in 2004/05 to 57.9 per 1,000 in 2008/09).[15]

## Occupational pay gaps

Providing opportunities to work and enhancing the skills that will increase the chances of finding work (and finding better paid work) will only impact on income inequality if work is sufficiently well paid. At present, work does not pay well for everyone. Table 6.1 has already demonstrated that women in full-time employment are less well paid than men. This table also highlights the scale of the differences in typical pay across occupational groups. For example, men working in 'sales and customer service' in Scotland are typically paid £306 per week; men in 'professional occupations' are paid more than double this amount (£719 per week). Incidentally, the typical weekly pay for a man in 'sales and customer service' is well below the poverty threshold for a couple with two children aged five and 11 (Table 3.2). Such families would be reliant either on the state to lift them out of poverty (eg, through child benefit or tax credits) or on a second household income.

In recent years, public ire at variations in occupational pay has increasingly been directed at executive-level pay and the excessive financial packages that stretch pay inequality by increasing pay at the upper extreme. However, there has also been growing recognition among the anti-poverty sector that low pay is a significant problem in its own right. The Scottish Living Wage Campaign seeks to address this problem and presents evidence that (in 2008) over 370,000 workers in Scotland were low paid, 43 per cent of low-paid workers were women in part-time jobs, while young men in full-time jobs were more likely than young women in full-time jobs to be low paid.[16]

A 'living wage' in 2010 was defined as £7.15 per hour. The Scottish government's own analysis on the impact of introducing a 'living wage' for low-paid workers in the public sector suggests that it would 'not have a significant impact on the proportion of income accruing to households in the bottom three income deciles'.[17] However, while it is estimated that raising the amount of the national minimum wage (from October 2010, £5.93 per hour for workers aged 21 and over and £4.92 per hour for those aged 18–20) to a living wage (£7.15 per hour in 2010[18]) would increase the take-home pay of a lone parent with a child aged under five living in local authority accommodation by 'only' 5 per cent, it could be argued that 'only' 5 per cent would be a significant increase for these households. In other words, this same data suggests that significant increases in income for those earning the least would accrue from a living wage.

Tangible steps have been taken to tackle low pay in Scotland in recent years. The longstanding agreement to commit to gender pay equality (through single status) has been followed in Scottish local government by practical steps to revalue competencies previously undervalued through job evaluation, although there are concerns that this is too often done on the basis of 'levelling down' rather than 'levelling up'.[19] Announcements in the Scottish Budget of autumn 2010 of the government's intention to freeze public sector pay were also tempered with some measures in place to protect the incomes of the lowest paid.[20]

Although far from welcome, the current financial climate seems to afford an opportunity to make tentative steps toward greater equality in pay. Regrettably, this may only be achieved by maintaining the income of the lowest paid and allowing the income of middle-to-high earners (on aggregate) to fall. Whether these adjustments will be sustained as the economy recovers is less clear. It may be more of a temporary austerity measure, rather than a concerted attempt to rebalance the value of underpaid work to ensure a future Scotland with less income inequality.

## Welfare benefit entitlement and take-up

The UK White Paper of November 2010 that gave notice of the Welfare Reform Bill outlined proposals for far-reaching changes to the welfare benefits system.[21] The changes that were proposed were not well received by anti-poverty campaigners, coming as they did on the back of Budget and Comprehensive Spending Review cuts to the social security budget totalling £18 billion. Notwithstanding the difficulties these changes will present to the most financially vulnerable, the government suggests that proposed simplifications to the benefits system could offer the means to tackle one of the most persistent and perplexing problems that exacerbates income inequality – low take-up of welfare benefits.

The Department for Work and Pensions (DWP) estimates that, for the UK as a whole, there was between £6,930 million and £12,700 million worth of unclaimed income-related benefits in 2008/09, a take-up rate of between 75 per cent and 85 per cent. Despite many local initiatives to increase take-up, the DWP's lower estimate suggests that take-up may have fallen from 77 per cent in 2007/08 to 75 per cent in 2008/09.[22]

Scotland is not immune from this low take-up. The same DWP estimates suggest that Scotland's share of entitled non-recipients of income-related benefits in Great Britain is 10 per cent for income support/income-related employment and support allowance, 8 per cent for both pension credit and council tax benefit, 7 per cent for housing benefit and 6 per cent for jobseeker's allowance. Although, on the whole, take-up is higher in Scotland than in other parts of Britain (for all but income support and income-related employment and support allowance), Scotland's share of entitled non-recipients of income-related benefits is lower than its share of entitled recipients. Clearly, there is still a significant problem of non-take-up of welfare benefits in Scotland. This, along with the low financial value of benefits to which people are entitled, is undoubtedly exacerbating income inequality.

## Conclusion

Income inequality has been a persistent problem in Scotland. There is no sign of this inequality lessening and no convincing evidence that, without significant policy shifts to address low pay, skills gaps, welfare adequacy and benefit take-up, the key drivers of change will lead to a significant reduction in income inequality in the years ahead. However, even in a time of overall pay restraint and labour market 'restructuring', it may be possible to make progress against the solidarity purpose target if sufficient attention is paid to protecting and increasing the relative share of overall pay, and wider income distribution, of those in the bottom three deciles.

### Notes

1  See www.scotland.gov.uk/about/scotperforms/purposes/solidarity
2  See note 1
3  Strictly speaking for 'income inequality' in the UK, reference to the 'poorest tenth' refers to the 10% of households with the lowest household income. As this data has not been equivalised, a degree of caution is required in interpretation.
4  Note that this comparison used Scottish government data and compares it with Eurostat data.
5  See www.scotland.gov.uk/topics/statistics/browse/social-welfare/incomepov erty/poverty-analysis-0809

6   Caution is required with this statistic, given that it is based on a low number of women providing income data.

7   There is a need for cautious interpretation of this data with low returns for all occupational groupings.

8   Scottish Government, *Equal Pay/Closing the Gender Pay Gap*, available at www.scotland.gov.uk/topics/people/equality/18500/13414

9   Scottish Government, *Gender Equality Scheme, 2008–2011*, 2008

10  Office for National Statistics, *Regional Labour Market Summary: seasonally adjusted*, 2010, Webtable 18sa, available at www.statistics.gov.uk/statbase/product.asp?vlnk=8281

11  Scottish Further and Higher Education Funding Council, *Scotland's Colleges: a baseline report March 2010*, 2010, p4

12  Scottish Government, 'College places for 4,000', Press Release, 20 March 2010, available at www.scotland.gov.uk/news/releases/2010/03/22085412

13  See www.scotland.gov.uk/news/releases/2010/11/17080954

14  Scottish Funding Council, *Scottish Participation in Further and Higher Education 2004/05 to 2008/09*, 2010, Table 3.6.2

15  See note 14, Table 4.6.1

16  See http://povertyalliance.org/slw-home.asp

17  Scottish Government, *Low Pay and Income Inequality in Scotland: a living wage*, 2010

18  The Scottish Government analysis was undertaken when the 'living wage' was estimated at £7 per hour, prior to its uprating to £7.15.

19  D Watson, C Judge and P Hunter, *Single Status and Equal Pay in Local Government*, MSP Briefing 124, Unison,

20  See note 13

21  Department for Work and Pensions, *Universal Credit: welfare that works*, Cmnd 7957, The Stationery Office, 2010, available at www.dwp.gov.uk/docs/universal-credit-full-document.pdf

22  Department for Work and Pensions, *Income-related Benefit Estimates of Take-up in 2008–09*, 2010

# Seven
# Who lives in poverty?
*John H McKendrick*

## Summary

- Children are at significantly greater risk of poverty than either working-age adults or pensioners, with more than one in four of Scotland's children growing up in poverty in 2008/09 (26 per cent), compared with 19 per cent of working-age adults and 11 per cent of pensioners.
- Since 1994/95, Scotland has experienced little change in the overall number of adults of working age who are living in poverty. After housing costs, the *number* has actually risen by 40,000 (7 per cent), although the *risk* of poverty is only 1 per cent higher than in 1994/95 due to population increase.
- Lone parents are more than twice as likely to be living in poverty compared with couples with children.
- Gender-based poverty is most marked among people of pensionable age – 17 per cent of Scotland's female pensioners are living in poverty.
- Poverty is unevenly distributed across Scotland. The highest numbers of people living in poverty are found in Scotland's largest cities, although poverty and household income deprivation are also prevalent in rural Scotland.

This chapter identifies which groups are at particular risk of poverty in Scotland. The risks of poverty are not spread evenly and, as was discussed in Chapter 4, there are many causes of poverty, some of which impact more strongly on particular groups.

Poverty varies across the lifecycle, by family and household type, by social status and according to where we live. The distribution of poverty across each of these four domains is considered for different groups of the population. Children, youth, working-age adults and pensioners are considered for the *lifecycle*; lone parents, partnered parents and childless adults are considered for *families and households*; work status, gender, ethnicity and disability are considered for *social status*; and local authorities and urban/rural areas are considered for *place*. The aim of the chapter is to provide information on the likelihood of living in poverty among different groups (risk rate) and on how much of Scotland's poverty is experienced by these groups (poverty composition).

It is important to remember that no group is homogenous and that real people share characteristics across these groupings that may increase or reduce the amount of poverty that they encounter. For example, although children in lone-parent households are, on the whole, at greater risk of experiencing poverty than children in two-parent households (50 per cent of children in lone-parent households are living in poverty, compared with 24 per cent of children in two-parent households – see Table 7.2),[1] the risk rate of a child experiencing poverty is far lower in a lone-parent household in which the lone parent works full time, than it is in a couple household in which both adults do not work and the head of household is unemployed (21 per cent, compared with 75 per cent – see Table 7.2). Similarly, it must also be understood that belonging to one of the groups with a higher at-risk rate of poverty does not in itself cause poverty. As Chapter 4 explained, poverty is caused by the interaction of political, social, economic and personal factors. However, some groups in Scotland are at greater risk of poverty, and this chapter aims to provide key information on these variations.

Where possible, this chapter uses the Scottish government's analysis of the *Households Below Average Income* (HBAI) data series. This provides a measure of income poverty for children, working-age adults and pensioners in Scotland.[2] More limited data on child poverty and disability is also drawn from the analysis undertaken by the Scottish government in the autumn of 2010 to inform the child poverty consultation.[3] Where there is an absence of readily available data for Scotland, reference is made to the original HBAI data for the UK to describe variation within groups – eg, to identify which groups of children are at greatest risk of experiencing poverty in Scotland.[4] Although using UK data to understand poverty in Scotland is not unproblematic, commentary is limited to that data which is considered to provide insight into poverty in Scotland. Finally, reference is also made to more broadly based measures of area multiple deprivation in Scotland. Once again, this data is used carefully, as it does not strictly describe poverty, but rather communities with high levels of household deprivation.

## Poverty across the lifecycle

### Overview

Projections over the next 25 years suggest that the population of Scotland will rise (to just over 5.54 million in 2033). Thereafter, the population is projected to continue rising through until 2048 (5.57 million), before slowly declining to 5.52 million by 2078.[5] This projected growth will reflect an excess of births over deaths through until 2026 and a net in-migration flow, with more people migrating to Scotland, than emigrating from it.

The number of people of working age is expected to increase to 2018 (3.36 million), before falling back to a level in 2033 that is just 2 per cent higher than in 2008 (3.31 million in 2033, compared with 3.24 million in 2008). There will be similar trends for children, with their number rising from 910,000 in 2008 to 920,000 in 2018, before falling steadily to 900,000 in 2033. In contrast, there will be a steady increase in the number of people of pensionable age (from 1.02 million in 2008 to 1.34 million in 2033).

People's risk of poverty and the particular barriers to escaping that poverty vary considerably over the lifecycle (Table 7.1). Although children are at the highest risk of poverty, there are particular problems associated with each age stage. Many young people continue to face particular disadvantage through exclusion from education, employment or training after school. Least progress has been made in reducing poverty among working-age adults, while the progress in tackling pensioner poverty may be undermined by the value of pensions in the years ahead. However, we should avoid over-simplifying poverty to simple statements of particular challenges to be faced at a set of discrete life stages – experience of poverty at one stage in the lifecycle can also have a significant impact on an individual's risk of poverty later on.

Table 7.1 illustrates that the most marked reductions in poverty in Scotland are for pensioners, while significant, although less dramatic, reductions are also evident for children. On the other hand, over the same period, there has been no significant change in the risk of poverty among working-age adults. These figures demonstrate the impact that policy interventions can have on rates of poverty; while children and pensioners have benefited from governments' anti-poverty targets and strategies, those of working age have not.

Table 7.1:

**Age-based variation in populations living in households with below 60 per cent UK median income (after housing costs), including self-employed, Scotland, 1994/95 to 2008/09**

| Year | Children | Working-age adults | Pensioners | All individuals |
|------|----------|--------------------|------------|-----------------|
|      | %        | %                  | %          | %               |
| 1994/95 | 30 | 18 | 29 | 23 |
| 1995/96 | 32 | 18 | 31 | 23 |
| 1996/97 | 33 | 19 | 33 | 25 |
| 1997/98 | 31 | 18 | 28 | 22 |
| 1998/99 | 31 | 19 | 27 | 23 |
| 1999/00 | 32 | 20 | 28 | 24 |
| 2000/01 | 32 | 22 | 25 | 24 |
| 2001/02 | 31 | 19 | 24 | 22 |
| 2002/03 | 27 | 20 | 25 | 23 |
| 2003/04 | 27 | 18 | 21 | 21 |
| 2004/05 | 25 | 18 | 16 | 19 |
| 2005/06 | 24 | 19 | 16 | 20 |
| 2006/07 | 25 | 18 | 15 | 19 |
| 2007/08 | 24 | 19 | 16 | 19 |
| 2008/09 | 26 | 19 | 11 | 19 |

Source: Scottish Government, *Poverty and Income Inequality in Scotland, 2008/09*, 2010, Table A1

Note: Figures are derived from the *Family Resources Survey*. The modified OECD equivalisation scales have been used in the calculations and the figures refer to income after housing costs.

## Children

Despite significant improvements over time that were discussed in Chapter 5, children are still at significantly greater risk of poverty than either working-age adults or pensioners, with more than one in four of Scotland's children growing up in poverty in 2008/09 (26 per cent), compared with 19 per cent of working-age adults and 11 per cent of pensioners (Table 7.1).

However as Table 7.2 shows, the risk of children experiencing poverty in the UK varies hugely on account of family type, number of siblings, the work status of parents or carers, and the age of the youngest

Table 7.2:

**Variation among children in measures of living in households with below 60 per cent median income (after housing costs), UK, 2008/09**

| | Risk rate | Composition of children in low-income households |
|---|---|---|
| | % | % |
| **Family type** | | |
| Lone parent | 50 | 40 |
| Couple | 24 | 60 |
| **Family type and work status** | | |
| Lone parent, in full-time work | 21 | 4 |
| Lone parent, in part-time work | 29 | 6 |
| Lone parent, not working | 75 | 29 |
| Couple, one or more self-employed | 30 | 11 |
| Couple, both in full-time work | 3 | 1 |
| Couple, one in full-time work, one in part-time work | 7 | 5 |
| Couple, one in full-time work, one not working | 29 | 18 |
| Couple, one or more in part-time work | 60 | 11 |
| Couple, both not in work | 75 | 14 |
| **Number of children in household** | | |
| 1 | 27 | 25 |
| 2 | 27 | 40 |
| 3 or more | 40 | 35 |
| **Age of youngest child in household** | | |
| Under 5 | 34 | 49 |
| 5–10 | 28 | 27 |
| 11–15 | 29 | 20 |
| 16–18 | 21 | 4 |

Source: Department for Work and Pensions, *Households Below Average Income, 2008/09*, Corporate Document Services, 2010, Tables 4.3-4.6.

child. Risk rates are particularly high in lone-parent households (50 per cent), particularly when that lone parent is not working (75 per cent), in couple households with part-time (but not full-time) work (60 per cent), in couple households in which no one works (75 per cent) and in households with three or more children (40 per cent).

Higher risks of poverty need to be understood in the context of the overall numbers of children experiencing poverty in the UK. Thus, it also important to note that more than one-half of children in poverty live in households in which an adult is working (57 per cent of children experiencing poverty); most children experience poverty in households headed by a couple (60 per cent); and most child poverty is found in households with either one or two children (65 per cent) (Table 7.2). Indeed, it is only when households are classified according to the age of youngest child that the risk rate and proportionate share of children experiencing poverty coincide – poverty is clearly more likely to be a characteristic feature of households with very young children (Table 7.2).

## Young adults

As poverty data tends to be collected at the level of the household, as opposed to the individual, young people's poverty is often concealed by household circumstances. Disentangling young people's circumstances from household circumstances is intriguing. For example, while some young people must remain in the parental home because they cannot afford to move, others whose personal income may be adequate, may be classified as living in poverty on account of their parents' or carers' circumstances.

The primary focus of government concern over young people and poverty is to reduce the numbers who are described as being not in education, employment or training (NEET), or the 'more choices, more chances' (MC2) group as they are known in Scotland. Figure 7.1 shows that following a steady increase in the MC2 group from 1997 to 2001, a downward trend from 2001 to 2008. However, ominously, the proportion of Scotland's 16–19-year-olds who are not in education, training or employment rose sharply between 2008 and 2009.

## Working-age adults

Adults of working age in contemporary Scotland are no less likely to be living in poverty than their counterparts in the mid-1990s (Table 7.1). As for children, risk rates vary among adults of working age and risk rates are higher in the UK among the youngest adults – 27 per cent of adults without children and 61 per cent of adults with children aged under 25 years of age are living in poverty (Table 7.3).

Figure 7.1:

**16–19-year-olds not in education, employment or training,
Scotland, 1996 to 2009**

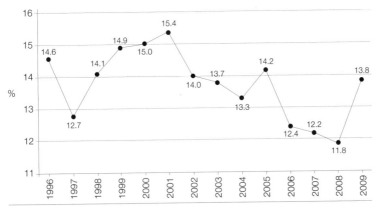

Source for 2004–2009: Scottish Government, drawn from *Annual Population Survey*, Table 4.1. Data for
1996–2002 is drawn from the *Labour Force Survey*. Data for 2003 is drawn from the *Annual Scottish Labour
Force Survey* (Scottish booster to *Labour Force Survey*). Data from 2004 is drawn from the new integrated
*Annual Population Survey*.

Table 7.3 also shows that being a parent – particularly being a lone parent
– and being in a household with less work, is associated with living in
poverty for adults of working age in the UK (48 per cent of lone parents).
These conclusions are predictable, but the proportion of workless working-age adults at risk is notable; two-thirds of households with unemployed adults are living in poverty (68 per cent).

Yet, once again, we must guard against reducing our understanding
of poverty in the UK to the most at-risk groups. More than half of working-
age adults living in poverty are from households without children (57 per
cent), and more than half are living as a couple (52 per cent) either with children (31 per cent) or without children (21 per cent). One-half of working-age
adults living in poverty live in households in which at least one adult works
(52 per cent). Similarly, working-age adult poverty is not limited to youth;
almost one-quarter of all working-age adults living in poverty are in their 40s
(23 per cent) and almost one-quarter are in their 50s or older (24 per cent).

Table 7.3:

## Variation among working-age adults in measures of living in households with below 60 per cent median income (after housing costs), UK, 2008/09

|  | Risk rate | Composition |
|---|---|---|
|  | % | % |
| **Presence of children in household** | | |
| None | 19 | 57 |
| Some | 26 | 43 |
| **Household composition** | | |
| Couple, no children | 13 | 21 |
| Lone man, no children | 26 | 22 |
| Lone woman, no children | 27 | 14 |
| Couple, with children | 22 | 31 |
| Lone parent | 48 | 12 |
| **Family type and work status** | | |
| Single/couple, one or more full-time self-employed | 23 | 11 |
| Single/couple, both in full-time work | 5 | 8 |
| Couple, one in full-time work, one in part-time work | 6 | 4 |
| Couple, one in full-time work, one not working | 24 | 14 |
| Single/couple, no full-time, one or more in part-time work | 35 | 16 |
| Workless, one or more aged over 60 | 34 | 4 |
| Workless, one or more unemployed | 68 | 13 |
| Workless, other inactive | 57 | 31 |

| Age of adult | without children | with children | without children | with children |
|---|---|---|---|---|
| 16–19 | 30 | 61 | 6 | 6 |
| 20–24 | 24 | – | 11 | – |
| 25–29 | 15 | 32 | 5 | 5 |
| 30–34 | 14 | 26 | 3 | 6 |
| 35–39 | 16 | 24 | 3 | 9 |
| 40–44 | 19 | 23 | 4 | 9 |
| 45–49 | 17 | 18 | 5 | 5 |
| 50–54 | 17 | 22 | 6 | 3 |
| 55 and over | 19 | 27 | 13 | 2 |

Source: Department for Work and Pensions, *Households Below Average Income, 2008/09*, Corporate Document Services, 2010, Tables 5.4, 5.5, 5.7 and 5.8

Notes:
1. Figures are derived from the *Family Resources Survey*.
2. The modified OECD equivalisation scales have been used in the calculations and the figures refer to income after housing costs.

## Pensioners

In the five years between 1996/97 and 2001/02, Scotland experienced a significant reduction in the number of pensioners living in poverty. Current data suggests that there has been another marked reduction in the number of pensioners living in poverty between 2007/08 and 2008/09. Indeed, the latest data from the Scottish government suggests that pensioners are now less likely than adults of working age to experience poverty in Scotland (Table 7.1).

## Families and households

### Overview

In addition to demographic population change, social changes also alter the shape of the households in which we live. Among the most significant socio-population changes over the last few decades have been: a decrease in family size; a decline in the number of couples who marry; more children being born outside marriage, the majority to cohabiting couples; an increased divorce rate; and growth in the number of lone-parent households.

The number of adults living on their own in Scotland is expected to increase by almost 50 per cent from 840,790 in 2008 (36 per cent of all households) to over 1.25 million by 2033 (45 per cent of all households). The number of lone-parent households is also projected to rise from 162,880 households in 2008 to over 237,680 households in 2033, while households containing two or more adults with children is expected to fall from 433,420 (19 per cent of all households) in 2008 to 314,970 in 2033 (11 per cent).[6]

### Lone parents

The routes into lone parenthood are many and the characteristics of lone-parent families are varied. There are more than 160,000 lone parents with dependent children in Scotland, more than one-quarter of all family households (27.3 per cent).[7] However, lone parenthood is often not a permanent status, but is rather a stage in family life lasting on average around five and a half years.[8] It has been estimated that one-third to one-half of all children in Scotland will spend some time in a lone-parent family.[9] The vast majority of lone parents are women (confirming common understanding), but often the reality of lone parenthood is at odds with some popular perceptions, with most lone parents having previously been married and the median age of lone parents being 36 (contrasting the image of lone parents as single young mums).[10] At any point in time, less than 3 per cent of lone parents are teenagers and only 15 per cent have never lived with the father of their child.[11]

Lone parents are disproportionately represented among families experiencing poverty in the UK. They are more than twice as likely to be poor compared with couples with children (Table 7.3). One-half of lone-parent households are living in poverty (48 per cent). Indeed, Scottish-level data suggests that the risk of poverty in lone-parent households might even be greater than the HBAI data suggests for the UK.[12] The Scottish government's recent analysis of relative poverty across Scottish local authorities estimated, using before housing costs data, that 41 per cent of lone-parent households were living in relative poverty, compared with 12 per cent of small two-parent family households and 14 per cent of large two-parent family households. In this analysis, lone-parent households had the highest risk of poverty among all household types (the risk rate for single-pensioner households was 36 per cent and it was 24 per cent for single-adult households).

## Partnered parents

Although lone-parent households are more likely to experience poverty (Table 7.3), the poverty experienced in two-parent households must not be overlooked. For example, poverty is experienced in one in every five two-parent households in the UK (Table 7.3). Furthermore, almost one-third of the adults living in poverty in the UK are from two-parent households (31 per cent) – approaching three times the number of adults living in poverty in lone-parent households (12 per cent) (Table 7.3). Thus, although the risk rate of poverty is higher for lone parenthood, there is more poverty in two-parent households in the UK.

## Social status

Patterns of poverty are not only determined by the stage in life which we are at, or our family status. Cross-cutting these factors are a range of social factors, which are associated with the likelihood of living in poverty. Significant here is the impact of work status, gender, ethnicity and disability.

## Workers/non-workers

Those in work in the UK are less likely to face poverty. Unsurprisingly, the risk of poverty is lower for households which are 'work-rich' (all adults working) than for households which are 'work-poor' (no-earner couples or for couples where part-time work is the only experience) (Table 7.3). Half of the households with adults of working age who are living in poverty are without work (48 per cent), with the risk rate of poverty being even more marked (at 68 per cent) for households in which the head of the household is unemployed (Table 7.3). However, these observations should not be taken to imply that poverty is absent from households with work. After all, half of adults of working age who are living in poverty in the UK are from households with work (52 per cent). This poverty is spread across a range of household types (defined by work status), with a significant proportion of 'all households in poverty made up of adults of working age' being of the self-employed (11 per cent); where one of a couple is working full time and the other is not working (14 per cent); and where no one is engaged in full-time work, but one or more adults is engaged in part-time work (16 per cent). It is also significant to note that a number of adults experiencing poverty in the UK reside in households in which all adults are engaged in full-time work (8 per cent). Adult poverty is not solely a result of worklessness (entry into the labour market does not guarantee a route out of poverty).

## Gender

In the UK, more women live in poverty than men, with a greater difference in the risk rate between men and women evident in the later years (Table 7.4); women of pensionable age are more likely than men of pensionable age to live in poverty (17 per cent, compared with 14 per cent). The difference in risk rate between men and women (Table 7.4), allied to the fact

Table 7.4:

**Gender variation in living in households with below 60 per cent of median income (after housing costs), UK, 2008/09**

|  | Risk rate | Composition of low-income households |
|---|---|---|
|  | % | % |
| **Adults by gender and children, individuals** | | |
| Men | 19 | 33 |
| Women | 21 | 38 |
| Children | 30 | 29 |
| **Pensioners, individuals** | | |
| Men | 14 | 33 |
| Women | 17 | 67 |

Source: Department for Work and Pensions, *Households Below Average Income, 2008/09*, Corporate Document Services, 2010, Tables 3.3, 3.5, 6.3 and 6.5

Notes:
1. Figures are derived from the *Family Resources Survey*.
2. The modified OECD equivalisation scales have been used in the calculations and the figures refer to income after housing costs.

that women live to a longer age than men, come together to create a situation where women comprise two-thirds of people of pensionable age who live in poverty in the UK (Table 7.4). For far too many women, later life is one that is characterised by poverty.

## Disability

As Table 7.5 shows, in the UK, the risk rate of poverty is broadly comparable between disabled pensioners and non-disabled pensioners (15 per cent, compared with 17 per cent). Indeed, the risk rate of poverty is greater among non-disabled pensioners than disabled pensioners. In contrast, disability is associated with a higher risk of poverty among children (36 per cent of disabled children, compared with 30 per cent of non-disabled children) and adults of working age (33 per cent, compared with 20 per cent of non-disabled adults).

Scottish government analysis of the HBAI dataset demonstrates that disability increases children's risk of poverty.[13] Based on a before

Table 7.5:

**Variation by disability in living in households with below 60 per cent of median income (after housing costs), UK, 2008/09**

|  | Risk rate | Composition of low-income households |
|---|---|---|
|  | % | % |
| **Disability, whole population (by age stage)** | | |
| Disabled children | 36 | 2 |
| Disabled working-age adults | 33 | 12 |
| Disabled pensioners | 15 | 8 |
| Non-disabled children | 30 | 27 |
| Non-disabled working-age adults | 20 | 45 |
| Non-disabled pensioners | 17 | 8 |
| **Disability, children (by household composition)** | | |
| No disabled adults, no disabled child | 28 | 71 |
| No disabled adults, 1 or more disabled child | 35 | 8 |
| 1 or more disabled adults, no disabled child | 40 | 16 |
| 1 or more disabled adults, 1 or more disabled child | 42 | 6 |
| **Disability, adults of working age (by household composition)** | | |
| No disabled adults, no disabled child | 19 | 71 |
| No disabled adults, 1 or more disabled child | 28 | 3 |
| 1 or more disabled adults, no disabled child | 29 | 25 |
| 1 or more disabled adults, 1 or more disabled child | 38 | 2 |
| **Disability, pensioners (by household composition)** | | |
| No disabled pensioners | 17 | 47 |
| 1 or more disabled pensioners | 15 | 53 |

Source: Department for Work and Pensions, *Households Below Average Income, 2008/09*, Corporate Document Services, 2010, Tables 3.3, 3.5, 4.3, 4.5, 5.6, 5.9, 6.3 and 6.5

Notes:
1. Figures are derived from the *Family Resources Survey*.
2. The modified OECD equivalisation scales have been used in the calculations and the figures refer to income after housing costs.

housing costs analysis, more than one in three children who live with a disabled adult in Scotland live in poverty (35 per cent, compared with 19 per cent of children who do not live with a disabled adult). Similarly, one in four families with disabled children in Scotland live in poverty (26 per cent, compared with 19 per cent of families with non-disabled children).

## Ethnicity

Information about minority ethnic populations in Scotland is still scarce. The paucity of data is significant, particularly given the small numbers of minority ethnic populations in Scotland and the very different histories of ethnic integration and immigration in Scotland and the rest of the UK. To ensure that the sample size is sufficient to make robust estimates in Scotland would require the use of minority ethnic groupings that lack cultural coherency and the use of longer time-series data to verify accuracy. Scottish government analysis shows that the risk of poverty was greater among minority ethnic groups from 2002/03 to 2008/09.[14] Compared with 21 per cent of children from White ethnic groups, the risk of poverty was 40 per cent for children in Asian households and 34 per cent for children in households of 'Other ethnic groups'.

Data on the risk rate of poverty and composition of people experiencing poverty by ethnic background is available for the UK. Here, we find a higher risk rate of poverty among those of minority ethnic origin at each life stage (Table 7.6). For example, pensioners who are of minority ethnic origin are much more likely to be living in poverty, compared with those of White ethnic origin (49 per cent for Bangladeshi/Pakistani pensioners, compared with 17 per cent). However, it is important not to over-generalise the experience of poverty among minority ethnic groups. Half of adults of working age (56 per cent) and two-thirds of children (66 per cent) of Pakistani/Bangladeshi ethnic origin are living in poverty, compared with around one-quarter of adults of working age (26 per cent) and one-third of children (36 per cent) of Indian ethnic origin. Furthermore, given the very different histories and scale of minority ethnic immigration to Scotland, it cannot be assumed that these UK patterns pertain to Scotland.

## Place

## Local authorities

Glasgow has more than its fair share of Scotland's poverty (Table 7.7). One-quarter of households in Glasgow were judged to be income deprived in the last *Scottish Index of Multiple Deprivation* (25.7 per cent) and a similar proportion of the city's households were judged to be living in poverty when

Table 7.6:

## Variation by ethnic group in living in households with below 60 per cent of median income, after housing costs, UK, 2008/09

| | Risk rate | Composition by ethnic group in low-income households |
|---|---|---|
| | % | % |
| **Whole population (ethnicity based on adult head of household)** | | |
| White | 20 | 82 |
| Mixed | 35 | 1 |
| Asian or Asian British | 43 | 9 |
| *Of which, Indian* | *(29)* | *(3)* |
| *Of which, Pakistani/Bangladeshi* | *(60)* | *(5)* |
| Black or Black British | 41 | 5 |
| Chinese or other ethnic group | 37 | 2 |
| **Children (ethnicity based on adult head of household)** | | |
| White | 27 | 77 |
| Mixed | 41 | 1 |
| Asian or Asian British | 54 | 12 |
| *Of which, Indian* | *(36)* | *(3)* |
| *Of which, Pakistani/Bangladeshi* | *(66)* | *(8)* |
| Black or Black British | 50 | 6 |
| Chinese or other ethnic group | 46 | 2 |
| **Adults of working age (ethnicity based on adult head of household)** | | |
| White | 19 | 82 |
| Mixed | 34 | 1 |
| Asian or Asian British | 39 | 9 |
| *Of which, Indian* | *(26)* | *(3)* |
| *Of which, Pakistani/Bangladeshi* | *(56)* | *(5)* |
| Black or Black British | 37 | 5 |
| Chinese or other ethnic group | 34 | 3 |
| **Pensioners** | | |
| White | 17 | 93 |
| Mixed | – | 0 |
| Asian or Asian British | 35 | 3 |
| *Of which, Indian* | *(31)* | *(2)* |
| *Of which, Pakistani/Bangladeshi* | *(49)* | *(2)* |
| Black or Black British | 31 | 2 |
| Chinese or other ethnic group | 30 | 1 |

Source: Department for Work and Pensions, *Households Below Average Income, 2008/09*, Corporate Document Services, 2010, Tables 3.3, 3.5, 4.3, 4.5, 5.5, 5.8, 6.3 and 6.5

Notes:
1. Figures are derived from the *Family Resources Survey*.
2. The modified OECD equivalisation scales have been used in the calculations and the figures refer to income after housing costs.
3. The data is based on three-year averages.

the Scottish government used the *Scottish Household Survey* to estimate local rates of poverty in Scotland (23 per cent).[15] The more broadly based idea of multiple deprivation also shows that Glasgow's problems are highly concentrated; approaching one-half of small areas in Glasgow are found to be among the 15 per cent most deprived areas in Scotland (43.5 per cent), with almost one-quarter of small areas in Glasgow being among the 5 per cent most deprived areas in Scotland (22.8 per cent). Almost one in three of Scotland's most deprived areas are found in Glasgow alone (30.9 per cent). Although there has been a significant reduction in Glasgow's share of the area deprivation concentration since 2004, Glasgow still has a disproportionate share of Scotland's most deprived areas.

Although poverty and deprivation is most prevalent in the City of Glasgow, Glasgow's neighbouring authorities of West Dunbartonshire, Inverclyde, North Lanarkshire, Renfrewshire and South Lanarkshire are among those in Scotland with the highest rates of income poverty and household poverty. Further exacerbating West Coast poverty are the high rates of poverty evident in North and East Ayrshire. Clackmannanshire and the City of Dundee are the only local authorities from the east coast of Scotland to feature prominently in the 'league table' of the local authorities with more of Scotland's poverty and income deprivation.

It is important to identify the parts of Scotland in which rates of poverty are most prevalent. However, sight must not be lost of local authorities with better than average rates of poverty, but in which reside sizeable numbers of people living in poverty.[16] For example, more people are income deprived in Edinburgh (55,900) and Fife (51,450) than in every other authority in Scotland except for Glasgow and North Lanarkshire. The City of Aberdeen and Highland are also authorities with relatively favourable rates of poverty and income deprivation, but high numbers of people experiencing these conditions – eg, with 22,170 and 27,250, respectively, of income-deprived people living in these areas.

The over-concentration of Scotland's most deprived areas in the City of Glasgow (referred to previously) also results in the virtual absence of 'deprived areas' in more rural authorities. For example, while 7.9 per

Table 7.7:

**Estimates of area-based poverty in Scottish local authorities for population (2005–2008) and deprived data zones (2009)**

| Local authority | Population | | National share of deprived areas | Local share of deprived areas (data zones) in each local authority area | | |
|---|---|---|---|---|---|---|
| | % income deprived | % households in relative poverty | 15% most deprived data zones | 5% most deprived areas % | 10% most deprived areas % | 15% most deprived areas |
| Glasgow City | 25.7 | 23 | 30.9 | 22.8 | 34.9 | 43.5 |
| West Dunbartonshire | 21.3 | 20 | 3.2 | 5.9 | 15.3 | 26.3 |
| Inverclyde | 20.6 | 21 | 4.3 | 15.5 | 30.9 | 38.2 |
| Dundee City | 20.4 | 24 | 5.5 | 10.1 | 22.3 | 30.2 |
| North Ayrshire | 19.2 | 23 | 4.4 | 5.6 | 14.5 | 24.0 |
| East Ayrshire | 18.2 | 18 | 2.8 | 6.5 | 13.0 | 17.5 |
| North Lanarkshire | 18.2 | 20 | 9.1 | 5.0 | 11.7 | 21.3 |
| Clackmannanshire | 16.3 | 18 | 1.2 | 3.1 | 10.9 | 18.8 |
| Renfrewshire | 15.9 | 17 | 4.4 | 5.6 | 13.6 | 20.1 |
| South Lanarkshire | 15.2 | 20 | 5.9 | 2.3 | 8.0 | 14.6 |
| Eilean Siar | 15.1 | 25 | 0 | 0 | 0 | 0 |
| SCOTLAND | 15.1 | 19 | | | | |
| South Ayrshire | 15.0 | 22 | 1.8 | 4.1 | 6.1 | 12.2 |
| West Lothian | 14.4 | 16 | 1.9 | 0 | 2.8 | 9.0 |
| Dumfries and Galloway | 14.3 | 22 | 1.1 | 1.6 | 4.7 | 5.7 |
| Fife | 14.3 | 21 | 5.2 | 1.8 | 6.2 | 11.3 |
| Falkirk | 13.9 | 20 | 1.7 | 1.5 | 5.6 | 8.6 |
| Angus | 12.8 | 20 | 0.6 | 0 | 1.4 | 4.2 |
| Midlothian | 12.6 | 16 | 0.4 | 0 | 0.9 | 3.6 |
| Highland | 12.5 | 17 | 1.6 | 1.4 | 3.1 | 5.5 |
| Argyll and Bute | 12.3 | 20 | 1.0 | 1.6 | 5.7 | 8.2 |
| Edinburgh City | 11.9 | 19 | 6.1 | 4.0 | 7.7 | 10.9 |
| Scottish Borders | 11.4 | 18 | 0.5 | 0 | 1.5 | 3.8 |
| East Lothian | 11.3 | 20 | 0.3 | 0 | 0 | 2.5 |
| Moray | 11.2 | 21 | 0.1 | 0 | 0 | 0.9 |
| Stirling | 11.1 | 18 | 0.7 | 2.7 | 4.5 | 6.4 |
| Aberdeen City | 10.6 | 15 | 2.9 | 1.9 | 5.2 | 10.5 |

| | | | | | |
|---|---|---|---|---|---|
| Orkney Islands | 10.3 | 21 | 0 | 0 | 0 | 0 |
| Perth and Kinross | 9.9 | 16 | 0.6 | 1.1 | 2.3 | 3.4 |
| East Renfrewshire | 8.9 | 14 | 0.5 | 0.8 | 0.8 | 4.2 |
| East Dunbartonshire | 8.5 | 16 | 0.4 | 0.8 | 1.6 | 3.1 |
| Shetland Islands | 8.5 | 15 | 0 | 0 | 0 | 0 |
| Aberdeenshire | 7.9 | 16 | 0.4 | 0.3 | 0.7 | 1.3 |

Source: Scottish Government, *Scottish Index of Multiple Deprivation 2009*, 2009, Tables 3.1 to 3.4 and Scottish Government, *Relative Poverty in Scottish Local Authorities*, 2010, Table 3

Notes
1. Estimate by Scottish government using *Scottish Household Survey* data for 2005-2008, before housing costs.
2. The *Scottish Household Survey* data used by the Scottish government to provide an estimate of the proportion of the population living in relative poverty has the status of 'data being developed' and should be used with caution (particularly for local authorities with a small sample in the *Survey*).

cent of Aberdeenshire's households are 'income deprived', only 1.3 per cent of Aberdeenshire's small areas are among Scotland's 15 per cent most deprived areas (Table 7.7). The dispersion of deprivation and poverty is most striking for Eilean Siar. Although the proportion of the income deprived in Eilean Siar is at the average for Scotland (15.1 per cent), none of Scotland's 15 per cent most deprived areas are found in this authority.

The poverty of place also cannot be reduced to discrete macro-geographies of affluence and poverty. Although a disproportionate share of Scotland's poverty is found in the City of Glasgow and neighbouring authorities, these swathes of poverty sit alongside East Dunbartonshire and East Renfrewshire, two of the authorities in Scotland in which poverty and income deprivation is least prevalent – less than one in 10 working-age adults are income deprived in these authorities, compared with one in four in the City of Glasgow.

## Urban and rural

As the discussion of poverty across Scotland's local authorities emphasises, poverty is most prevalent in urban settings. Table 7.8 reports that almost half of Scotland's 779,250 income-deprived population live in large urban areas (45.8 per cent) and more than one-quarter live in smaller urban areas (30.8 per cent).

However, the urban basis of Scotland's poverty should not disguise the fact that poverty is also prevalent in rural Scotland. Almost 100,000

Table 7.8:

**Income deprivation in urban and rural areas, Scotland, 2009**

| Year | No. of income-deprived | % of population who are income-deprived | % of income-deprived people in 15% most deprived areas |
|---|---|---|---|
| Large urban | 357,300 | 18 | 50 |
| Other urban | 240,380 | 15 | 30 |
| Accessible small towns | 60,830 | 13 | 14 |
| Remote small towns | 26,820 | 14 | 16 |
| Accessible rural | 57,770 | 9 | 5 |
| Remote rural | 36,140 | 11 | 4 |
| SCOTLAND | 779,250 | 15 | 34 |

Source: Scottish Government, *Scottish Index of Multiple Deprivation 2009*, 2009, Table 3.7

people in rural Scotland are income deprived, amounting to one in 10 of the rural population. Chapter 18 explores the phenomenon of rural poverty in more detail. Sight must also not be lost of the fact that more than two of every five of Scotland's poor live between the extremes of city and country (in small towns and other urban areas).

## Conclusion

This chapter has highlighted how the risk of poverty for people in Scotland is related to their age, the kinds of households in which they live, their social status and the places where they live. Marked and important variations are apparent depending on these factors. However, it is also clear that poverty impacts on people to a greater or lesser extent regardless of how old they are, who they live with, their gender, ethnicity, work status or geographical location. It is, therefore, important to examine risk of poverty alongside the overall proportion of the population who make up these different groups and places – the people and places with the highest risk of poverty do not necessarily account for the greatest numbers of people living in poverty.

### Notes

1   Although this poverty gap has reduced since the first edition of In *Poverty in Scotland 2007* (from 28% to 26%), lone parents' risk of poverty has actually

increased (from 48% to 50%). The improvement is only 'relative', as the risk of living in poverty has increased at a greater rate for children in two-parent families over the same period (from 20% to 24%).

2 Scottish Government, *Poverty and Income Inequality in Scotland, 2008/09*, 2010

3 Scottish Government, *Child Poverty in Scotland: a brief overview of the evidence*, 2010

4 Department for Work and Pensions, *Households Below Average Income, 2008/09*, Corporate Document Services, 2010

5 Registrar General for Scotland, *Projected Population of Scotland, 2008-based*, 2009

6 See note 5

7 See note 5

8 One Parent Families Scotland, *One Parent Families: a profile*, 2009, available at www.opfs.org.uk/files/one-parent-families_a-profile_2009.pdf

9 See note 8

10 See note 8

11 See note 8

12 Scottish Government, *Relative Poverty Across Scottish Local Authorities*, 2010, Figure 3. The *Scottish Household Survey*-based estimate (before housing costs) of 41% compares to a before housing costs estimate of 33% for lone-parent households in the UK

13 See note 3, p10

14 See note 3, p3

15 Note that these Scottish Household Survey-based estimates of poverty are calculated using a before housing costs measure.

16 Scottish Government, *Scottish Index of Multiple Deprivation 2009*, 2010, Table 5.1

# Eight

# What is life like for people experiencing poverty?

*John H McKendrick*

## Summary

- Some aspects of financial wellbeing have improved for low-income households in recent years, although the gap between low-income and high-income households remains marked.
- Exposure to the risk of fuel poverty is highly skewed by household income, with virtually all households with the lowest income experiencing fuel poverty, in contrast to virtually none of the highest earning households.
- For both adults and children, living on a low income is associated with lower levels of mental wellbeing. Similarly, it is associated with shorter lives and more years with ill health.
- It is problematic to 'blame the poor' for adverse health outcomes, with living on a low income sometimes being associated with more positive health behaviours – eg, lower levels of alcohol consumption.
- Living in a deprived area is generally associated with less neighbourhood satisfaction, although there is a slightly higher level of satisfaction with public transport services.
- Children from deprived areas are consistently reported to have poorer access to local opportunities for safe play and to participate in fewer activities, compared with children living beyond these areas.

## Introduction

This chapter considers the experience of living in poverty in contemporary Scotland, one of the wealthiest countries in the world. It focuses on the here and now. It does not speculate on the long-term consequences of living in poverty, or claim that people currently experiencing poverty will be forevermore condemned to a life of adversity. The chapter only draws on quantitative data. Numbers cannot fully capture the reality of what life is like for people living in poverty. In particular, the numbers that are available to us are unable to tell us what people think or how people experiencing poverty make sense of this condition. However, numbers are not without value. Quantitative evidence enables us to understand how some negative consequences of poverty are broadly experienced in Scotland. The experience of low income and deprivation in Scotland is described in terms of financial wellbeing, health, community life and children's leisure lives.

The chapter draws on household income data and data comparing people living in and beyond multiply deprived areas. Without identification of the point at which low income reflects poverty for different household types, distribution of household income data does not measure poverty. Similarly, living in a multiply deprived area does not imply living in poverty (nor does living outside a multiply deprived area imply an absence of poverty). Care is taken in interpreting this data when discussing poverty in Scotland.

## Financial wellbeing

'Poverty is being skint.'[1]

For people living on a low income, a lack of money leads to a fragile existence that involves the threat of falling into debt, being forced to choose between one necessity and another, going without, being caught frequently in a cycle of 'dead-end' jobs, and being unable to save money.

National survey data reinforces these observations. Although more people from low-income households report that they 'manage financially well' than not (34 per cent, compared with 22 per cent of those households with an annual net income of less than £10,000), it is much more likely that those in Scotland who report that they are not managing their finances well are from low-income households (the 22 per cent compares with only 4 per cent of those in households with more than £30,000 annual net income).[2]

The Scottish government has been active in promoting financial inclusion and there has been significant progress in accessing the means of financial management in recent years. In *Poverty in Scotland 2007*, we reported that 81 per cent of those from households with the lowest annual net income (less than £10,000 per annum) had a bank or building society account.[3] Just four years on, and only 2 per cent of these households are without someone who has a bank, building society, credit union or Post Office card account (see Table 8.1). However, there are differences in the financial products to which households have access, with those on higher incomes being almost three times as likely to have access to a building society account, while those on the lowest incomes are four times as likely to have a Post Office card account (Table 8.1). There is also a geographical expression to this, with one in five households in Scotland's most deprived areas not having access to a bank account. Credit unions are also more likely to be used in Scotland's most deprived areas, although their generally lower uptake among low-income households poses the question of whether or not higher uptake in deprived areas reflects uptake among the higher income households living in these areas (Table 8.1).

A similar pattern of response is found to having any savings or investments – more low-income households in 2011 than in 2007 report that they have savings or investments, but there are still fewer low- than high-income households with savings or investments in 2011. As Table 8.1 shows, households with the lowest annual net income are three times as likely not to have savings or investments (36 per cent of those with an annual income of less than £10,000, compared with 12 per cent of those with an annual income of £30,000 or above). Thus, an unacceptable and disproportionate share of low-income households in Scotland do not have the financial means which lend themselves towards stability and which enable them to fend off unforeseen financial crises.

Living on a low income is also associated with less ready access to those resources which are important to participate fully in contemporary Scotland, including accessing the world of work. As Table 8.2 shows, households in Scotland with the lowest net income are most likely not to have home internet access, home broadband access and access to a car for private use. Thus, the majority of households with an annual net income of less than £6,000 do not have access to a car for private use (57 per cent) compared with a tiny minority of households with an annual income of over £40,000 (2 per cent). Similar proportions also do not have access to the internet at home (58 per cent, compared with 3 per cent), or do not have home broadband internet access (60 per cent, compared with 5 per cent). Consumption that is pertinent to accessing the world of work does throw a consistent 'glitch' at the lower end of the household income scale in that those on the very lowest income (£0 – £6,000 per

Table 8.1:

**Financial resources by net annual household income and deprivation area status, Scotland, 2009**

| | £0–£10,000 | £10,001–£20,000 | £20,001–£30,000 | Over £30,000 | 15% most deprived | Rest of Scotland | Scotland |
|---|---|---|---|---|---|---|---|
| | % | % | % | % | % | % | % |
| **Respondent or partner has bank or building society account** | | | | | | | |
| Bank | 87 | 90 | 94 | 96 | 82 | 92 | 91 |
| Building society | 13 | 17 | 23 | 35 | 10 | 24 | 22 |
| Credit union | 1 | 2 | 3 | 4 | 4 | 2 | 2 |
| Post Office card | 13 | 9 | 4 | 3 | 14 | 6 | 7 |
| None | 2 | 1 | 1 | 0 | 4 | 1 | 1 |
| Refused to say | 2 | 2 | 3 | 2 | 4 | 3 | 3 |
| *Base* | *1,792* | *3,458* | *2,096* | *2,595* | *1,339* | *8,937* | *10,276* |
| **Respondent or partner has any savings or investments** | | | | | | | |
| Yes | 50 | 56 | 64 | 74 | | | 61 |
| No | 36 | 32 | 23 | 12 | | | 26 |
| Refused to say | 11 | 11 | 12 | 12 | | | 11 |
| Don't know | 3 | 1 | 1 | 1 | | | 2 |
| *Base* | | | | | | | *9,965* |

Source: Scottish Government, *Scotland's People: Annual Report from the 2009 Scottish Household Survey*, Scottish Government, 2010, Figure 6.4 and Table 6.12

Notes:
1. Without identification of the point at which low income reflects poverty, distribution of household income data does not measure poverty. Furthermore, the income data presented in this table is not equivalised. Care has to be taken in interpreting this data when discussing poverty in Scotland.
2. Living in a multiply deprived area does not imply living in poverty (nor does living outside a multiply deprived area imply an absence of poverty). Care has to be taken in interpreting this data when discussing poverty in Scotland.

annum) have higher consumption than those with a 'slightly higher' low income (£6,001 to £10,000).[4]

Trend data also suggests some complexities. While access to a car has grown for those with the very lowest household incomes (from 35 per cent in 2007 to 43 per cent for those with less than £6,000 per annum), car ownership has fallen for many other low-income households over the

Table 8.2:

**Aspects of consumption by annual household income, Scotland, 2009**

| | £0–£6,000 | £6,001–£10,000 | £10,001–£15,000 | £15,001–£20,000 | £20,001–£25,000 | £25,001–£30,000 | £30,001–£40,000 | Over £40,000 | Scotland |
|---|---|---|---|---|---|---|---|---|---|
| | % | % | % | % | % | % | % | % | % |
| **Cars available for private use** | | | | | | | | | |
| Yes | 43 | 39 | 48 | 67 | 83 | 89 | 95 | 98 | 70 |
| No | 57 | 61 | 52 | 33 | 17 | 11 | 5 | 2 | 30 |
| *Base* | *702* | *1,810* | *2,667* | *2,073* | *1,576* | *1,274* | *1,804* | *1,765* | *1,3671* |
| **Home internet access** | | | | | | | | | |
| Yes | 42 | 34 | 44 | 62 | 78 | 84 | 91 | 97 | 66 |
| No | 58 | 66 | 55 | 38 | 22 | 16 | 9 | 3 | 34 |
| *Base* | *555* | *1,435* | *2,074* | *1,604* | *1,228* | *966* | *1,392* | *1,366* | *1,0620* |
| **Home broadband internet access** | | | | | | | | | |
| Yes | 39 | 31 | 42 | 58 | 74 | 80 | 89 | 95 | 63 |
| No | 60 | 68 | 58 | 42 | 25 | 19 | 10 | 5 | 37 |
| *Base* | *555* | *1,435* | *2,074* | *1,604* | *1,228* | *966* | *1,392* | *1,366* | *1,0620* |

Source: Scottish Government, *Scotland's People: Annual Report from the 2009 Scottish Household Survey*, Scottish Government, 2010, Tables 8.2, 9.6 and 9.9

Note: Without identification of the point at which low income reflects poverty, distribution of household income data does not measure poverty. Furthermore, the income data presented in this table is not equivalised. Care has to be taken in interpreting this data when discussing poverty in Scotland.

same period (those earning between £10,001 and £25,000 are now less likely to report that they can access a car for private use). Indeed, there is now a minority of car owners in the income band £10,001 to £15,000 (48 per cent in 2009, compared with 55 per cent in 2003/04).[5] As might be expected given the emerging technology, home internet access has grown for all income groups in Scotland, with the highest rates of growth between 2007 and 2011 evident for low-income households, as ownership reaches saturation point for the higher income households.

If we step back to consider the basic necessities of existence, we find unacceptable deprivations among Scotland's poorest people. As Table 8.3 shows, fuel poverty is almost absent among households in

Scotland with a net weekly income of over £700. In sharp contrast, almost all of those with a net weekly income of less than £100 and four-fifths of those households with a net weekly income of between £100 and £199 experience fuel poverty, as do two in every five households with a net weekly household income of between £200 and £299.

Financial wellbeing in Scotland will undoubtedly be challenged as the austerity cuts announced in the autumn of 2010 are introduced. Although not markedly different from other national regions in the UK, Scotland will be vulnerable to the proposed welfare reforms, given that the majority of households in Scotland are in receipt of some form of benefit (59 per cent) and a significant minority are in receipt of tax credits (14 per cent) (see Table 8.4). If the contraction in car ownership among Scotland's lower to middle income earners between 2007 and 2011 is a sign of financial stress among this population strata, the proposed tax credit cuts (which will impact most on this income group) may have a greater impact on financial stress in Scotland than is envisaged.

## Health

'Your worth is all about money, money, money.'

The problems caused by living on a low income extend far beyond the ability to consume, with people living in poverty sensing that their worth is often rated (adversely) on economic terms. Being seen to be poor is to be seen to be less worthy, and leads to low self-esteem. People living on a low income experience stigmatisation on account of their poverty, a lack of emotional and practical support that could be provided by those in more powerful positions, and a feeling of being unable to participate fully in one's community.

Mental wellbeing is, not surprisingly, less than satisfactory among low-income households in Scotland. Table 8.5 shows evidence of psychological health of adults and children using standard measurement tools from the *Scottish Health Survey*. For each measure of mental distress among adults, and at each income level, more women report mental distress than men. For example, anxiety is reported by 17 per cent of women and 10 per cent of men in the households with the highest income; suicide is reported to have been attempted by 8 per cent of women and 3 per cent of men in households with 'average' income; and depression is reported

Table 8.3:

**Household fuel poverty and extreme fuel poverty by weekly household income, Scotland, 2009**

| Weekly net household income | Not fuel poor | Fuel poor | Extreme fuel poor | Fuel poverty within household income band % |
|---|---|---|---|---|
| Less than £100 | 2,000 | 81,000 | 68,000 | 99 |
| £100 – £199.99 | 79,000 | 333,000 | 121,000 | 81 |
| £200 – £299.99 | 275,000 | 195,000 | 35,000 | 41 |
| £300 – £399.99 | 263,000 | 77,000 | 12,000 | 23 |
| £400 – £499.99 | 220,000 | 28,000 | 6,000 | 11 |
| £500 – £699.99 | 345,000 | 38,000 | 1,000 | 10 |
| £700 or more | 378,000 | 12,000 | 1,000 | 3 |
| All Scotland | 1,578,000 | 766,000 | 242,000 | 33 |

Source: S Walker and others, *Scottish Housing Condition Survey: key findings for 2009*, Scottish Government, 2010, Table 24

Notes:
1. The definition of fuel poverty that is used is that specified by the Scottish Executive in the Fuel Poverty Statement of 2002. Households are defined as 'fuel poor' if they would be required to spend more than 10% of household income on fuel. Households in extreme fuel poverty would be required to spend more than 20% of their household income on fuel.
2. Without identification of the point at which low income reflects poverty, distribution of household income data does not measure poverty. Furthermore, the income data presented in this table is not equivalised. Care has to be taken in interpreting this data when discussing poverty in Scotland.

by 34 per cent of women and 15 per cent of men in the lowest income households (Table 8.5). More than this, gender differences become most marked among low-income households – for men, mental health improves steadily as household income level rises, whereas for women, there is a sharp difference between women living in households with the very lowest household income levels (lowest 20 per cent) and all others.

Gender differences are less marked for children, suggesting that these may emerge in adulthood or as it is approached in the later years of childhood. However, mental distress is more prevalent among both young boys and girls living in low-income households, suggesting that the strains of living on a low income do not only impair the quality of life of adults. For example, while the majority of boys aged 4 to 12 in the lowest income households are judged to have 'psychological wellbeing' (83 per cent), levels are notably lower than their peers from the highest income house-

Table 8.4:

## Households receiving different types of benefits by national region in the UK, 2008/09

| | Scotland | England | Wales | Northern Ireland | UK |
|---|---|---|---|---|---|
| | % | % | % | % | % |
| Working tax credit | 5 | 5 | 5 | 7 | 5 |
| Child tax credit | 13 | 14 | 15 | 15 | 14 |
| Income support | 5 | 5 | 6 | 8 | 5 |
| Pension credit | 6 | 5 | 6 | 6 | 6 |
| Housing benefit | 13 | 11 | 11 | 11 | 11 |
| Council tax benefit | 17 | 15 | 17 | 3 | 15 |
| Retirement pension | 25 | 25 | 28 | 21 | 25 |
| Widows' benefits | – | – | – | – | – |
| Jobseeker's allowance | 2 | 2 | 3 | 2 | 2 |
| Incapacity benefit | 5 | 3 | 6 | 5 | 4 |
| Severe disablement allowance | 1 | 1 | 1 | 1 | 1 |
| Attendance allowance | 3 | 3 | 3 | 3 | 3 |
| Carer's allowance | 1 | 1 | 2 | 2 | 1 |
| Disability living allowance (care component) | 7 | 6 | 9 | 10 | 6 |
| Disability living allowance (mobility component) | 7 | 5 | 9 | 10 | 6 |
| Industrial injuries disablement benefit | – | 1 | 1 | 1 | 1 |
| War disablement or war widow's pension | – | – | 1 | – | – |
| Child benefit | 21 | 22 | 24 | 26 | 22 |
| On any income-related benefit | 20 | 18 | 21 | 21 | 19 |
| On any non-income-related benefit | 56 | 57 | 62 | 59 | 57 |
| All in receipt of benefit | 59 | 60 | 66 | 62 | 60 |
| All in receipt of tax credits | 14 | 14 | 16 | 17 | 14 |
| All not in receipt of state support | 41 | 40 | 34 | 37 | 40 |
| Sample size | 4,869 | 20,942 | 1,311 | 2,285 | 29,407 |

Source: S Clay and others, Family Resources Survey 2008/09, Department for Work and Pensions, 2010, Table 2.7

Notes:
1. There were very few employment and support allowance (ESA) cases in the 2008/09 *Family Resources Survey*. Contributory ESA cases are treated as incapacity benefit, and income-related ESA cases as income support.
2. Owner-occupiers in Northern Ireland can access a 'rent rebate'.

holds (95 per cent have 'psychological wellbeing' in households with the highest income). The overarching conclusion from Table 8.5 is that living on a low income is associated with higher levels of mental distress.

Physical health is also affected by living on a low income. Men and women from less deprived areas live longer and enjoy more years in good health (see Figure 8.1). The harsh realities of life expectancy statistics and healthy life expectancy statistics make for unpalatable reading. Men in the most deprived places in Scotland can expect to spend 10 of their 69 years in ill health, compared with men in the most affluent places who can expect to spend under six of their 80 years in ill health. Although women live longer, they can also expect to spend more years than men in ill health. Thus, women in the poorest places in Scotland can expect to spend over 14 of their 76 years in ill health, compared with women in the most affluent places who can expect to spend just over six of their 83 years in ill health. Indeed, expressed as area statistics, these figures most probably underestimate the different life experiences and expectancies of Scotland's rich, comfortable and poor.

Clearly, deprivation and low income prevent men and women from enjoying healthy lives. There is a train of thought that would apportion blame to 'the poor' for living an unhealthy life. Indeed, there is some evidence that men and women living in households with the lowest income are living less healthy lifestyles than those in the most affluent households.[6] However, it is too simplistic to reduce health behaviours to lifestyle choice and 'blame the poor' for three reasons. First, a culture of 'poor bashing' tends to marginalise the structural barriers and opportunity constraints that make it more difficult to live a healthy lifestyle. Second, 'blaming the poor' is a wholly inadequate response to the health of children. Whether or not adult guardians are to 'blame' for children's health conditions should not be used as a reason to absolve from responsibility local service providers for improving health among children in low-income households. For example, although evidence suggests that both boys and girls in low-income households have a poorer quality diet (Table 8.6), it must be acknowledged that not all of their food consumption is within the household and that breakfast clubs, school lunches and after-school

Table 8.5:

## Mental distress and psychological ill health by household income groups (quintiles), across age and sex, Scotland, 2008/09

| | 20% lowest income household | Quintile 2 | Quintile 3 | Quintile 4 | 20% highest income household |
|---|---|---|---|---|---|
| | % | % | % | % | % |
| **Adults, depression** | | | | | |
| Men | 15 | 13 | 9 | 7 | 9 |
| Women | 34 | 19 | 17 | 9 | 10 |
| **Adults, anxiety** | | | | | |
| Men | 23 | 19 | 11 | 9 | 10 |
| Women | 32 | 21 | 19 | 17 | 17 |
| **Adults, attempted suicide** | | | | | |
| Men | 10 | 7 | 3 | 1 | 1 |
| Women | 15 | 5 | 8 | 3 | 1 |
| **Psychological wellbeing among children, aged 4 to 12** | | | | | |
| Boys, SDQ of 02–13 | 83 | 84 | 92 | 94 | 95 |
| Girls, SDQ of 02–13 | 80 | 93 | 91 | 97 | 97 |

Source: J Corbett and others, *Scottish Health Survey 2009*, Scottish Government, 2010, Tables 1.9 and 1.15

Notes:

1. Without identification of the point at which low income reflects poverty, distribution of household income data does not measure poverty. Furthermore, the income data presented in this table is not equivalised. Care has to be taken in interpreting this data when discussing poverty in Scotland.

2. The mental health measure of depression used is as follows: Percentage of adults who have a symptom score of 2 or more on the depression section of the Revised Clinical Interview Schedule. See J Corbett and others, *Scottish Health Survey 2009*, Scottish Government, 2010, for details.

3. The mental health measure of anxiety used is as follows: Percentage of adults who have a symptom score of 2 or more on the anxiety scale of the Revised Clinical Interview Schedule. See J Corbett and others, *Scottish Health Survey 2009*, Scottish Government, 2010, for details.

4. The following question was used in the *Scottish Health Survey* to record attempted suicide: Have you ever made an attempt to take your own life, by taking an overdose of tablets or in some other way? See J Corbett and others, *Scottish Health Survey 2009*, Scottish Government, 2010, for details.

5. The Strengths and Difficulties Questionnaire (SDQ) was answered by parents on behalf of children 4–12 years. The SDQ comprises 25 questions covering aspects such as consideration, hyperactivity, malaise, mood, sociability, obedience, anxiety, and unhappiness. These can be condensed into five component symptom scores corresponding to emotional symptoms, conduct problems, hyperactivity, peer problems and pro-social behaviour, ranging in value from 0 to 10. A total SDQ score (referred to here as a 'total deviance score') was calculated by summing the scores from each domain, with the exception of pro-social behaviour, ranging from 0 to 40. For each, values can be classified as 'normal', 'borderline' and 'abnormal'.

clubs each have a role to play in enhancing the quality of children's diet. Finally, not all of the evidence suggests that people in low-income households lead a less healthy life. For example, and in sharp contrast to the

Figure 8.1:

**Life expectancy and healthy life expectancy by sex and deprivation area status, Scotland, 2007/08**

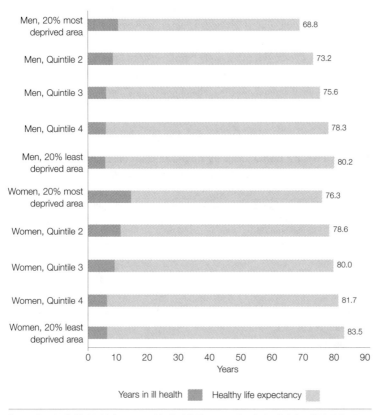

Source: Scottish Public Health Observatory, *Healthy Life Expectancy Deprivation Quintiles*, 2010, Tables 1 and 2, available at www.scotpho.org.uk

Notes:
1. Uses 'self-reported health' as a measure of ill health.
2. Living in a multiply deprived area does not imply living in poverty (nor does living outside a multiply deprived area imply an absence of poverty). Care has to be taken in interpreting this data when discussing poverty in Scotland.

public persona of people experiencing poverty, consumption of alcohol above recommended levels is lower for both men and women from low-income households, with drinking at a level considered to be 'harmful' being twice as likely for both men and women in the highest, compared with the lowest, income households (Table 8.6).

The complexities of understanding the relationship between low income and health outcomes is further demonstrated in Table 8.7, which considers healthy weight issues. Although gender differences are evident across the income range for both children and adults, there are interesting patterns for low-income households. Thus, while boys from low-income households are more likely than girls from low-income households to be overweight (35 per cent, compared with 23 per cent for those from the 20 per cent lowest income households), women are more likely than

Table 8.6:

**Selected health behaviours by household income groups (quintiles), across sex and age, Scotland, 2008/09**

|  | 20% lowest income household | Quintile 2 | Quintile 3 | Quintile 4 | 20% highest income household |
|---|---|---|---|---|---|
|  | % | % | % | % | % |
| **Drinking, men** |  |  |  |  |  |
| Non-drinker | 20 | 14 | 9 | 6 | [4] |
| Moderate | 56 | 65 | 60 | 63 | 59 |
| Harmful | 16 | 17 | 24 | 25 | 30 |
| Hazardous | 9 | [5] | 7 | 6 | 7 |
| **Drinking, women** |  |  |  |  |  |
| Non-drinker | 23 | 17 | 12 | 9 | 7 |
| Moderate | 61 | 68 | 69 | 69 | 66 |
| Harmful | 10 | 13 | 16 | 18 | 22 |
| Hazardous | 6 | [3] | [3] | [4] | 4 |
| **Diet Quality Index, mean** |  |  |  |  |  |
| Boys | 43.6 | 46.7 | 47.0 | 47.6 | 51.7 |
| Girls | 45.3 | 46.6 | 47.0 | 49.2 | 51.0 |

Source: J Corbett and others, *Scottish Health Survey 2009*, Scottish Government, 2010, Table 3.3

Notes:

1. Without identification of the point at which low income reflects poverty, distribution of household income data does not measure poverty. Furthermore, the income data presented in this table is not equivalised. Care has to be taken in interpreting this data when discussing poverty in Scotland.

2. See J Corbett and others, *Scottish Health Survey 2009*, Scottish Government, 2010 for details of how problem drinking was classified.

3. See J Corbett and others, *Scottish Health Survey 2009*, Scottish Government, 2010 for details of the Diet Quality Index.

Table 8.7:

**Weight problems, by household income groups (quintiles), across sex and age, Scotland, 2008/09**

|  | 20% lowest income household | Quintile 2 | Quintile 3 | Quintile 4 | 20% highest income household |
|---|---|---|---|---|---|
|  | % | % | % | % | % |
| **Obesity (central obesity, using waist-hip ratio)** | | | | | |
| Men | 44.1 | 36.2 | 32.2 | 41.7 | 27.3 |
| Women | 56.2 | 44.3 | 36.9 | 35.9 | 31.4 |
| **Overweight** | | | | | |
| Boys | 34.8 | 29.7 | 33.0 | 31.1 | 30.4 |
| Girls | 23.2 | 31.4 | 26.3 | 23.6 | 29.2 |
| **Underweight** | | | | | |
| Boys | 2.2 | 2.2 | 1.6 | 1.3 | 1.0 |
| Girls | 1.6 | 1.6 | 3.0 | 0.7 | 0.4 |

Source: J Corbett and others, *Scottish Health Survey 2009*, Scottish Government, 2010, Tables 7.7 and 8.5

Notes:
1. Without identification of the point at which low income reflects poverty, distribution of household income data does not measure poverty. Furthermore, the income data presented in this table is not equivalised. Care has to be taken in interpreting this data when discussing poverty in Scotland.
2. Waist-hip ratio is a measure of central obesity (abdominal fat). See J Corbett and others, *Scottish Health Survey 2009*, Scottish Government, 2010, Table 7.2.4 for details.
3. BMI is used to estimate under- and overweight for children. See J Corbett and others, *Scottish Health Survey 2009*, Scottish Government, 2010, Table 8.2 for details.

men to be overweight from the same household income group (56 per cent of women, compared with 44 per cent of men). At the heart of these contrasting trends are differences for children from the lowest income households. Thus, for boys, there is a marked increase in the incidence of being overweight between those from lowest income households and highest income households (35 per cent, compared with 30 per cent of boys from the highest income households), while in contrast for girls, there is a marked decrease in the risk of being overweight among this group (23 per cent, compared with 29 per cent of girls from the highest income households). Being underweight is more characteristic of both boys and girls from the lowest income households, with boys being twice as likely as those from the highest income households to be underweight (2.2 per cent, compared with 1 per cent) and girls being four times more likely than girls from the highest income households (1.6 per cent, compared with

0.4 per cent). Taken together, whereas boys from low-income households are less likely to have a healthy weight than boys from the highest earning households, the opposite is true for girls.

## Community life and environment

'There is no chance for people like us to make improvements in our lives.'

People experiencing poverty are more likely to be living in deprived areas with inadequate services and facilities. Their physical environments are often badly cared for and 'depressing', and they are more likely to feel unsafe in their neighbourhood.

Table 8.8 uses information from the *Scottish Household Survey* to

Table 8.8:

**Perceptions of personal safety by deprivation area status, Scotland, 2009**

|  | 15% most deprived areas | Rest of Scotland | Scotland |
|---|---|---|---|
|  | % | % | % |
| **How safe respondent feels walking alone at night** | | | |
| Safe (very, fairly) | 60 | 77 | 75 |
| Unsafe (bit, very) | 37 | 19 | 22 |
| Don't know | 4 | 3 | 3 |
| *Base* | *1,231* | *7,871* | *9,102* |
| **How safe respondent feels at home at night** | | | |
| Safe (very, fairly) | 94 | 98 | 97 |
| Unsafe (bit, very) | 6 | 2 | 3 |
| Don't know | 0 | 0 | 0 |
| *Base* | *1,231* | *7,871* | *9,102* |

Source: Scottish Government, *Scotland's People: Annual Report from the 2009 Scottish Household Survey*, Scottish Government, 2010, Table 4.21

Note: Living in a multiply deprived area does not imply living in poverty (nor does living outside a multiply deprived area imply an absence of poverty). Care has to be taken in interpreting this data when discussing poverty in Scotland.

Table 8.9:

**Evaluation of neighbourhood environment, by deprivation area status, Scotland, 2009**

|  | 15% most deprived areas | Rest of Scotland | Scotland |
|---|---|---|---|
|  | % | % | % |
| **Selected aspects of neighbourhood that are particularly liked** | | | |
| Pleasant environment | 45 | 60 | 57 |
| Safe environment | 9 | 22 | 20 |
| Good public transport | 24 | 20 | 21 |
| Good amenities | 41 | 46 | 45 |
| Sense of community/friendly people | 56 | 74 | 71 |
| Like nothing about the area | 13 | 3 | 4 |
| **Selected aspects of neighbourhood that are particularly disliked** | | | |
| Unpleasant environment | 37 | 29 | 30 |
| Unsafe environment | 11 | 2 | 4 |
| Poor public transport | 2 | 6 | 5 |
| Poor amenities | 16 | 12 | 12 |
| No sense of community/problem residents/substance abuse | 42 | 16 | 20 |
| Dislike nothing about the area | 25 | 32 | 31 |

Source: Scottish Government, *Scotland's People: Annual Report from the 2009 Scottish Household Survey*, Scottish Government, 2010, Tables 4.5 and 4.8

Note: Living in a multiply deprived area does not imply living in poverty (nor does living outside a multiply deprived area imply an absence of poverty). Care has to be taken in interpreting this data when discussing poverty in Scotland.

compare perceptions of night-time safety at home and in the wider neighbourhood. On the whole, the majority of people in Scotland perceive themselves to be safe in their own homes at night, and there is little significant difference between those living in the most deprived areas and the rest of Scotland in the proportion who feel unsafe in their own home. However, there is a marked difference in perceived safety in the wider neighbourhood at night. Twice as many people from the most deprived areas in Scotland do not feel safe walking alone at night in their neighbourhood (37 per cent, compared with 19 per cent of those living outside the most deprived areas).

Local area differences extend beyond perceptions of safety. As

Table 8.9 shows, people living in the most deprived areas of Scotland (also the areas with a disproportionate share of people experiencing poverty in Scotland) are more likely to express displeasure over problems in their neighbourhood (42 per cent are concerned with the lack of a sense of community, problem residents and substance abuse, compared with 'only' 16 per cent expressing such concern outside areas of deprivation). Similarly, residents of multiply deprived areas are less likely to express pleasure at aspects of their neighbourhood (13 per cent reported that they liked nothing about their area, compared with only 3 per cent of those living outside deprived areas). On the other hand, people living in deprived areas commented favourably on public transport.

Life on a low income means one is less able to participate fully in society. Whether such participation is manifest in education or leisure, political participation or having a voice in local/national decision making, it is a fundamental right to which many people experiencing poverty have less experience of, and access to. As Table 8.10 shows, those living in households with lower incomes are also less likely to give up time to assist as a volunteer or organiser – eg, 19 per cent of those in households with an annual income of less than £10,000, compared with the Scottish average of 28 per cent. This data is suggestive that the UK coalition govern-

Table 8.10:

**Whether gave up time to help as a volunteer/organiser in the last 12 months by annual household income, Scotland, 2009**

|  | £3,000 – £6,000 | £6,001 – £10,000 | £10,001 – £15,000 | £15,001 – £20,000 | £20,001 – £25,000 | £25,001 – £30,000 | £30,001 – £40,000 | Over £40,000 | Scotland |
|---|---|---|---|---|---|---|---|---|---|
|  | % | % | % | % | % | % | % | % | % |
| Yes | 19 | 19 | 20 | 26 | 27 | 33 | 34 | 40 | 28 |
| No | 81 | 81 | 80 | 74 | 73 | 67 | 66 | 60 | 72 |
| *Base* | *360* | *948* | *1,313* | *984* | *736* | *588* | *820* | *772* | *6,521* |

Source: Scottish Government, *Scotland's People: Annual Report from the 2009 Scottish Household Survey*, Scottish Government, 2010, Table 12.4

Note: Without identification of the point at which low income reflects poverty, distribution of household income data does not measure poverty. Furthermore, the income data presented in this table is not equivalised. Care has to be taken in interpreting this data when discussing poverty in Scotland.

ment's idea of a 'big society' is yet some way from being achieved in Scotland's most deprived areas.

## Growing up in deprived areas

It is widely recognised that having adequate opportunities to play and participating in a range of activities is beneficial for children.[7] New data from the *Scottish Household Survey* provides some insight into the impact on play and activity participation for children living in multiply deprived areas.

Compared with other children, those from deprived areas in Scotland are reported to have less ready access to different types of play space in their local area; there are greater parental concerns for children's safety travelling to these play spaces; there is more concern for children's safety at these play areas; and children must reach an older age before parents consider it to be safe for them to visit these areas without supervision (Table 8.11). Clearly, there are more concerns over children's play in Scotland's most deprived areas.

The single finding that places children from deprived areas on a par with their counterparts from non-deprived areas is access to games pitches (41 per cent are reported to have safe access to such play space among both populations). Otherwise, children from deprived areas are reported to be disadvantaged at every turn. Of particular note is the dearth of access to natural and wooded areas for play (44 per cent have no local access to such space, compared with 22 per cent of those from non-deprived areas). This may be less concerning to parents (although disconcerting to play professionals given the value of natural play environments), as concerns about being harmed by children and particularly adults are highest in these areas – eg, 59 per cent are concerned about bullying from other children in natural/wooded areas, compared with 38 per cent of those outside deprived areas. There is a broad consensus that children's safety to visit independently local play spaces emerges in the later years of primary school, although once again, it is perceived that children from deprived areas must wait a little longer before their parents/guardians perceive that it is safe. For example, 10.3 years is judged to be the age at which it is safe for them to visit their local park without supervision, compared with 9.8 years for children outside these deprived areas. This is not to

Table 8.11:

## Opportunities for children's play, by deprived area status 2009

| | Playground % | Park % | Games pitch (including football) % | Field/open space % | School playground % | Natural/wooded area % | Street/road % | Base % |
|---|---|---|---|---|---|---|---|---|
| **Availability of play area** | | | | | | | | |
| Deprived area | 42 | 47 | 41 | 37 | 34 | 22 | – | 1,274 |
| Non-deprived area | 46 | 52 | 41 | 47 | 40 | 44 | – | 6,486 |
| **Safe for children to walk or cycle to play area on their own** | | | | | | | | |
| Deprived area | 51 | 45 | 55 | 46 | 58 | 31 | 37 | 293 |
| Non-deprived area | 68 | 59 | 64 | 64 | 68 | 49 | 44 | 2,602 |
| **Safe to visit play area with two or three friends** | | | | | | | | |
| Deprived area | 58 | 55 | 62 | 54 | 65 | 37 | 40 | 293 |
| Non-deprived area | 74 | 68 | 71 | 71 | 73 | 55 | 46 | 2,602 |
| **Concerns of bullying by children in play area** | | | | | | | | |
| Deprived area | 55 | 54 | 55 | 54 | 49 | 59 | 47 | 293 |
| Non-deprived area | 41 | 42 | 40 | 36 | 34 | 38 | 29 | 2,602 |
| **Concerns of children being harmed by adults in play area** | | | | | | | | |
| Deprived area | 42 | 48 | 44 | 45 | 42 | 59 | 42 | 293 |
| Non-deprived area | 33 | 38 | 35 | 36 | 28 | 44 | 28 | 2,602 |
| **Youngest age at which it would be safe for child to visit play area without supervision** | | | | | | | | |
| Deprived area | 9.6 | 10.3 | 10.3 | 10.3 | 9.8 | 11.2 | 9.6 | 448 |
| Non-deprived area | 9.2 | 9.8 | 9.8 | 9.6 | 9.3 | 10.5 | 9.3 | 2,736 |

Source: Scottish Government, *Scotland's People: Annual Report from the 2009 Scottish Household Survey*, Scottish Government, 2010, Tables 7.6–7.11

Note: Living in a multiply deprived area does not imply living in poverty (nor does living outside a multiply deprived area imply an absence of poverty). Care has to be taken in interpreting this data when discussing poverty in Scotland.

be underestimated; six months in the life of a primary-school child is a significant length of time.

Disadvantage is not only associated with play space. Parents also report that children and young adults from deprived areas participate less frequently in a whole range of leisure activities (Table 8.12). Some of the

Table 8.12:

**Activities of young people aged 8-21 by deprivation area status, Scotland, 2009**

| | 15% most deprived areas | Rest of Scotland | Scotland |
|---|---|---|---|
| | % | % | % |
| Music or drama | 17 | 27 | 26 |
| Other arts | 5 | 6 | 6 |
| Sports or sporting | 45 | 56 | 54 |
| Other outdoor activity | 15 | 22 | 21 |
| Other groups or clubs | 20 | 24 | 23 |
| Representing young people's views | 2 | 3 | 3 |
| Mentoring or peer education | 1 | 3 | 3 |
| *Base* | *340* | *1,991* | *2,331* |

Source: Scottish Government, *Scotland's People: Annual Report from the 2009 Scottish Household Survey*, Scottish Government, 2010, Table 7.12

Note: Living in a multiply deprived area does not imply living in poverty (nor does living outside a multiply deprived area imply an absence of poverty). Care has to be taken in interpreting this data when discussing poverty in Scotland.

differences in rates of participation are quite striking: 27 per cent of those living outside deprived areas participate in music or drama, compared with only 17 per cent from deprived areas (this is of relevance to Chapter 19). Similarly, while the majority outside deprived areas participate in sport (56 per cent), this is a minority experience within deprived areas (45 per cent).

## Conclusion

This chapter has demonstrated that low income and living in deprived areas have far-ranging impacts on Scotland's adults and children. A lack of money directly leads to insecurity and an inability to meet life's basic necessities. Poverty also strips people of their dignity and is associated with mental ill health. Physical ill health is also more prevalent among the men, women, boys and girls of Scotland's lower income households.

Lower life expectancies (and lower healthy life expectancies) look set to continue as Scotland's more deprived communities are more likely to be less pleasant places to live in and to be places in which concerns for personal safety are heightened. Finally, children from more deprived areas in Scotland are consistently disadvantaged in terms of access to safe play and participation in activities.

Although a bleak picture has been portrayed of life on a low income and in deprived places in contemporary Scotland, we should not lose sight of the continuing resilience of people living in some of Scotland's poorest communities. As well as highlighting the difficulties people face, we must also recognise the quality in many people's lives, their desire to get on, get heard and overcome. The present conditions that many experience need not determine their futures, if we can find effective means to support and enable Scotland's most disadvantaged communities and tackle the underlying poverty that too often undermines their resilience.

## Notes

1   All epigraphs are quotations drawn from people experiencing poverty, who participated in the Get Heard project. L Burnett, *Dignity Shouldn't Have to be Earned*, Poverty Alliance, 2006

2   Scottish Government, *Scotland's People: Annual Report from the 2009 Scottish Household Survey*, Scottish Government, 2010, p49, Table 6.2

3   L Burnett and J H McKendrick, 'Living in Poverty', in *Poverty in Scotland 2007*, CPAG, 2007, Table 5.1, p83

4   The glitch may reflect difficulties in obtaining accurate data for the most severely income-deprived households. Indeed, this problem is acknowledged in the technical report that accompanies the substantive research findings report (Scottish Government, 'Limitations of the Data', *Scottish Household Survey: methodology and fieldwork outcomes, 2007/08*, 2010, section 6). Thus, it is likely that the glitch is an anomaly and that there is total consistency of lower consumption across the household income spectrum (without a glitch at the lower end).

5   See note 2, p72, Table 8.2

6   C Bromley and others, *Scottish Health Survey 2003*, Vol 2, Scottish Executive, 2005, Tables 1.4, 1.9, 2.7, 2.11, 3.4 and 4.7

7   B Manwaring and C Taylor, *The Benefits of Play and Playwork*, Skills Active, 2007

# Section Four

## Scotland in focus: 2007–2011

# Nine

# Presenting and representing poverty

*Gerry Mooney and Sharon Wright*

## Introduction

This book is concerned with understanding poverty in Scotland: what it is and what it is caused by; what it means for people; how it can be measured; and how levels have changed over time. Before we move on (in Chapter 10) to consider the specifics of how poverty is tackled by policies, practices and service provision, we consider another important aspect of poverty in Scotland – how it is presented in public debates and popular culture. We reflect on examples from political debate, television entertainment and autobiography to illustrate a variety of ways in which poverty has been drawn to the attention of the public. Each of these examples offers a different viewpoint from which to interpret poverty, demonstrating that, far from being a neutral issue, poverty continues to elicit strong reactions from a wide spectrum of commentators. We can take two lessons from this observation: first, that there is a wide gap between established research-based knowledge and political rhetoric and, second, that poverty continues to capture the public consciousness, albeit in ways that are not always or everywhere progressive and helpful. In this chapter, we explore the implications of these different representations for people experiencing poverty.

## 'The poor' as 'the problem'

Diverse and multiple aspects of poverty are represented publically on a daily basis, with lesser or greater degrees of sympathy. It is beyond the scope of this chapter to offer a comprehensive overview of interpretations of poverty. Instead, we have selected a small number of examples to illustrate what we believe to be significant viewpoints from a spectrum of opinion, some of it influential in shaping policy outcomes. The first of these is the public presentation of poverty in contemporary political debates. Here, we focus centrally on the ways in which the main UK governing party, the Conservatives, presented poverty in Scotland in its campaigning for the 2008 Glasgow East by-election and the 2010 general election.

The context for presenting poverty in political debates in 2010 was very different from the last time the Conservative Party held power (1979–1997), when some right-wing politicians denied the very existence of poverty in the UK. One of New Labour's most notable achievements in this field when in government (1997–2010) was to shift the parameters of debate by recognising the existence of poverty and the need for state action to eradicate it. Although not all Labour politicians sang from the same hymn sheet in recognising the structural causes of poverty (particularly in relation to adult benefit recipients and 'welfare reform' debates), there were indications that research evidence had informed some policy discussions. This was especially true in relation to the clear goal of eradicating child poverty by 2010, presented along with transparent and independent methods of assessing progress.[1] Although the chosen policies and government funding proved inadequate to meet the ultimate goal,[2] unprecedented progress was made initially in lowering exceptionally high child poverty rates and, crucially for our discussion here, poverty was re-established as a central concern for government.

## Did 'Shettleston man' 'break' Scotland?

In contrast to evidence-based discussions of child poverty in the New Labour era, recent political campaigning has brought a revival of moralistic scapegoating. A new political appetite has grown for the condemnation of 'poor' places and people. Politicians have painted the set of sizeable elements of Scottish society as 'broken' and cast 'the Shettleston man' – a stereotypical work-shy 'folk devil' – as the perpetrator.[3] A key moment in this new mythology was the 2008 Glasgow East by-election. The hotly contested Westminster seat, previously a Labour stronghold, attracted much attention for the power struggles between New Labour and Gordon Brown and the Scottish National Party (SNP) and Scottish First Minister Alex Salmond. However, it was not just the political battle that attracted the spotlight. Politicians and the media brought the people of Glasgow East themselves to centre stage for public judgement.[4]

The presentation of Glasgow East was overwhelmingly negative, giving voice to a type of thinking that has long featured prominently in the reporting of poverty in disadvantaged urban areas across the UK in constructing particular locales as 'problem' places and 'welfare ghettoes'.[5] Dramatic headlines focused on premature death rates and persistently high and long-term unemployment. The new language of 'worklessness' (a term coined by New Labour) became commonplace as an oversimplification of benefit receipt, bundling together a range of distinct circumstances that previously counted as legitimate grounds for absence from the labour market – eg, disability or acute, severe and terminal ill health and substantial informal caring commitments. This use of the term 'worklessness' is potentially stigmatising because it does not recognise unpaid work (such as essential care work), which is an activity of obligation at least as much as choice, and limits the time and energy available for paid employment. The term is also problematic because it implies that the 'lacking' is on the part of the individual who does not have work, rather than the labour market, which does not provide it.

Such representations offered inadequate acknowledgement that the East End of Glasgow suffered from long-term economic decline in the second half of the twentieth century, following the dismantling of much of Scotland's heavy and manufacturing industries. Journalists were quick to comment on other 'problems' in the area. In the *Independent*, one commentator spoke of the 'desolation' of Easterhouse, and of 'broken families', that this is a 'broken society'.[6] Glasgow East was viewed as a place of misery, of apathy and despair (read 'demoralisation' or 'moral inadequacy'), a place containing 'wasted highlands'.[7] The *Times* journalist Melanie Reid, while perhaps using the most headline-grabbing language, was not out of step with many other journalists in making the following comment:[8]

> Glasgow East is a part of the world that defies exaggeration. Desultory buses head out from the city centre towards some of the worst areas of concentrated poverty in the Western world: Shettleston, Barlanark, Garthamlock, Easterhouse, Parkhead... communities that figure with monotonous regularity both on the charge sheet at Glasgow Sheriff Court and at the top of the lists of the most socially deprived wards in Britain. They might as well be called Guantanamo. For many thousands of welfare prisoners on sink estates, marooned by bad housing, violence, addiction, unemployment, ill health and shattered relationships, there is little chance of escape.

In this way, media and political commentary acted to influence and shape one another.[9] Visits to the Glasgow East constituency by David Cameron (now Prime Minister) and Iain Duncan Smith (now Secretary of State for Work and Pensions in the UK Conservative/Liberal Democrat coalition government) played a key role in shaping much of the social commentary of the media during the election. Duncan Smith had visited the area in February 2008 to launch a Centre for Social Justice report, *Breakthrough Glasgow*, detailing what he identified as the key problems afflicting the area.[10] Using a language that was soon to be the staple of many of the newspaper reports of the by-election, Glasgow East was held up to represent the 'broken society'. Following Smith to Glasgow to launch the Conservative general election campaign, Conservative leader David Cameron also invoked Smith's 'broken society' image and together they were instrumental in representing the people of Glasgow East in very disparaging terms. Notable here was the figure of 'Shettleston man' who was regarded as a particular problem subject:[11]

> This individual has low life expectancy. He lives in social housing, drug and alcohol abuse play an important part in his life and he is always out of work. His white blood cell count killing him directly as a result of his lifestyle and its lack of purpose.

Elsewhere, Smith makes reference to 'Shettleston man's' 'couch potato' lifestyle.[12] The clear message was that ill health, unemployment and poverty are primarily matters of individual failure and also of personal responsibility. David Cameron also spoke of the 'dangers' of 'demoralisation' in areas such as Glasgow East:[13]

> The thread that links it all together passes, yes, through family breakdown, welfare dependency, debt, drugs, poverty, poor policing, housing, and failing schools but it is a thread that goes deeper, as we see a society that is in danger of losing its sense of personal responsibility, social responsibility, common decency and, yes, even, public morality.

> We as a society have been far too sensitive. In order to avoid injury to people's feelings, in order to avoid being judgemental, we have failed to say what needs to be said. We have seen a decades-long erosion of responsibility, of social virtue, of self-discipline, respect for others, deferring gratification instead of instant gratification…

Instead we prefer moral neutrality, a refusal to make judgements about what is good and bad behaviour. Bad. Good. Right. Wrong. These are words that our political system and our public sector scarcely dare to use any more.

It is clear from such commentary that welfare provision is identified as the factor generating the kinds of social problems that have been highlighted above:[14]

For too long, people have been allowed to languish, trapped in a dependency culture that held low expectations of those living there and made no demands of them either. You only need to look at the social housing system that successive governments have pursued to realise why, on so many of these estates, lone parenting, worklessness, failed education and addiction are an acceptable way of life. Over the years we have put all the most broken families, with myriad problems, on the same estates. Too few of the children ever see a good role model: for the dysfunctional family life is the norm.

Worse still, visiting vast Estates like Easterhouse... you realise that incentives to remain dependent far outweigh anything else...

To rectify this we need to accept that the welfare system has become part of this breakdown, giving perverse incentives to too many people. It needs to be changed. It needs to have a simple purpose: to move people from dependence to independence...

At the heart of this lies work. The system must help people to not only find work but also to remain in work, to get the 'work habit'.

The label 'broken Britain' has succeeded in entering wider and popular discourses about the social and moral health of UK society today and, in particular, has increasingly featured across a range of stories about the state and future of welfare. As with many other anti-welfare narratives over recent decades, part of the potency and pervasiveness of the broken society idea is that it is a very flexible notion, able to be deployed without evidence as an explanation of a range of social problems and popular social ills. For Conservatives such as Duncan Smith and the Centre for Social Justice, there is an explicit argument that the broken and falling apart society has its roots in 'broken families'. Teenage pregnancies, increasing numbers of one-parent households caught, of course, in a 'dependency culture', feature prominently in this account. The Centre for Social Justice identifies five poverty 'drivers': family breakdown, welfare dependency, educational failure, addiction to drugs and alcohol and serious personal debt. However, marriage and a stable two-parent family life are presented as key to 'mending' 'broken Britain', thereby reducing levels of poverty.

## 'The poor' as freak show?

The second example of how poverty is presented in contemporary Scotland is provided by the four-part BBC reality television programme *The Scheme*, the first two parts of which were broadcast in May 2010. In this example, the community of a largely deprived housing scheme, Onthank in Kilmarnock, was presented for public consumption as entertainment. The series provoked a great deal of debate and controversy across Scotland and beyond, reflected in considerable press coverage and presence on social networking sites and online discussion forums. *The Scheme* purported to offer a 'warts and all' 'reality-based' documentary account of life in this particular housing scheme. It positioned the viewer in judgement over the behaviour and lifestyles of those exhibited.[15] In showcasing the problematic or dysfunctional aspects of family relationships, unemployment, alcohol or drug taking and violence, without insight into the underlying causes (such as the devastating economic change in this part of East Ayrshire) or contexts (of widening social inequalities) of social problems, programme makers have created a modern day equivalent of the 'freak show'.

The case of the representation of the population of Glasgow East in *The Scheme* connects in important ways with wider narratives and stories about welfare 'in crisis' in the contemporary UK.[16] As we have seen here, there is a virulent and potent anti-welfarist message being presented and this is perhaps most explicitly captured today in the 'broken society' idea, that we briefly explored above.

One of the most forceful criticisms of *The Scheme* – and 'poverty porn' more generally – is that it provides a view of poverty and people experiencing poverty out of context – ie, it offered a vision, and a very partial and flawed understanding of poverty, which did not consider the underlying social and economic factors that work to generate and reproduce poverty over time. Instead, the focus was on one housing scheme, and on particular individuals and families within it, in isolation from the wider issues around poverty, disadvantage and inequality across Scotland and the UK today. In this respect, *The Scheme* (which is perhaps now the best known programme of its kind) represents but one example of this genre. It relies on a largely cultural and behaviour-centred perspective, focusing on the individual and family, and on the generation of specific cultural and behavioural norms and lifestyles, which work to keep people in poverty.

There is an increasing interest among poverty researchers in what is now being referred to as 'poverty porn'. This refers to the offering up of poverty and of 'poor people' for public entertainment and titillation. While some of this is played out on social networking sites, as well as in the popular press, more significant and potent is the manner in which the televisual media have begun to see in poverty – and its associated conditions – a means to cheap, popular and populist entertainment. *The Jeremy Kyle Show* and *Tricia* represent one end of this spectrum – and perhaps some of the best known examples of TV-based poverty porn. These are supplemented by a whole host of 'makeover' and 'self-improvement' shows, as well as other programmes which offer the wealthy a chance to express their philanthropy by dispensing money to good causes (*Secret Millionaire*), or to live among poor people to 'experience what poverty is really like' (*How the Other Half Live*).

## An outbreak of moral behaviourism?

In recent years, there has been a steady development of what might be usefully termed a 'psychologisation' of social problems in Scottish and UK society, driven by a renewed emphasis on the individual. In recent years, for example, the Department for Work and Pensions has discussed introducing 'talking treatment' for unemployed people in a hope that this will make them more attractive to potential employers. Elsewhere, there have been proposals that cognitive behaviour therapy might offer new ways of challenging poverty – and challenging 'the poor'. In all of this, there is an emphasis on individual psychology, aspirations, happiness and mental wellbeing. Behavioural psychology increasingly appears to lie at the centre of where social welfare is heading across the UK – and Scotland – today. Other observers have written critically of the growth in the 'happiness' industry and emerging 'therapy' culture in Scotland.[17] Central to some of this activity has been the work of the Scottish Centre for Confidence and Well-Being, and its director, Carol Craig. Craig argues that a 'crisis of confidence' (reflected in the prevalence of a 'dependency culture' across parts of Scottish society) is preventing ordinary Scots from reaching their potential and therefore from prospering.[18]

That the Scottish people apparently suffer from a 'crisis of confidence' is seen here as reflecting a deep-seated problem at the heart of the nation's psyche, the supposedly introvert Scot contrasted with the more extraverted English person, for instance. But the national psyche is also characterised, Craig claims, by a collectivism that stifles enterprise and entrepreneurship, generates a lack of enthusiasm for business and so on. There is then, an 'attitude problem', a lack of aspirations that lies at the root of Scotland's many social ills, poverty and poor health included. The adoption of much more positive attitudes is the way not only to personal, but national, salvation.

Craig's initial work has been roundly criticised.[19] This has not prevented Craig from returning more recently in a book that focuses much more explicitly on Glasgow and West Central Scotland.[20] In *The Tears That Made the Clyde*, Craig once again is concerned with an assorted multitude of 'pathologies' that are seen as inflicting the residents of the city. Glaswegians herein represent a 'pathological population' on a level with Maoris, Native Americans and Australian aborigines.[21] Addictive behaviours, strained personal, familial and social relationships and a 'feeling of oblivion' are seen as rife in the city. There has been much concern in policy circles, especially with regard to questions of morbidity and mortality, of the so-called 'Glasgow effect'. Referring to ill health and other social ills, Craig comments:[22]

> We are used to seeing all these types of problems as the result of deprivation but this on its own does not help us to account for poor health. Should we not begin to ask if it is in the breakdown of so many families and relationships which may be a causal factor? Could it be the case that these personal relationships in Glasgow were poor anyway and that de-industrialisation undermined them even more?

The idea of family 'breakdown' is somewhat ambiguous to put it mildly, reflecting many problematic value judgements. What are 'poor' personal relationships? What we are left with is a view of 'pathology' in West Central Scotland that emerges from a combination of low self-esteem and unhappiness, albeit that there is some awareness in the book of long-term economic decline.

In such thinking, any idea that inequalities of wealth, income, power

and life chances play a role in shaping people's lives is immediately relegated to a secondary position, if acknowledged at all. A focus on individual deficiencies, family 'dysfunctioning' and assorted behavioural traits of
one kind or another is central. There are, then, once again echoes of the
portrayal of poor families in *The Scheme* as we highlighted above.

Some examples of the way in which structural factors are recognised but simultaneously relegated have also found expression in other
contexts. At a conference on 'Transcending Poverties' in Glasgow in
February 2007, organised by the Royal Society of Edinburgh (and supported by the Roman Catholic Church in Scotland), there were repeated
references to the need for those experiencing poverty to take 'responsibility' for their own wellbeing, to spend their money on things other than
cigarettes and alcohol. Scottish historian Tom Devine captured the thrust
of the conference claiming that:[23]

> This conference is important because it moves outside the orthodoxy of
> improving aspects such as employment, area regeneration or health cam-
> paigns and tries to look at the extent to which there must be cultural and
> indeed even spiritual underpinnings for this malaise...
>
> We can examine why the majority with means are unwilling to be taxed. If
> you are dealing with a straightforward transfer of surplus from the better-off
> to the less well off there is always the possibility of dependency.
> Redistribution of wealth in itself might not be the cure and simply perpetu-
> ate the malaise. I don't think the old methods of taxing the rich to help the
> poor will really work.

Such is the steady drift towards a more punitive and harsher understanding in much of the discussion and representation of poverty in Scotland in
recent years.

## 'Othering' people experiencing poverty

The first two presentations of poverty in Scotland, 'the poor' as 'the problem' and 'the poor' as 'freak show' share an approach that is based on
viewing poverty from the outside. Those concerned with developing a
more progressive understanding of poverty, that is an understanding and
appreciation of poverty as rooted in questions and issues of inequality,
equalities and social justice, face a continual battle to reject such 'other-

ings' – that is the stigmatisation, marginalisation and denial of voice to those experiencing poverty today (see Chapter 1).[24] This belies the potency of anti-poor narratives and ideas within society today. Since the mid-1960s, in particular, our understanding of poverty and its causes has developed apace. Yet alongside the development of more sophisticated theories and elaborate systems of measurement, the idea that poverty is the product of 'problem' behaviour and of the limitations of people experiencing poverty has remained ever-present and, arguably, in the context of the deepening financial crisis that has gripped the country today, has become even more pronounced.

Poverty researchers, as well as many campaigning organisations and groups of poverty activists, have long understood that the media plays a particularly significant role in helping to reproduce the view of poor people – and of poor places – as in some ways culpable in their own predicament.[25] This thinking was in the largely discredited (though ever potent) 'culture of poverty' and 'cycle of deprivation' theories in the 1970s – and also echoed in the 'underclass' arguments of the 1980s and 1990s. However, ideas such as these find a home in other approaches to poverty. During the period when New Labour formed the UK government, a recurring distinction was drawn between the 'hard working' and the 'inert', with frequent pronouncements about inadequate parenting, dysfunctional lifestyles and behaviours. Once again then, we can only too readily see the hardening of attitudes to poverty and to people experiencing poverty in recent times. But there are other ways in which poverty has been understood – and presented.

## Poverty as context: social justice for the future

The third example is very different from the first two. Cathy McCormack's 2009 book, *The Wee Yellow Butterfly*, offers a fresh view of poverty. Drawing on her own personal experience of childhood poverty, McCormack shows how structural forces operate to constrain individual choices. In this presentation of poverty, the focus is on compassionate understanding, rather than judgemental moralising, offering hope for the future of a social justice approach. McCormack lays out in graphic ways the impact that poverty has on people's lives, and the struggle to cope – as well as the capacity to fight back and campaign for a more just society. However, McCormack also questions the role of what has generally been referred to as the 'poverty industry' – ie, policy makers, academics and others who make a living out of 'poverty'. She also highlights that poverty is about 'non-material' dimensions, but that these are crucially dependent on an understanding that the material is at the root cause of poverty and that tackling income and wealth inequalities, through redistribution, is also a central element of the war on poverty:[26]

> There has to be redistribution from the haves. There must also be a change of consciousness among the wealthy about the consequences of their wealth making.

McCormack is clear that the voices of those experiencing poverty have to be given prominence in any meaningful attack on poverty itself. As we have seen from the discussion in this chapter and elsewhere in this collection, all too often such voices are at best, marginalised, but more often misrepresented and/or completely overlooked. 2010 was declared the European Year for Combating Poverty and Social Exclusion. As part of its involvement in this, the Poverty Alliance commissioned three short films to raise awareness of poverty in Scotland from the perspectives of young, adult and older people.[27] *Making a Difference* graphically captures the experiences of different groups of people living in, and fighting against, poverty across Scotland. It stands in very sharp contrast to the misrepresentations of people in poverty explored above. Importantly, what these films portray are voices that are all too often hidden and which must take centre stage in the fight against poverty.


## Conclusion

In this chapter, we have explored three examples of the public presentation of poverty. The first demonstrated how media reports and political debates surrounding the Glasgow East by-election in 2008 and the 2010 general election campaign constructed poverty as the individual responsibility of those most affected by it. This approach was not well grounded in research evidence and encouraged the stereotyping of benefit recipients, embodied in the image of the 'Shettleston man'. Similarly, our second example of the presentation of poverty, in the reality television series *The Scheme*, positioned viewers in judgement over the context-free lives of people in a disadvantaged community. Such unsympathetic presentations could be expected to harden attitudes towards poverty and emphasise anti-'welfare' sentiments. They offer an overwhelmingly culture-centred explanation of poverty as a disciplining technique, highlighting aspirational and other numerous and diverse deficits, flawed patterns of consumption and problem behaviours.

Cathy McCormack's *The Wee Yellow Butterfly*, our third example of how poverty is presented in Scotland, offers a counterbalance to the moral condemnation that is evident in some political debates and television portrayals. Grounded in personal experience, McCormack offers insight and compassion in an account that seeks to understand the balance between structural constraints and personal action. This approach offers hope for better connections between debate and research evidence and fuels anti-poverty campaigning.

## Notes

1   T Ridge and S Wright (eds), *Understanding Inequality, Poverty and Wealth: policies and prospects*, The Policy Press, 2008

2   L Harker, *Delivering on Child Poverty: what would it take?* A Report for the Department for Work and Pensions, The Stationery Office, 2006; D Hirsch, *Ending Child Poverty in a Changing Economy*, Joseph Rowntree Foundation, 2009

3   S Cohen, *Folk Devils and Moral Panics*, Routledge, 2002

4   G Mooney, 'The 'Broken Society' Election: class hatred and the politics of poverty and place in Glasgow East', *Social Policy and Society* Vol 8, issue 4, 2009, pp437–50

5   F Nelson, 'The tragedy of welfare ghettoes', *The Spectator*, 6 February 2009

6   J Rentoul, 'The Prime Minister's nightmare scenario', The *Independent*, 13 July 2008

7   M Reid, 'Labour's Glasgow fortress may succumb to apathy', *The Times*, 8 July 2008

8   M Reid, 'A political timebomb in Glasgow's Guantanamo', *The Times*, 3 July 2008

9   J H McKendrick, S Sinclair, A Irwin, H O'Donnell, G Scott and L Dobbie, *Media, Poverty and Public Opinion in the UK*, Joseph Rowntree Foundation, 2008

10  Centre for Social Justice, *Breakthrough Glasgow: ending the costs of social breakdown*, Centre for Social Justice, 2008

11  I Duncan Smith, 'Why talk alone will never end the misery I saw in Glasgow East', *Mail on Sunday*, 13 July 2008

12  I Duncan Smith, 'Living and dying, on welfare in Glasgow East', *The Daily Telegraph*, 13 July 2008

13 D Cameron, 'Fixing our broken society' at www.conservatives.com, 7 July 2008

14 See note 12

15 L Brooks, 'Exotic, extreme, engrossing: tune in to channel poverty', *The Guardian*, 27 May 2010; M McLaughlin, 'The Scheme: a brutal eye-opener or 'poverty porn'?' *The Scotsman*, 28 May 2010; P Kane, 'It's not about people or poverty. The Scheme is quite simply porn', *Sunday Herald*, 23 May 2010; G Mooney and L Hancock, 'Poverty Porn and the Broken Society', *Variant*, 39/40, Winter 2010, pp14–17

16 G Mooney and S Neal, "Welfare Worries': mapping the directions of welfare futures in the contemporary UK', *Research, Policy and Planning*, Vol 27, issue 3, 2009/10, pp141–50

17 C Clark, 'From Self to Structure: challenging the 'happiness industry'', *Variant*, 27, 2006; I Ferguson, 'An Attitude Problem? Confidence and well-being in Scotland', in N Davidson, P McCafferty and D Miller (eds), *Neoliberal Scotland*, Cambridge Scholars Publishing, 2010, pp295–313

18 C Craig, *The Scots' Crisis of Confidence*, Big Thinking, 2003

19 See I Ferguson, 'An Attitude Problem? Confidence and well-being in Scotland', in N Davidson, P McCafferty and D Miller (eds), *Neoliberal Scotland*, Cambridge Scholars Publishing, 2010, pp295–313

20 C Craig, *The Tears That Made The Clyde*, Argyll Publishing, 2010

21 See note 20, p285

22 See note 20, p41

23 T Devine, 'Glasgow could be a laboratory to test how we tackle the ills of modern society', *The Herald Society*, 30 January 2007, p10

24 See also R Lister, *Poverty*, Polity Press, 2004; G Mooney, 'The Disadvantaged Working Class as 'Problem' Population: the 'broken society' and class misrecognition', *Concept*, Vol 1, No. 3, 2010, available at http://concept.lib.ed.ac.uk/index.php/Concept/issue/current

25 S Sinclair, J H McKendrick and P Kelly, 'Taking the High Road? Media and public attitudes toward poverty in Scotland', *Scottish Affairs*, 67, 2009, pp70–91

26 C McCormack, *The Wee Yellow Butterfly*, Argyll Publishing, 2009, p261

27 Poverty Alliance, *Making a Difference*, 2010 (DVD)

# Ten

# Combating poverty through policy, practice and the provision of services

*Gerry Mooney and Sharon Wright*

## Introduction

The continuing existence of poverty in a country as wealthy as Scotland can be seen as a dramatic failure of the measures taken to combat it. Anti-poverty action has a long history. It has been more than 60 years since the UK government introduced a comprehensive welfare state that was intended to eliminate 'want' and more than a decade since the ground-breaking commitment by Westminster (subsequently endorsed by Holy-rood and enshrined in law) to eradicate child poverty by 2020.

Why then, despite these stated intentions, does poverty still persist with such prevalence and intensity in Scotland today? The explanation is that straightforward anti-poverty policies that have proven effective in other com-parable countries (such as ensuring benefits, taxes and wages are at levels that allow people to afford basic necessities and social participation) have not been implemented in Scotland. Instead, Scotland, to a large extent reliant on UK decisions on funding and policies relating to income (witness the October 2010 Comprehensive Spending Review, for instance), has continued to tol-erate an experience of poverty that is exceptional and unnecessary.

The authors in Section Five of this book outline the profound effects of this for different groups, assess the success of different approaches to policy and practice and make suggestions for more effective ways of com-bating poverty in Scotland.

## The Scottish context

The context of poverty in Scotland is particular – widening income inequal-ities have seen a rise in income and assets for the richest in the population, while poverty has been widespread. In this respect Scotland is similar to the rest of the UK, but very different from most rich nations.[1] Existing inequalities were exposed and hardened in the aftermath of industrial decline in the late twentieth century. Within living memory, Scotland's economy was transformed from a leading world manufacturer to a largely service sector economy. This meant a major change in the type of jobs available, which reduced traditional opportunities for working-class men. (In Chapter 19, Richard Holloway highlights the impact of this for young men in ex-industrial communities.)

However, despite the challenges of a reshaped labour market, people in Scotland have lived up to their hard-working reputation. Directly before the 2008 recession (triggered by global financial crisis), record numbers of people were in employment in Scotland[2] – at a higher rate than the UK as a whole (also at its highest ever rate) and outperforming most European and Organisation for Economic Co-operation and Development (OECD) countries.[3] Two lessons can be drawn from this observation. Firstly, that simply attaining a very high employment rate is not a solution to poverty (as implied by the UK approach to welfare reform) (see also Chapter 21). Secondly, the widespread representation of many people in Scotland as 'work-shy' (see Chapter 9) is without basis in evidence.

Overall, it is therefore not a lack of employment or a lack of wealth that has caused poverty in Scotland – both have been in abundance – but a failure of the policies that should reward paid employment adequately and distribute resources fairly among the population. The outcome is a Scotland in which less affluent children are denied opportunities to fulfil their educational potential (see Chapter 12) and lives are cut short prematurely (see Chapter 11).

## Key issues for policy, practice and service provision

The following chapters (11–22) explore key issues of policy, practice and service provision.

Carol Tannahill and Bruce Whyte (Chapter 11) show that, although health is improving overall, inequalities are increasing, especially for men. Health inequalities have grown to such a level that men in the wealthiest parts of Glasgow can expect to live up to 28 years longer than those in the most deprived areas.[4] Ultimately, poverty leads to early death for large numbers of people in Scotland. The Scottish government has recognised the severity of health inequalities in its report *Equally Well*.[5] Policy solutions, and subsequent implementation, need to maintain a clear focus on the underlying causes of these inequalities and avoid drifting towards an over-emphasis on behavioural change and lifestyle 'solutions' to the problem. While there have been important steps forward, as with the example of paid employment above, individual behaviour is not enough without intervention to address the social determinants of ill health and early death. Addressing the structural causes of inadequate income and health inequalities would, as Wilkinson and Pickett argue, benefit the whole society, not just those on a low income.[6]

Bronwen Cohen (Chapter 12) demonstrates that, since children face the highest risk of poverty in Scotland, access to early years' services, together with improvements to maternity pay and leave, can play a crucial role as part of an effective anti-poverty strategy. The commitment to eradicate child poverty by 2020 has raised the profile of measures to intervene in early years. She points out that targeting services on the disadvantaged can create stigmatisation. Lessons from international research show that fully integrated services – in terms of access, funding, workforce, regulation and co-ordination – combined with a universal entitlement approach and capping of fees to parents are more effective in reaching families with poor educational backgrounds and bring particularly big gains for children under three – the age group most at risk of poverty.

In Chapter 13, John Dickie takes up the issue of poverty for children of all ages, demonstrating its damaging large-scale effects. The landmark commitment to eradicate child poverty by 2020 has, since the 2007 edition of *Poverty in Scotland*, been enshrined in law. Unfortunately, policies have not yet proven fully fit for purpose, and new approaches and investment in families will be necessary in order for the goal to be achieved. Key policy changes are suggested: a living wage; family-friendly work practices; increases to benefits and tax credits; and a better balance between universal and targeted support. Progress is recognised in relation to tax credits (especially in contributing towards the costs of childcare); the positive effects of the national minimum wage; opportunities for flexible working arrangements to support parents in their role as workers; and free school meals. However, since half of children in poverty live in households where at least one adult is in paid work,[7] just getting a job is not enough to eradicate child poverty. Concerns are raised over increasing work conditions for parents and the declining value of benefits, which are often difficult to claim. Rising unemployment levels as a result of the recession are likely to increase levels of child poverty. An increase in the numbers of people who will have no alternative but to claim increasingly restricted benefits and tax credits is predicted, pointing to a crucial role for welfare rights advice to ensure that people, both in and out of work, receive their entitlements.

Gaps in life expectancy and severe health problems are also combined with attainment gaps between different income groups, with poverty acting as a barrier to children and young people achieving their educational potential. Claire Telfer, in Chapter 14, shows that the attainment gap has remained static in recent years, resulting in thousands of young people leaving school with no, or low, qualifications and skills. Underachievement in education is estimated to cost around £1 billion a year in Scotland. *A Curriculum for Excellence* recognises the issue of underachievement and seeks to increase choice for children and young people, particularly those from disadvantaged backgrounds.[8] Another key strategy was to reduce class sizes for the earliest years of primary school. Commitments to extend entitlement to pre-school education have also been made. Explicit action to improve the educational attainment of children living in poverty still needs to be developed at the heart of the Scottish government's child poverty strategy.

Income is a fundamental aspect of poverty and in Chapter 15 Tommy Gorman reinforces the need for effective welfare rights advice, particularly for ill and disabled people in Scotland, in order to maximise income through take-up of benefits and tax credits. The focus is on people coping with cancer and the challenges presented by changes from incapacity benefit to employment and support allowance, which have made it more difficult to access financial support through the benefit system. The extra costs of illness and disability are highlighted, along with the drop in income and subsequent hardship that has been found to follow the onset of long-term illness. Another important challenge is how to ensure financial stability when moving in and out of employment (because of either ill health or insecure employment). The issue of maintaining stability is also important for people who claim benefits in other circumstances – eg, as lone parents following relationship breakdown.

In Chapter 16, Keith Dryburgh focuses on debt, which is often experienced by people living in poverty because their income (from work or benefits) is insufficient to meet basic necessities. This reinforces the message from several other chapters that paid employment cannot guarantee a route out of poverty unless a living wage is paid, and that benefits and tax credits need to be increased so that recipients can avoid poverty. Scottish government initiatives have increased access to vital debt solutions. There have also been improvements in UK government policy on financial inclusion, but progress towards combating poverty has been undermined by the 2010 Westminster coalition government's approach to reducing public expenditure (see also Chapter 1). Effective intervention to tackle debt issues is not just about ensuring that people on low incomes have bank accounts, but that incomes are adequate and low-cost credit options are available where appropriate as an alternative to high-interest doorstep lending.

In Chapter 17, Eurig Scandrett explores the relationship between poverty and environmental injustice, which includes living in poorer physical environments, with greater reliance on public transport, which is less available in rural areas. There are calls for better consultation in development processes to ensure the development of more just policies.

In Chapter 18, John McKendrick investigates rural poverty in Scotland. One in seven people in rural Scotland live in poverty.[9] Good progress was made in both recognising rural poverty (in the Scottish government's *Achieving Our Potential* strategy) and in lowering income poverty between 2005/06 and 2007/08. Several challenges remain in rural areas: higher costs of living; higher levels of consumption; fewer earning opportunities; dispersed or 'invisible' deprivation; a culture of self-sufficiency; gender pay issues; the costs of transport; and access to services.

Issues of housing disadvantage (eg, homelessness) are explored by Richard Grant and Zoe McGuire in Chapter 22. Among their policy recommendations is a demand for an improvement in the quality and the quantity of social housing.

## Conclusion

Across the contributions in Section Five, there is acknowledgement of significant progress in recognising and responding to poverty (particularly, but not only, child poverty) at UK and Scottish levels. Good practice has been identified in consultative processes, the passing of the Child Poverty Act 2010, and a range of initiatives to tackle debt, rural poverty, child poverty (including, for example, improved access to free school meals) and inequalities in education and health.

Several authors also indicate ongoing challenges, particularly in relation to addressing income poverty since policies do not yet guarantee that paid employment is a route out of poverty (see Chapter 21 by Kendra

Strauss and Peter Kelly), and low rates of benefit payment ensure that many recipients live in poverty – and, in any case, jobs do not exist for everyone who needs them. Insufficient income therefore continues to be a key cause of poverty in Scotland, but the main mechanisms for addressing it are controlled by Westminster, where the priority of the 2010 Conservative/Liberal Democrat coalition government is to cut public expenditure. The combination of a UK government influenced heavily by free-market values and a recession that has been taken to justify widespread cuts (rather than to prompt the end of 'fat cat' bonuses or income tax increases for the wealthy), risks a serious undermining of the very real progress towards combating poverty that was made in the early twenty-first century.

Other challenges are thrown up by the issue of participation. In Chapter 20, Peter Kelly challenges policy makers and the Scottish government to resource effective participation, recognising that a lack of resources is one of the key factors that serve to undermine a commitment to participation. Through measures such as this, he argues, voices of people experiencing poverty are more likely to be heard.

There is substantial scope for the Scottish government to lead the way in UK anti-poverty action, particularly in relation to services such as health, education and childcare – and also in relation to questions of voice and participation. Several authors also identify international examples of effective anti-poverty policy, within which services play a crucial role in supporting parents to work and ensuring that children's needs are met. Such an approach would involve a 'whole society' view of the causes and consequences of poverty. Action to address the structural causes of income, health and attainment inequalities could benefit Scottish society as a whole.

A 'whole society' approach could also involve all citizens in Scotland offering greater dignity and respect to each other. The parameters and underlying assumptions of political and media debates can be changed to reflect more accurate understandings of social issues, such as poverty. There is scope for reporting on poverty to be more compassionate towards people living in vulnerable situations, without the judgemental moralisation that has been tolerated in a number of arenas (see Chapter 9).

## Notes

1   OECD, *OECD Employment Outlook*, OECD, 2007
2   Comparable records go back to 1971.
3   Eurostat, *Employment*, Eurostat, 2008, available at http://epp.eurostat.ec.

europa.eu; National Statistics, *Employment*, 2008, available at www.statistics. gov.uk; OECD, *OECD Employment Outlook*, OECD, 2007

4   World Health Organization, *Closing the Gap in a Generation: health equity through action on the social determinants of health*, World Health Organization, 2008

5   Scottish Government, *Equally Well: report of the Ministerial Task Force on Health Inequalities*, Scottish Government, 2008; available at www.scotland.gov. uk/publications

6   R Wilkinson and K Pickett, *The Spirit Level: why more equal societies almost always do better*, Penguin, 2010

7   L Harker, *Delivering on Child Poverty: what would it take?* A report for the Department for Work and Pensions, The Stationery Office, 2006

8   Scottish Government, *A Curriculum for Excellence*, Scottish Government, 2010

9   Scottish Government, *Scottish Government: poverty analysis*, 2009, available at www.scotland.gov.uk, accessed 26 October 2010

# Section Five

## Issues and future challenges

# Eleven
# Inequalities in health

*Carol Tannahill and Bruce Whyte*

## Introduction

Many studies have demonstrated links between health and socio-economic disadvantage. In Scotland, a series of national and local health profiles have shown differences of health across the whole deprivation gradient.[1] In the period 2004 to 2006, male life expectancy in the 10 per cent most deprived areas in Scotland was more than 13 years lower than that in the 10 per cent least deprived areas[2] and when smaller areas are compared even greater differences are seen. The 28-year gap in male life expectancy at birth (1998–2002) between Calton (in East Glasgow) and North Lenzie has been cited internationally as an example of the scale of socio-economically determined health inequalities, even in countries with well-developed universal services.[3] The size of the health gap in Scotland varies by gender (generally greater for men), age group (being largest among working-age adults) and cause of death.[4]

The relationship between poverty and health is complex. While health in Scotland has been improving and poverty reducing *overall*, health inequalities remain a major challenge, and some have been widening. Furthermore, it has been argued that relative income inequality is harmful, not only for those in the poorest circumstances but also for society as a whole. Wilkinson and Pickett demonstrate consistently strong associations internationally between inequality in society and a wide range of health and social outcomes, arguing that the wealthy too would experience benefits from a less unequal income structure.[5]

Focusing on the West of Scotland through the 1980s to 2000, Glasgow became a more affluent and 'middle-class' city, but there were widening health inequalities, particularly among men.[6] It is often argued that Glasgow's health record is a consequence of the change in its economy and employment base, but comparative studies of the West of

Scotland with other post-industrial regions across Europe suggest that while de-industrialisation has had an impact, there are clearly other factors involved.[7] Moreover, although income deprivation is no worse in Glasgow than in Liverpool or Manchester, mortality rates are higher.[8] Importantly, this excess mortality is observed across the whole spectrum of deprivation and among all ages, except the very young. In short, despite the strong and pervasive links between poverty and ill health, income deprivation does not in and of itself explain Glasgow's, and Scotland's, poor health. Other factors – as yet undetermined – seem to be at play.

## The policy context for tackling health inequalities in Scotland

Health sits as a devolved power to the Scottish parliament. Although there remains a number of dimensions that require UK or European Union-level negotiation and action (eg, NHS terms and conditions, the GP contract, aspects of food policy, and communicable disease control), the Scottish government has significant discretion to tailor health policy to Scotland's context and particular health challenges. As a consequence, there is a growing divergence between Scotland and the other countries of the UK in terms of NHS structures and governance processes. The Scottish parliament arguably places greater weight on public health issues – as illustrated by being the first legislature in the UK to ban smoking in public places and, more recently, in its cross-government commitment to addressing health inequalities.

*Equally Well*, the report of the Ministerial Task Force on Health Inequalities, is the first Scottish policy focused exclusively on delivering more equal health outcomes in Scotland.[9] It recognises that approaches to improving the health of the whole population will not necessarily result in its more equal distribution. Those who are hardest to reach, or have the least resources (whether material, social or psychological), are likely to be disadvantaged as they often require a different, or more intensive, service or intervention.

*Equally Well* contains 78 recommendations to 'improve health and other life outcomes for particularly vulnerable groups of people, who need a cross-government and cross-sector approach from the service they rely on'.[10] All government directorates, not just health, have a role in delivery.

In 2010, the Task Force reconvened to review progress and linkage to other aspects of social policy, and to consider whether the recommendations remained relevant and deliverable in the current financial context. This review emphasised that early intervention sits at the heart of this policy agenda, and restated the need for transformational change and collaborative approaches across different public services.[11] In addition, the case was made for fostering and promoting people's assets and capacities for health and wellbeing.[12]

It is important briefly to highlight two other dimensions of the policy context. First, a focus on equalities issues (including the impacts of socio-economic circumstances on health) is now evident across a range of Scottish health policies.[13] Second, there are a number of issue-specific policies, strategies and frameworks focused on priority public health challenges (alcohol, obesity and so on) that recognise the need for targeted, as well as universal, approaches.

## Delivering better health outcomes for people in poverty

*Equally Well* represents a strong policy context for action to reduce health inequalities in Scotland. It does not simply represent 'more of the same'. It emphasises early intervention, reflects the chronic nature of the stresses that lead to worse health outcomes for those in poverty, seeks to re-orientate public services to deliver differently across the population, and builds on current intelligence about priority issues and effective practice. It has also secured 'buy-in' from across government – and therefore a degree of leverage in all government directorates. There are no 'quick wins' in any of this, however, as these approaches are to be implemented against the backdrop of no improvement over decades in life expectancy in our poorest communities.

In our view, the primary challenges concern leadership and implementation. A particular sort of leadership will be required. Its characteristics would include giving health and social outcomes an equal (or greater) weight to that given to economic outcomes, and leading debate about the type of society we want for Scotland in the future, recognising trade-offs between efficiency and equity. Many of the established policy levers – such as a focus on delivering cost-effective interventions and achieving numerical targets – effectively militate against equitable outcomes by placing a premium on the 'number' (eg, the number of cases seen) regardless of its composition (the level of need of those cases). Cost-effectiveness is clearly important and will become increasingly so as resources become more scarce, but other considerations need to be given weight alongside it. Leadership will need to be durable and sustainable across political and organisational divides. That will require clarity and consensus around a suitably broad set of principles that should underpin decision making for population health.[14]

The implementation challenges are rather different. Awareness of the health needs of people in poverty – and of the pathways between poverty and health – is not sufficiently widespread. The implications of these needs for services, and how they are delivered, are not yet well enough articulated. Greater value needs to be put on the skills involved in working with different sectors and with communities. The incentives that reinforce behaviours that disadvantage poorer people should be challenged. The *Equally Well* test sites are seeking to do this in their different ways. Learning from such approaches needs to be spread widely. In addition, the danger of 'lifestyle drift' needs to be avoided whereby, despite policy recognition of the structural and social determinants of health inequalities, implementation focuses on individual behaviours.[15]

It is too early to say whether *Equally Well*, together with the two other social policy pillars (*Getting it Right for Every Child* and *Achieving Our Potential*) will deliver better health outcomes for people in poverty. But it is already clear to us that, despite the favourable policy context, major challenges exist in relation to implementation. Government has an important role to play in this too.

## What more could be done?

Above all else, it needs to be emphasised that the health of Scotland's poorest people will not be improved, or health inequalities reduced, through a series of programmatic interventions. Our policy prescription (which reflects not only good public health intelligence but also current economic realities) is therefore not about new initiatives, but about the choices that need to be made to protect and support good health among the most vulnerable in society.

First, there is scope for a renewed focus on the 'social'. By this we mean the place of social enterprise; the ways in which public spaces are used; the fostering of volunteering and different employment models; the accessibility of cultural and leisure activities; the building of social capital; attention to intergenerational links and facilities; and much more. All of these can contribute to the health of individuals, and also to community and population health.

Linked to this is the need to foster community-led approaches to health, accompanied by attention to models of governance and community leadership. There is growing recognition of the limited potential of current models of support and care to achieve good health for all. Community-led approaches can supplement public services, be empowering to those involved, and be directly relevant and responsive to community needs and circumstances. At the time of writing, the Chief Medical Officer is advocating that increased attention be paid to 'assets' and the releasing of individual potential – crucially recognising these approaches as a part of the remedy for reducing health inequalities.

Third, policy needs to be future-oriented. Aspects of our way of life and our current pattern of service provision are simply unsustainable, both environmentally and economically. Examples include our ways of travel, the growth in hospital-based healthcare, and our eating patterns. All have implications for Scotland's health, and there is an urgent need to establish alternatives that support better health outcomes for all.

Lastly, Scotland should continue to lead the way with brave public health policy, emphasising early intervention and sustaining the policy focus across parties and political terms. Scotland's policy focus on health inequalities has been regarded as an international exemplar. We need to maintain that in order for our health outcomes to be regarded in the same way.

## Notes

1  Glasgow Centre for Population Health, *Community Health and Wellbeing Profiles for Greater Glasgow*, 2008, available at www.gcph.co.uk/publications; Scottish Public Health Observatory, *ISD Community Health and Wellbeing Profiles*, 2008, available at www.scotpho.org.uk

2  Scottish Government, *Equally Well: report of the Ministerial Task Force on Health Inequalities*, 2008, available at www.scotland.gov.uk/publications/2008/06/25104032/0

3  Commission on Social Determinants of Health, *Closing the Gap in a Generation: health equity through action on the social determinants of health*, Final Report of the Commission on Social Determinants of Health, World Health Organization, 2008

4  A H Leyland, R Dundas, P McLoone, F A Boddy, *Inequalities in Mortality in Scotland 1981–2001*, Medical Research Council Social and Public Health

Sciences Unit Occasional Paper Series No.16, Medical Research Council Social and Public Health Sciences Unit, 2007

5  R Wilkinson and K Pickett, *The Spirit Level: why more equal societies almost always do better*, Penguin, 2009

6  P Hanlon, D Walsh and B Whyte, *Let Glasgow Flourish*, Glasgow Centre for Population Health, 2006

7  D Walsh, M Taulbut and P Hanlon, *The Aftershock of Deindustrialisation: trends in mortality in Scotland and other parts of post-industrial Europe*, Glasgow Centre for Population Health, 2008

8  D Walsh, N Bendel, R Jones and P Hanlon, *Investigating a 'Glasgow Effect'*, Glasgow Centre for Population Health, 2010

9  See note 2

10 See note 2, p3

11 Scottish Government, *Equally Well Review 2010: report by the Ministerial Task Force on implementing Equally Well, the Early Years Framework, and Achieving Our Potential*, 2010

12 See note 11, pp7–8

13 For example, Scottish Government, *Healthcare Quality Strategy for NHS Scotland*, 2010

14 A Tannahill, 'Beyond Evidence – to Ethics: a decision-making framework for health promotion, public health and health improvement', *Health Promotion International*, Vol 23(4), 2008, pp380-90

15 D J Hunter, J Popay, C Tannahill and M Whitehead, 'Getting to Grips with Health Inequalities at Last?' *British Medical Journal*, Vol 340, 2010

# Twelve

# Early years: getting it right for Scotland's youngest citizens

*Bronwen Cohen*

## Poverty in the early years

The highest levels of poverty in Scotland can be found in families with young children.[1] Indeed, young children account for nearly one-half of all children and young people in poverty.[2] After housing costs are taken into account, young children's risk of poverty is much higher than that of any other major population group, including pensioners, and that risk is not diminishing.[3] Furthermore, many young children have endured poverty all their young lives. The 2010 Growing up in Scotland report found that one-quarter of three- and four-year-olds and one-fifth of five- and six-year-olds were living in 'persistently poor' families over the four-year study period.[4] There was little change in child poverty rates in Scotland between 2004/05 and 2008/09.[5]

## Childrearing costs

Having a baby and providing care during the early years has a big impact on the income of families, and on women in particular. Maternity and parental leave provisions still do not adequately compensate for the loss of income during the child's first year. While leave entitlement is potentially long (up to a year), the period of relatively well-paid maternity leave is short (six weeks at 90 per cent of pay).

In the months after birth, the income of many families is affected by the difficulty in accessing and affording childcare services. An annual survey on the costs of raising a child has charted a 43 per cent increase in costs between 2003 and 2010.[6] In Scotland, between 2008 and 2009, the cost of a day nursery place for children aged two and under rose by

12 per cent.[7] Childcare (for all ages) is the biggest single cost incurred by families, and the loss of child benefit as a universal entitlement for every child will compound the problem for some.

Although Scotland, in common with the rest of the UK, has high overall attendance rates for children in services for three- to five-year-olds, UK statistics show that of working-age women with children aged under five, 57 per cent were in employment, compared with 71 per cent of those whose youngest child was aged five to ten.[8] Thirty-eight per cent of all women with dependent children worked part time – often in work that is lower paid than men.

If work is available, it needs to cover the costs of childcare to make it worthwhile. Scottish parents spend, on average, more than £600 a month for 25 hours of childcare a week, compared with Norway, where parents' fees are capped at 2,250 Norwegian krone – equivalent to £387 a month for a full-time place.[9]

It is important to remember that some families (eg, those with a child with additional support needs) will face extra costs and an increased challenge of finding childcare, while those living in rural areas face increased transport costs to access services for children.

## Recent policy affecting poverty in early childhood

While child poverty figures have remained relatively static over the last five years, much has been done over the last decade at a UK level to improve parental leave and to support childcare in order to lift children out of poverty by making it easier for parents of young children to continue to work, or return to work. The introduction of tax credits and increased benefits raised the incomes of the 'working poor' and the unemployed alike.

Pledges on eradicating child poverty were associated with substantial amounts of funding through the Treasury's Sure Start programme, increases to maternity and paternity leave and pay, and extending entitlement to universal, free, part-time nursery education for three-year-olds in 2004. There was also a two-year (2006–2008), limited, centrally funded scheme offering free nursery places for disadvantaged two-year-olds in Scotland.

In December 2008, the Scottish government and the Convention of Scottish Local Authorities published the *Early Years Framework*. This was developed within the new context of the concordat, which set out a new working relationship between national and local government and brought the government-controlled ring-fencing of funds to an end. The framework calls for 'a new level of ambition in early years', which 'cannot be achieved by a business as usual approach. Transformational change is required.' It asks for 'a renewed focus on services from pregnancy through to age three as the period of a child's development that shapes future outcomes'.[10] The framework comes with no additional funds, however, and its success will be measured by whether local authorities meet agreed targets in their single-outcome agreements. In June 2010, Scottish government ministers reaffirmed their commitment to the early years by inviting other top officials and frontline staff to sign a pledge to improve outcomes for children, despite the financial climate.

The UK emergency Budget delivered by the coalition government in autumn 2010 pledged not to *reduce* child poverty, but rather to ensure it would *not increase*. The UK-funded health in pregnancy grant was abolished and child benefit was frozen for three years.

## Critical review of policy on poverty in early childhood

Early years' services and the workforce that staff them continue to be divided between zero to two-year-olds (care) and three-year-olds to school age (education). Those making up the workforce of the services for under-three-year-olds (such as childminders and nursery staff) are often themselves the 'working poor', with unstable and low incomes. Responsibility for early years' services development, crucial to strategic planning, is also effectively split between Holyrood and Westminster, as the Westminster Department for Work and Pensions provides tax credits to help families in paid employment pay for childcare, while services are the responsibility of the Scottish government. This makes any strategic attempt to cap costs to parents and invest in more and higher quality provision very difficult, if not impossible.

When a child does reach the age of three, the fragmented nature of local early education and care often means parents must invest time and money into a patchwork of childcare to make work possible. The fact that there are limited part-time jobs (which often pay less than full-time work) means it is not possible and not financially feasible for some parents, particularly lone parents, to return to work.

The emergency Budget relies on an increase in child tax credit to mitigate cuts and price rises elsewhere. However, credits have to be applied for and there is evidence that many families fail to take up tax credits because they fear the consequences of overpayments that need repaying and subsequently push families into debt.[11]

Targeting services on those most at risk of poverty is frequently advocated – and the current economic climate has reinforced this. But, as the OECD *Starting Strong II* report pointed out (echoed by Penn in her later report for the European Commission), 'targeted programmes segregate, may stigmatise and generally fail to provide for many of the children eligible for special programmes'.[12] The latest Growing up in Scotland report states that four in ten children experienced poverty at least once during a four-year period, which suggests that poverty touches more children than other point (or indeed place)-in-time studies imply, and that many might be missed from traditional means of targeting support.

## Policy prescriptions for 2011 and beyond

So what should be done? Nothing less than a transformation in early years' policy and service delivery, which is nothing more than is stated in the *Early Years Framework*. However, in order to achieve such change, there needs to be full integration of services for the early years in terms of access, funding, workforce, regulation and co-ordination. Research carried out for the European project *Working for Inclusion* found that countries with low levels of child poverty also had the highest levels of early childhood education and care services.[13] These were delivered by a fully integrated government system, with high take-up of universal entitlement at a lower capped cost to parents, and by a highly qualified, well-paid and integrated workforce. Such services are more effective in reaching families with poor educational backgrounds and offer particularly high gains for children under three – the age group most at risk of poverty.

Can this happen in Scotland? It will require a more determined approach to developing a fully integrated system, as well as revised devolutionary arrangements to allow the Scottish government to invest directly in early years' education and care services, and cap their costs to parents. Scotland might do worse than look to the way Norway has developed its services – with a national goal to offer a kindergarten place, as a right, to all children from the age of one (now achieved) and ring-fenced funding to local authorities during the development stage (now ended).

And the experience of those countries that offer the best provision seems to suggest that taxpayers perceive this as a good use of their local and national income tax. For countries such as Sweden, this is central to their vision of the role of early years' services in delivering a 'knowledge' and 'equal' society. The current debate on new powers for the Scottish government and an early years' framework that highlights the need for transformational change offers an opportunity to bring our services into the twenty-first century and our youngest citizens out of poverty. Let us hope we take it.

## Notes

1　Children in Scotland analysis of *Households Below Average Income* data; House of Commons Committee of Public Accounts, *Tax Credits and PAYE: eighth report of session 2007/08*; and *Scottish Neighbourhood Statistics*

2　Cabinet Office, *State of the Nation Report: poverty, worklessness and welfare dependency in the UK*, 2010, available at www.cabinetoffice.gov.uk

3　Scottish Government, *Poverty and Income Inequality in Scotland, 2008–2009*, 2010, Table A1

4　Scottish Government, *Growing up in Scotland: the circumstances of persistently poor children summary report*, 2010. Poverty risk may be even higher among the very youngest children. The longitudinal nature of this study, and the small sample sizes of Scotland-wide data, means that there is no currently published, disaggregated data on the numbers of children under the age of three or under two experiencing poverty.

5　See note 3

6　Centre for Economics and Business Research for Liverpool Victoria, *Cost of a Child*, January 2010

7　Children in Scotland/Daycare Trust, *Childcare Costs in Scotland Survey*, Children in Scotland, 2009

8　Office for National Statistics, *Labour Force Survey*, 2008

9　Currency conversion on 4 October 2010, with 1 NOK = 0.107728 GBP. To equivalise spend, this currency conversion also takes account of purchasing parity power (OECD estimates that 160% of GBP are required to purchase the same volume of goods with NOK. See www.oecd.org/dataoecd/48/18/18598721.pdf. £242 rises to £387 after purchasing parity power, an outlay that is still considerably less than in Scotland.

10　Scottish Government, *The Early Years Framework*, 2009, Section 5 (Priorities for Action), available at www.scotland.gov.uk/publications/2009/01

11　'Working tax credit' at www.wikipedia.org, 2010

12　OECD, *Starting Strong II: early childhood education and care*, OECD, 2006, p17; H Penn, *Early Childhood Education and Care: key lessons from research for policy makers*, European Commission/NSSE, 2009, p61

13 Children in Scotland, *Working for Inclusion: an overview of European Union early years services and their workforce*, Children in Scotland, 2010, available at www.childreninscotland.org.uk/wfi

# Thirteen
# Child poverty

*John Dickie*

## Introduction

One in four of Scotland's children still live in poverty. Behind this dry statistic are tens of thousands of children whose health is being damaged,
education undermined and lives cut short because families lack the
resources needed to give their children a fair start in life. Such ongoing
poverty damages not just children themselves, but society as a whole. It
undermines social cohesion and wider wellbeing and imposes huge financial costs, with an estimated £1.5 billion of additional social expenditure
and lost tax revenue in Scotland alone.[1]

There is nothing inevitable about child poverty; it has been much
lower in the past, and is much lower across Europe today. This chapter
explores to what extent government at every level has tackled child poverty since 2007 and sets out the action needed if targets to eradicate child
poverty in Scotland by 2020 are to be met.

## Child poverty policy since 2007

In *Poverty in Scotland 2007* it was argued that four key policy changes
were needed if child poverty was to be abolished: a greater focus on tackling low pay and family-unfriendly practice in the workplace; increases in
benefits and tax credits; a rebalancing of targeted and universal support;
and greater attention to the role played by income inequality. Four years
on, what policy changes have we seen, and to what extent do they reflect
these four necessary shifts?

Paid work has continued to be the key focus of child poverty policy.
Tax credits, including support with childcare (see Chapter 12), the nation-

al minimum wage and action to increase flexible working arrangements have played a positive role, increasing the number of parents in work and the financial rewards of that work. Yet at the same time, welfare 'reforms' (ratcheting up the conditions attached to benefit entitlement and shifting people onto less generous benefits) have threatened family incomes and failed to grapple with the real barriers to work. Rising unemployment has since made accessing paid work even more problematic, particularly for those with ill health, a disability or caring responsibilities.

Meanwhile, for those able to find work, employment too often fails to provide a route out of poverty. Half of children in poverty in Scotland live in families where at least one adult is in work.[2] Pay distribution remains extraordinarily unequal, with women particularly disadvantaged, while inflexible employment patterns and lack of childcare limit the number of hours parents can work.

Proposals from the UK coalition government include positive ideas to reduce the financial barriers faced when moving into work (through increased income disregards and more gentle tapers, enabling people to keep more of their benefits as their earnings increase[3]), but continue to fail to address wider job barriers and the need to protect those unable to work.

In Scotland, work has also been at the heart of anti-poverty strategy. The Scottish National Party (SNP) government set out a joint framework with local authorities for tackling poverty, *Achieving Our Potential*.[4] This included key commitments to making work pay by scoping action on tackling pay inequalities in the public sector and promoting learning from previous approaches to removing barriers to work, such as Working for Families. Free school meals entitlement has also been extended to children in working families with the lowest incomes. However, there are significant concerns about the extent to which national ambitions are translating into action at local level, given that much ring-fencing of resources has been removed (such as those previously earmarked for the Working for Families initiative) and the lack of any clear alternative mechanisms for monitoring local spending decisions for their impact on child poverty. More positively, ministers have recently signaled a commitment to ensure that all directly employed Scottish government and NHS workers receive a 'living wage'.[5]

The four years leading up to the 2010 UK general election saw intermittent investment to boost benefits and tax credits. In Scotland, the government continued to promote welfare rights advice and information as an important way of maximising incomes through funding new models of provision linked to health services for young families and those affected by cancer, as well as through specialist second-tier support to frontline work-ers. However, concerns again remain about the adequacy of funding, and the comprehensiveness of reach, of advice provision at local level.

As a result of increases to benefits and tax credits, and action on employment, there were around 100,000 fewer children living in poverty in Scotland by 2008/09 compared with the mid-1990s.[6] By 2010/11, the UK government anticipated a fall in the number of children living in poverty across the UK by perhaps as much as a million since 1998/99.[7] Nevertheless, the current welfare safety net leaves many families well below the poverty line, and many still fail to get the financial support to which they are entitled – over one in six families failing to access tax cred-its worth £150 million in Scotland alone.[8] Worse still, the first coalition Budget in June 2010, and the subsequent October Spending Review, announced huge benefit cuts for those both in and out of work, impact-ing hardest on the poorest families.[9] Despite increases in the child element of child tax credit, these cuts are likely to increase child poverty, unless urgent action is taken to reverse their impact.

The years since 2007 also saw tentative moves towards providing more support through universal mechanisms that are more effective in boosting take-up and reducing stigma than means-tested support. Increases to child benefit, the introduction of health in pregnancy grants and piloting of universal free school meals had been announced by the previous UK Labour government, all of which would have played an important role in preventing poverty by targeting support at all parents. Meanwhile, in Scotland, the SNP government committed to rolling out free school meals to all P1–P3 pupils, following a successful pilot that signifi-cantly boosted take-up (including among those already entitled) and pos-itively impacted on family budgets.[10]

However, such positive developments are currently being under-mined. The Scottish government and local authorities have backtracked on the roll-out of universal free school lunches in Scotland, and the new UK government has proposed freezing and restricting entitlement to child benefit as well as abolishing health in pregnancy grants. Similarly, imple-mentation of Scottish government commitments to extend universal nurs-ery provision in Scotland (important in providing quality early years education and in giving parents greater flexibility to increase their hours at work) has been scaled back.

An important recognition of the role that underlying income inequal-ities play in driving poverty (including child poverty) came when a key sol-idarity target 'to increase overall income and the proportion of income earned by the three lowest income deciles as a group by 2017' was set within the Scottish government's economic strategy. However, this has not, so far, led to any change in the overall distribution of income.[11] At UK level there has been no specific commitment to address directly such inequality, with coalition measures to date likely to increase it.

Perhaps the most significant wider developments in policy since 2007, prior to the 2010 UK election, have been the embedding of the commitment to eradicate child poverty in law and an increased focus on the role of local government. The 2010 Child Poverty Act places a duty on the UK government to ensure targets to eradicate child poverty by 2020 are met, produce strategies setting out how it will do so, and report to Parliament on progress. The Act also places a duty on the Scottish government to produce strategies setting out the measures it will take to contribute towards UK targets. While legislation alone cannot eradicate poverty, the Act is important in ensuring that eradicating child poverty is a purpose of government, not just a particular ruling party, and that income is central to defining that poverty.

The Act puts on statute a growing emphasis on the role of local government, with English local authorities required to assess need and produce local child poverty strategies. In Scotland, however, such a duty does not apply. Instead, *Achieving Our Potential* is meant to act as the framework for local authority action with single-outcome agreements providing '... the vehicle for describing how poverty is being tackled at a local level'. However, while all single-outcome agreements discuss poverty, it is difficult to identify strategic approaches to tackling child poverty (or poverty generally). Only four councils explicitly state that tackling child poverty is a priority and only two set a local outcome to reduce child poverty. Only one refers to a child poverty strategy.[12] At the same time, commitments by local government and ministers to address poverty and reduce educational barriers through introducing a universal approach to free school meals and reviewing school clothing grants, with a view to more consistent and generous provision, have either been scaled back or stalled altogether.

## 2011 and beyond: what is needed now?

A policy agenda dominated by unprecedented spending cuts means the future for children in poverty may look bleak. However, the very real progress that had been made in reducing child poverty stalled even as the economy boomed and public spending rose. Just as a growing economy and rising public spending were not, in themselves, the solution to child poverty, recession, economic recovery and public spending cuts must not be a barrier to further progress. Politicians at every level need to ensure that, whatever the overall level of resources available, spending decisions and pay settlements focus on ensuring low-income families have a fairer share, and that services are delivered in a way that does not exclude children.

In the short term, stronger mechanisms need to be put in place to ensure Scottish government anti-poverty frameworks actually deliver at a local level, while at UK level coalition commitments to fairness and ending child poverty need to be backed by tax and spending decisions that contribute to, rather than undermine, such ambitions. Every level of government needs to pay as much attention to the tax levers at their disposal as they do to cutting spending, both to ensure adequate resources to protect citizens from poverty and to address the unfair tax burden on our poorest families.

Finally, politicians need to think beyond the immediate impact of policy and assess the extent to which decisions made in the short term will contribute to, or undermine, the creation of the conditions needed for a Scotland genuinely free of child poverty. International evidence suggests that a combination of high-quality labour markets, universal high-quality services (including childcare), and high levels of social security support are key conditions associated with low levels of poverty.[13] While crucial employment and social security levers remain at Westminster, Scottish and local government also have an important role to play in fostering these conditions, particularly in relation to improving the quality of employment opportunities, the distribution of pay, and the protection and development of universal approaches to service provision.

### Notes

1   D Hirsch, *Estimating the Cost of Child Poverty in Scotland: approaches and evidence*, Scottish Government Social Research, 2008
2   A Parekh, P Kenway and T MacInnes, *Monitoring Poverty and Social Exclusion in Scotland 2010*, Joseph Rowntree Foundation/New Policy Institute, 2010, p10, Figure 4
3   Department for Work and Pensions, *21st Century Welfare*, The Stationery Office, 2010
4   Scottish Government, *Achieving Our Potential: a framework to tackle poverty and income inequality in Scotland*, The Scottish Government, 2008

5  Scottish Parliament, *Minutes of Proceedings* Vol 3, No.70 Session 3, Thursday 29 April 2010

6  Scottish Government, *Poverty and Income Inequality in Scotland: 2008–09*, National Statistics, 2010, Annex 1, Table A1

7  *Ending Child Poverty: mapping the route to 2020*, 2010, p13

8  HM Revenue and Customs, *Child Benefit, Child Tax Credit and Working Tax Credit Take-up Rates 2007–08*, 2010, Table 9

9  J Browne and P Levell, *The Distributional Effect of Tax and Benefit Reforms to be Introduced Between June 2010 and April 2014: a revised assessment*, Briefing Note BN108, Institute for Fiscal Studies, 2010

10 Scottish Government, *Evaluation of the Free School Meals Trial for P1 to P3 Pupils*, Scottish Government Social Research, 2008

11 Scottish Government, *Scotland Performs*, available at www.scotland.gov.uk/about/scotperforms/purposes/solidarity, accessed September 2010

12 *Single Outcome Agreements 2009: an analysis by members of the campaign to End Child Poverty in Scotland*, 2009, available at www.cpag.org.uk/scotland/downloads/ECPSOAreport231109final/pdf

13 For example, E Hein, *Flexicurity: can Scotland learn from Denmark?* Presentation at 'Punching Above our Weight? Smaller nations and regions in the fight against poverty in Europe', 24 September 2009. For more information, see www.povertyalliance.org.uk

# Fourteen

# Education: closing the achievement gap

*Claire Telfer*

## The nature and scale of the problem

One of the starkest inequalities in Scottish society is the poorer educational outcomes of children living in poverty, compared with children from more affluent backgrounds. Low income in a family is a strong predictor of low educational performance. Inequalities in educational outcomes are apparent from the early years, with children living in poverty arriving at school with significant disadvantages. Evidence has shown that children's attainment is already structured by social class at 22 months.[1] By the age of three, children in poverty are lagging one full year behind their better-off peer group in terms of cognitive development, social skills and school readiness. Further, by age six, initially low-achieving children from more advantaged homes will tend initially to out perform high-achieving children from less advantaged homes.[2] Inequalities associated with poverty and area deprivation widen by the time a child is age 10 and about to leave primary school.[3]

By the time the most disadvantaged young people leave school, the achievement gap is considerable. The average tariff scores of S4 pupils decrease as deprivation increases.[4] In 2008/09 children living in the least deprived areas had much higher tariff scores (230) compared with those living in the most deprived areas (124).[5] This achievement gap has remained static for the last six years. Failure to reach their educational potential means that thousands of young people are leaving school with no, or low, qualifications and skills. The achievement gap represents a tremendous waste of talent. In economic terms, it has been estimated that the cost to public services of under-achievement in education is around £1 billion a year in Scotland.[6]

## Policy

The policy approach for combating the achievement gap must be seen in the broader context of the long-term goal to eradicate child poverty by 2020. While there has been no explicit focus or strategy at Scottish government level to reduce educational inequalities or to improve educational outcomes for children in poverty since 2007, addressing inequalities in attainment is noted as vital to meeting the 2020 goal in *Achieving Our Potential*.[7] Further, education is specified as one of the policy areas that must be considered in developing the Scottish government's strategy for combating child poverty – a commitment in the UK government's Child Poverty Act 2010. Supporting the poorest children to succeed at school and achieve their potential requires a cross-cutting and comprehensive policy approach that addresses both school and non-school factors.

In terms of non-school factors, research has found that the home environment and the ability of parents to engage in their children's learning are the key factors that determine young people's educational outcomes.[8] Therefore, overarching policy initiatives designed to improve outcomes for children and families and give children the best start in life (discussed in the previous two chapters) are also pertinent to education. Building on the 'Getting it Right for Every Child' approach for supporting children, there has been a major policy focus on improving outcomes for young children, and ensuring children reach school with the cognitive, emotional and social capacities to learn, through the Scottish government and the Convention of Scottish Local Authorities *Early Years Framework*.[9] This is in recognition that all the evidence points to the early years being the most significant in determining children's long-term outcomes (see Chapter 12). This policy recognises that the cycles of poverty and inequality can be broken in and through the early years, and that supporting parents and families in their parenting role is essential to nurturing positive developmental and educational outcomes for children. Further, there has been an explicit focus on increasing entitlement to formal pre-school education. All three- and four-year-olds are currently entitled to 12 hours a week of free pre-school education. The Scottish government committed to extending this to 15 hours a week by 2010.

In relation to school factors, the policy drive has focused on universal approaches that support all children to improve their educational outcomes. Key policies include rebalancing the curriculum away from knowledge to skills and wider achievement through implementing a 'Curriculum for Excellence'. This approach provides for a broader understanding of attainment and achievement. It recognises the need to address under-achievement and to provide more choices and more chances for all children and young people, particularly those from disadvantaged backgrounds. Another policy priority has been to reduce class sizes for the earliest years of primary school (P1 to P3). This is seen as a way of driving up standards for the youngest pupils.

## Critique

The broad approach that has driven policy implies that, by improving outcomes for all children, this will in turn benefit the poorest children. However, the persistence of the achievement gap implies that a 'one size fits all' approach at national level is not working. It suggests more targeted initiatives are needed. This would help focus the attention of key actors. A policy focus on tackling educational inequalities may also assist in articulating the role of education policy in eradicating child poverty. It is acknowledged that 'only by reversing the historic trend in the poorest achieving least at school can the government deliver the kind of impact needed to tackle child poverty and the inter-generational cycle of poverty.'[10]

Evidence strongly suggests that in order to reduce later low achievement, policy should focus on supporting parents to engage in their children's learning and to improve the home learning environment.[11] Therefore, the emphasis on delivering the *Early Years Framework* and supporting parenting is welcome. A comprehensive early years and prevention service in poor areas needs to be seen as a core part of tackling the achievement gap. Furthermore, research has shown a critical gap in evidence-based parent support programmes that impact on the poorest children's educational outcomes.[12] It is most often the parents from lower income groups who find it most difficult to engage in their children's education. This suggests that policy initiatives should look to address the gap between children's formal and informal learning opportunities, and support parents to engage in their children's learning to enhance their achievement at school. This is particularly important at key transition points – eg, on entering primary school. Expanding nursery provision is a welcome move, as good quality early education experiences can have a positive impact on children living in poverty and play a part in reducing later low achievement.[13] The commitment to extend universal entitlement to three- and four-year-olds to 15 hours a week from August 2010 has not been delivered across Scotland. In order to help prevent educational inequalities at an early stage, implementation of this policy should be prioritised.

In relation to the policy drive within schools, the objectives and over-arching approach to curriculum reform are welcome. Implementation is at an early stage and, therefore, it is too early to draw conclusions on the extent to which this is having a positive impact on the educational outcomes of children living in poverty. In addition to a policy focus, research has supported the case for extra resources to be directed towards pupils living in poverty. Studies have shown that this would impact directly on pupils' attainment and reduce the achievement gap if spent on initiatives that are known to work, such as pupil support, a varied curriculum, supporting transitions from nursery to primary school and parenting support.[14] There is some evidence that suggests that smaller class sizes make a positive difference in the first two years of school.[15] Delivering this policy remains a challenge. There is still considerable debate about whether this expensive policy is the most effective way of supporting children to succeed at school. Some local authorities have decided not to prioritise smaller class sizes, while others are committed to delivering it for at least some pupils – eg, giving priority to implementation in deprived areas. At national level, the Scottish government and the Convention of Scottish Local Authorities has agreed that at least 20 per cent of P1–P3 children are educated in classes of 18 pupils or less by 2010/11.[16]

## Recommendations

While education is often a route out of poverty, the evidence suggests that, for too many children, poverty is the route into educational under-achievement. There is no one 'magic bullet' to resolve the systemic nature of this, but existing evidence points to a number of steps that can be taken.

Firstly, there needs to be an explicit focus on improving the educational achievement of children in poverty. Further, the role of education in eradicating child poverty needs to be clearly articulated in the Scottish government's child poverty strategy.

Secondly, priority should be given to delivering evidence-based parenting programmes that support parents to engage in their children's learning. This would be more effective if delivered as part of a continuum of early years and parenting support. Government should look to identify and raise awareness of evidence-based parenting programmes that make a difference to children's educational outcomes.

Thirdly, further investment needs to be made in high-quality early education in deprived areas. This should begin with implementing the extension of nursery entitlement to three- and four-year-olds and extending nursery places to two-year-olds.

Fourthly, extra education investment needs to be directed towards children living in poverty. This should be based on improving outcomes and spent on interventions that have been proven to work.

Finally, schools and nurseries need to be more accountable for their role in the achievement of children living in poverty and school inspectors need to be more focused on the achievement of children living in poverty.

## Notes

1   L Feinstein, 'Inequality in the Early Cognitive Development of British Children in the 1970 Cohort', *Economica*, Vol 70, 2003, pp73-97

2   K Hansen and H Joshi (eds), *Millennium Cohort Study Second Survey*, Institute of Education, University of London, 2007

3   See note 1

4   The tariff score is an extended version of the Universities and Colleges Admissions Service (UCAS) Scottish tariff points system. Points are allocated according to the grade that a pupil achieves for different exams – eg, a standard grade at level 1 is equivalent to 38 points while a standard grade at level 4 is equivalent to 16 points. Tariff scores are used to compare levels of average attainment across different sub-groups of pupils.

5   Scottish Government, *SQA Attainment and School Leaver Qualifications in Scotland 2008/09*, 2010

6   D Hirsh, *Estimating the Cost of Child Poverty in Scotland*, Scottish Government, 2008

7   Scottish Government, *Achieving Our Potential: a framework to tackle poverty and income inequality in Scotland*, Scottish Government, 2008, available at www.scotland.gov.uk/publications/2008/11/20103815/0

8   D Hirsh, *Experiences of Poverty and Educational Disadvantage*, Joseph Rowntree Foundation, 2007

9   Scottish Government, *The Early Years Framework*, Scottish Government, 2009

10  D Hirsh, *What Will it Take to End Child Poverty?*, Joseph Rowntree Foundation, 2006

11  R Cassen, *Tackling Low Educational Achievement*, Joseph Rowntree Foundation, 2007

12 A Harris and J Goodall, *Helping Families Support Children's Success at School*, Save the Children, 2009

13 K Sylva and others, *The Effective Provision of Pre-school Education Project: findings from the pre-school period*, Department for Education and Skills, 2003

14 See, for example, A Bruan and others, *Final Report of the Evaluation of the Pupil Learning Credits Pilot Scheme*, Department for Education and Skills, 2005; H Chowdry and others, *The Pupil Premium: assessing the options*, Institute for Fiscal Studies, 2010

15 P Blatchford, *The Class Size Debate: is small better?* Open University Press, 2003

16 Scottish Government, 'More pupils in smaller classes', Press Release, 26 March 2010, available at www.scotland.gov.uk/news/releases/2010/03

# Fifteen

# Income maximisation: coping with the cost of cancer and disability in Scotland

*Tommy Gorman*

Scotland has an ageing population, which increasingly includes people living with cancer or some other disabling long-term health condition. With one in three people diagnosed with cancer at some point in their lives, the cost of disability is something a modern Scotland cannot ignore.

People affected by cancer need support to navigate the benefits system when their ability to do so is impaired through their illness. They often also need support to ascertain their entitlements.[1] That is why Macmillan is proactively developing advice partnerships throughout Scotland.

Most opinion, including, for example, that of the Centre for Social Justice, tends to support work as a route out of poverty and, more generally, to acknowledge the advantages for the individual and her/his family of earning money through gainful employment.[2] Despite some selective examples of professional benefit fraud, it remains the case that the benefits system is a safety net and not a route out of poverty. Consequently, there is a primary focus on tackling worklessness in the drive to eradicate poverty. What, however, of those who cannot work?

Employment and support allowance (ESA) was introduced in October 2008, replacing incapacity benefit and income support for people unable to work because of long-term ill health or disability. At the time, the government made assurances that the very sick or disabled (including chemotherapy patients and terminally ill people) would be protected and safeguards were included to protect these people. However, poor knowledge of the ESA rules within Jobcentre Plus offices, poor systems and poor understanding of cancer have resulted in many people with cancer getting a poor deal.[3]

For many people affected by cancer and other long-term disabling conditions, work is often not an option, and claiming the benefits to which they are entitled is often difficult because they do not know what to claim or how to apply.[4] This is reflected in the amount of benefits that remain unclaimed by older and disabled people in the UK – estimated at more than £16 billion (made up of £10.5 billion in means-tested benefits and £6.2 billion in tax credits) unpaid each year.[5]

Taking all six income-related benefits together for the UK,[6] there was between £6.9 billion and £12.7 billion left unclaimed in 2008/09 in the UK, compared with the £38.1 billion of benefits claimed, representing take-up by expenditure of between approximately 75 per cent and 85 per cent. In 2007/08, there was between £6.3 billion and £10.5 billion left unclaimed, compared with £35.2 billion that was claimed, representing take-up by expenditure of around 77 per cent to 85 per cent.[7]

Macmillan Cancer Support has expertise designing welfare benefits advice and financial support services for people affected by cancer and other long-term conditions. It has been established by Macmillan, CPAG and others that people affected by cancer and other disabling conditions often require financial advice and support on a wide range of issues, including employment rights, saving and borrowing, occupational pensions, as well as accessing welfare benefits and meeting all the extra costs associated with managing a serious illness. That is why Macmillan Cancer Support has developed advice partnerships throughout Scotland. These cancer-specific services should be viewed as 'pathfinders' that can be extended to support other vulnerable groups.[8]

## Financial concerns

Long-term illness frequently results in a drop in income as jobs are lost and savings are eroded. People of working age with a cancer diagnosis are six times more likely to report being unable to return to work because of their health. Cancer survivors, in general, are more likely to have a lower income and ongoing financial problems than the general population.[9]

Research has established that, for many people affected by cancer, financial concerns are a significant cause of stress, in some cases, second only to physical pain.[10] Ninety-one per cent of people affected by cancer in the UK experience a significant drop in income and an increase in daily living expenditure as a direct consequence of a cancer diagnosis. This is a situation also faced by many people who are affected by other long-term disabling conditions.[11] Managing a serious illness or disabling condition can be expensive. Daily living costs are likely to increase as a result of additional expenditure on, for instance, travelling to hospital, prescriptions, new clothing required because of sudden weight change, increased telephone bills and heating costs.

- Twenty per cent of all cancer patients experience difficulty in keeping up with housing costs (mortgage/rent), with 6 per cent of patients losing their homes as a direct consequence of their diagnosis.[12]
- People of working age with a cancer diagnosis are six times more likely to report being unable to return to work because of their health, and cancer survivors in general are more likely to have a lower income and ongoing financial problems than the general population.[13]

However, a significant amount of benefits are unclaimed by disabled people in Scotland, despite their legal entitlement to this financial safety net. For instance, research confirmed that 64 per cent of people with a terminal diagnosis did not access the benefits to which they were entitled.[14] Given that there is strong evidence of the need for this financial support, specialist welfare rights advice is vital for patients and families affected by serious illness.

## What has Macmillan delivered?

There is a clear demand for effective and responsive advice, advocacy and benefits navigation for cancer patients who are not receiving the financial support to which they are entitled. Macmillan Cancer Support aspires to ensure that every person who is diagnosed with cancer or experiences a long-term disabling condition has access to quality benefits advice as a systematic, integral and routine part of their patient journey. We aim to deliver early, targeted and ongoing interventions, with a focus on high-volume client groups, through utilising the existing expertise, knowledge and networks within partner organisations and augmenting, where appropriate, through formal training.

In partnership with colleagues in local government, Citizens Advice, NHS staff, the Pension, Disability and Carers Service, patient groups and other key stakeholders (including the Scottish government and Chest, Heart and Stroke Scotland), Macmillan services have delivered positive financial outcomes for people affected by cancer throughout Scotland, including remote and rural communities in the Highlands and Western Isles.

Since 2005, Macmillan advisers in Scotland have supported over

30,000 people affected by cancer to access over £90 million in benefits and allowances that would have largely gone unclaimed. Approximately 74 per cent of these service users achieved an increase in weekly income. One service led by West Dunbartonshire Council was launched at the Beatson Cancer Treatment Centre, Glasgow, and supported over 900 cancer patients to claim over £2 million in benefits and allowances in the first 13 months of its operation.

The purpose of these partnership projects is to improve the benefits advice given to cancer patients and to act as 'pathfinders' in the wider development of financial advice and support services across Scotland.

## Looking ahead

Problems faced by claimants experiencing cancer and other long-term conditions can only be addressed effectively if the revenue allocated to provide support for disabled people in Scotland is fully claimed by those with entitlement. They must have access to this safety net. In order to achieve the best outcome for these people we must accurately establish how much is being unclaimed, and by how many.

We also need to establish firm principles that affirm the rights to adequate financial support of disabled people. More specifically, there is a need to assert and promote awareness of the need for a statutory right to advice and support for:

- terminally ill people;
- people assessed as severely disabled;
- certain categories of disabled children.

More generally, questions need to be raised about the effectiveness of the distribution of the social security budget as it applies to people affected by cancer and other long-term conditions in Scotland, and whether there should be a greater fiscal role for Holyrood.

Financial stability in households dealing with the diagnosis and consequences of cancer or a long-term disabling condition is a critical prerequisite for supported self-management, vocational rehabilitation (including return to work) and the improvement of general health. Access to benefits is vital to this process. There are also confirmed advantages for local economies as a by-product of effective welfare rights interventions.[15]

Information must be made easy to access and focused appropriately to ensure that those affected by cancer and other long-term conditions are supported in the process of claiming the money to which they are entitled, or are simply empowered to manage their financial affairs. More people are living with disability than ever before and so improving the patient experience throughout this journey is crucial. In doing so, we can ensure that vulnerable citizens are not financially excluded as a result of circumstances beyond their control.

Scotland needs a well-informed national discussion with all key agencies and stakeholders participating, with a view to making a significant positive impact on the wellbeing of disabled people in Scotland. Financial stability must be an important factor in this debate.

## Notes

1 Macmillan Cancer Relief, *The Unclaimed Millions*, Macmillan Cancer Relief, June 2004. Macmillan's research into the extent of unclaimed disability living allowance and attendance allowance by people with a terminal diagnosis of cancer was the first of its kind.

2 Centre for Social Justice, *Breakthrough Britain: dynamic benefits, towards welfare that works*, Centre for Social Justice, 2009

3 Macmillan Cancer Support and Citizens Advice, *Failed by the System: why the employment and support allowance isn't working for people with cancer*, Macmillan/Citizens Advice, 2009

4 Macmillan Cancer Relief, *Access Denied: a better deal for people dealing with cancer,* May 2005. This study was commissioned by Macmillan Cancer Relief to build further understanding of the barriers faced by cancer patients trying to access disability living allowance and attendance allowance.

5 www.rightsnet.org.uk, accessed 3 February 2010

6 Income support, income-based jobseeker's allowance, income-related employment and support allowance, pension credit, housing benefit and council tax benefit.

7 See http://research.dwp.gov.uk/asd/income_analysis/jun_2010/0809_summ ary.pdf

8 Scottish Government, *Better Cancer Care: a discussion*, 2008

9 See note 8

10 A Quinn, *Macmillan Cancer Relief Study into Benefits Advice for People with Cancer*, University of Reading, 2002

11 Alzheimer Scotland confirms that approximately 71,000 people have dementia in Scotland in 2010. The numbers of people with dementia in Scotland are expected to rise to 127,000 by 2031. See www.alzscot.org

12 *The Observer*, 7 January 2008

13 See note 8

14 See note 1

15 Fraser of Allander Institute, *The Impact of Welfare Spending on the Glasgow Economy*, University of Strathclyde, 2001 and 2003. Their studies confirmed that welfare rights advice was a very effective form of job creation and that £10 million in additional benefits generated by Glasgow City Council's welfare rights service created an additional 258 mostly long-term jobs.

# Sixteen
# Poverty and debt

*Keith Dryburgh*

'It's my own fault really, but debt is so worrying and it does have an effect on the way you live, the way you think... and it does have a physical effect on you too because of the amount of stress it puts you under. So debt is a nightmare.'

Citizens Advice Bureau debt client in 2008[1]

If poverty is a trap into which individuals and families fall too easily, then debt is a weight on them that often prevents escape. On a typical day in Scotland, it is likely that 65 people will be made insolvent, Citizens Advice Bureaux will deal with nearly 400 new debt problems, while countless others will struggle to cope with mounting debts that affect their health and close relationships.[2]

Iain Duncan Smith, the Secretary of State for Work and Pensions, identified debt as one of the five key pathways into poverty.[3] However, this may be confusing cause and effect: poverty and low income are often a pathway into debt. Low income too often entails a lack of access to mainstream financial services and affordable credit; poorer access to debt solutions; and greater vulnerability to relationship problems and income shocks – all of which are major causes of debt.

Both the Holyrood and Westminster governments have introduced policy and legislation aimed at alleviating debt problems. This chapter examines the extent to which these have been successful, arguing that they have had a degree of success in addressing existing debt problems, but have failed to prevent problems from occurring by not addressing the causes of debt.

## Recent policy on debt

The Scottish government has concentrated on improving access to debt solutions for those stuck in a cycle of debt. A spectrum of debt solutions – including the debt arrangement scheme,[4] the 'low-income, low-assets' route to bankruptcy,[5] protected trust deeds[6] and the recent certificate for sequestration[7] – have been proactive in helping those in financial difficulty. In particular, the 'low-income, low-assets' route into bankruptcy gives those on a very low income the opportunity to make a fresh start without debt. Prior to these initiatives, those unable to repay their debts had to wait for their creditors to take formal action against them, a process that could take several years. The Scottish government has also made provisions to expand money advice through the Money Advice Training Resources, Information and Consultancy Service (MATRICS), run by Citizens Advice Scotland, and Money Advice Scotland, which has made a positive contribution to tackling debt problems.

The UK government has focused on addressing financial exclusion. People unable to access mainstream financial services face financial disadvantages which can lead to indebtedness, including higher interest credit, lack of insurance, having no account into which income can be paid and higher cost utilities.[8] The UK government set out its strategy to tackle financial exclusion in *Financial Inclusion: the way forward*.[9] The report outlines its belief that everyone should be able to manage their money effectively and securely through access to a bank account. The strategy also made provision to expand third-sector lending and money advice provision.

## Impact of policy

The Scottish government's initiatives on debt have increased access to vital debt solutions for many low-income households stuck in a cycle of debt. A growing number of people in debt (1,417 in 2009/10[10]) are successfully using the debt arrangement scheme to repay their debts. In 2009/10, over 6,500 people were made insolvent through 'low-income, low-assets',[11] the majority of whom would not have had access to a debt solution prior to its introduction in 2008. However, people with very low incomes are still struggling to access debt solutions because of the £100 fee required to access 'low-income, low-assets', and the high fees involved in protected trust deeds. Recent evidence has shown that 50 per cent of fees paid towards trust deeds are taken by insolvency practitioners, thereby making this debt solution unaffordable for many.[12]

While the Scottish government has had relative success in improving debt solutions for those on low incomes, there has been less focus on the causes of unmanageable debt. Research with Citizens Advice Bureaux found that over half of debt clients felt that low income was a main reason for their financial difficulties.[13] Debt problems also frequently arise from changes in family circumstances that reduce clients' incomes – job loss, relationship breakdown, health problems, and a higher cost of living can all turn manageable credit into unmanageable debt. Access to debt solutions can help alleviate the problems of debt, but does little to address the causes of debt for those on a low income.

The UK government's attempts to break the link between low income and debt through financial inclusion have been relatively successful in its stated aims. The proportion of people in Scotland with access to a bank account increased from 86 per cent to 91 per cent between 1999 and 2008,[14] thereby theoretically increasing access to affordable credit and the other benefits of financial inclusion.

However, it is questionable whether having a bank account constitutes true financial inclusion for those on low incomes. Despite an increase in the number of low-income consumers accessing mainstream financial services, their level of income and credit requirements mean that they are still less likely to have access to low-interest mainstream credit.[15] Instead, they have had to rely more on higher cost credit options, such as home credit and doorstep loans, high-interest credit cards, pay-day advances, cash converter lenders, and rent-to-own retailers. These sources of credit are expensive, with annual percentage rates commonly reaching three or even four figures, and can lead to intractable debt problems among those on a low income. The 'credit crunch' and the resulting recession have further tightened the availability of credit and are likely to lead to greater use of high-cost credit options. Greater access to mainstream financial services through basic bank accounts has yet to address the problem of access to affordable low-interest credit.

Indeed, being part of the financial mainstream can actually add to debt problems. Government policies and initiatives on debt have failed to address the ongoing problems of high overdraft charges. Legal proceedings between the Office of Fair Trading and UK banks ended in the Supreme Court in 2009, with a decision that confirmed the status quo and left consumers vulnerable to unfair charges.[16] Low-income consumers are disproportionately affected by overdraft charges as they are more likely to incur a charge and will have a greater proportion of their income taken by it.[17]

## Policy prescriptions

Recent UK and Scottish government policy has concentrated on the dual aims of improving access to debt solutions for those whose credit obligations have become unmanageable, and achieving financial inclusion for those on low incomes. Many of these initiatives have helped those on low incomes to escape debt and to gain a foothold in the financial mainstream. However, there has been too little policy intervention on many of the causes of debt – such as low income, lack of access to affordable credit, family breakdown and poor creditor behaviour – meaning that the flow of debtors has continued unabated. In a ten-year period, the number of clients approaching Citizens Advice Bureaux in Scotland with debt problems has doubled, while the amount of debt brought by these clients has increased more than ten-fold. Bureaux debt clients – most of whom are on a low income – have considerably more debt in relation to their income compared with five and ten years ago.[18]

Future policy and legislation on debt must continue to open access to debt solutions while addressing the causes of debt for those on low incomes. The process of financial inclusion must continue to ensure that those with a low income gain the full benefits of inclusion in the financial mainstream. Finally, in a country that is entering a period of austerity, money advice must be adequately resourced to deal with the increasing number of people who will be affected by redundancies and benefit cuts.

Poverty and debt are intrinsically linked, with one often leading to the other. It is only by dealing with the causes of debt that this link can be broken. Prevention remains the best remedy.

### Notes

1  M Gillespie, J H McKendrick, L Dobbie and F McHardy, *Drowning in Debt: report for Citizens Advice Scotland*, Scottish Poverty Information Unit, 2009
2  Estimates using Citizens Advice Scotland data from late autumn 2010.
3  I Duncan Smith, 'Welfare for the 21st Century' Speech, 27 May 2010, available at www.dwp.gov.uk/newsroom/ministers-speeches/2010/27-05-10.shtml
4  For information, see www.aib.gov.uk/services/das

5   For information, see www.aib.gov.uk/services/legislation/accessto bankruptcy/ debtorsapplication/lila

6   For information, see www.aib.gov.uk/services/ptd

7   For information, see A Bremnar and L Burgess, *SPICE Briefing: Home Owner and Debtor Protection (Scotland) Bill*, The Scottish Parliament, 2009, available at www.scottish.parliament.uk/business/research/briefings-09/SB09-73.pdf

8   L Mitton, *Financial Inclusion in the UK: review of policy and practice*, Joseph Rowntree Foundation, 2008, available at www.jrf.org.uk/publications

9   HM Treasury, *Financial Inclusion: the way forward*, The Stationery Office, 2007

10  Accountant in Bankruptcy, *Scottish Insolvencies in the First Quarter, 2010/11*, July 2010 available at www.aib.gov.uk

11  See note 10

12  For information, see www.aib.gov.uk

13  See note 1

14  *Scottish Household Survey 2007/08*, available at www.scotland.gov.uk/news

15  L Dobbie, *Understanding Financial Inclusion in the UK*, Briefing Paper, Scottish Poverty Information Unit, 2009

16  For information, see www.oft.gov.uk/shared_oft/personal-current-accounts/ oft1154

17  Office of Fair Trading, *Personal Current Accounts in the UK*, 2008

18  See note 1

# Seventeen
# Poverty and the environment: environmental injustice
*Eurig Scandrett*

## The environment and poverty

The environment has become part of public policy due to pressure from environmental campaigning groups. However, the worst environmental pollution is experienced by people who are poor or socially excluded, whose voices are largely absent from both policy making and environmental groups. In Scotland, 20 per cent of the most deprived population live within one kilometre of a source of industrial pollution, and the poorest decile are 65 times more likely to live close to a polluting energy installation than the richest decile.[1] The term 'environmental justice' was first used in the USA in campaigns against environmental racism, where toxic waste dumps are disproportionately located in black and minority communities.[2] Throughout the world, 'environmentalism of the poor' is regarded by some as a major global social force.[3]

In Scotland, the link between poverty and environmental damage became a significant issue for Jack McConnell's executive between 2002 and 2007 and was reflected in a number of speeches he gave as First Minister, couching environmental issues in the language of social democracy:[4]

> ... the people who have the most urgent environmental concerns in Scotland are those who daily cope with the consequences of a poor quality of life, and live in a rotten environment – close to industrial pollution, plagued by vehicle emissions, streets filled by litter and walls covered in graffiti... I believe the biggest challenge for the early twenty-first century [for democrats on the left of centre] is to combine economic progress with social and environmental justice.

While McConnell attempted to address the symptoms of environmental injustice by linking environmental and social policy, his executive failed to locate the causes of environmental injustice in economic decisions, so policies designed to deliver economic progress took no account of these. For the Scottish National Party (SNP) government, environmental policy has again been segregated from social and economic policy, and the interconnecting policy issue of environmental justice has disappeared from the political agenda. However, it is only by understanding environmental and social problems as interconnected with economic development that environmental justice can be addressed.

## The causes of environmental injustice

An important legacy of McConnell's executive is research into correlations between poverty and environmental damage in Scotland. In 2005, *Investigating Environmental Justice in Scotland* concluded:[5]

> For industrial pollution, derelict land and river water quality there is a strong relationship with deprivation. People in the most deprived areas are far more likely to be living near to these sources of potential negative environmental impact than people in less deprived areas... People living in the most deprived areas are more likely to experience the poorest air quality than those living in less deprived areas.

This research was a snapshot of the situation early in the twenty-first century and was not designed to identify the causes of these injustices. Economists have long recognised the tendency of markets to cause unintended costs to the environment, known as 'externalities'. Such costs are most likely to fall on people and places with the least influence on the market (the unemployed and low-waged) and the least valued, most vulnerable and already damaged environments.

The dominant approach to addressing externalities across Europe emphasises market solutions rather than publicly funded regulation. By attaching a price to polluting activity, businesses, public bodies and households have an economic incentive to reduce pollution. Such approaches may have some environmental benefits, although they do little to prevent costs being shifted onto the poor. Indeed, as costs rise and businesses look for the cheapest way to cut pollution, this approach may exacerbate the impact on the poor – eg, carbon offsetting through polluting 'development' projects in the global South.[6]

## Recent developments in environmental policy

Alex Salmond's government's record on environmental policy since 2007 has been inconsistent and has shown limited interest in the environmental impacts on the poor. On transport, for example, it has abolished bridge tolls, opposed road pricing and attempted to cancel Edinburgh's trams. Two-thirds of households earning under £10,000 have no access to a car and, according to transport pressure group Transform Scotland, 'transport policies that prioritise reliance on the use of cars will therefore adversely affect low-income groups'.[7] On the other hand, the government has backed the electrification of key rail routes and new line development. It has abolished development funds for both air and bus travel which would have benefited the wealthy and the poorest respectively.

Support for the SNP's first Budget allowed Green Party MSPs to lever the introduction of a £27.4 million Climate Challenge Fund, which has supported 250 community-based projects. Some of these incorporate anti-poverty initiatives, such as the North Edinburgh Trust, which has used Climate Challenge funding to build on its fuel poverty work, raising the issue of climate change using an anti-poverty approach. Through concerted lobbying, in May 2009, the Climate Change Act mandated demanding targets for carbon dioxide reduction. If achieved, these reductions would be good news for the world's poor who experience the main impact of climate change, although the government's first attempt to set annual targets was rejected in Parliament as being too weak. An Energy Assistance Package has been introduced, with a view to better target fuel poverty. However, where market instruments are used to identify the cheapest source of carbon reductions, this could be bad news for the poor in Scotland. The government has already delayed its energy efficiency action plan, that would benefit the poor, who spend a higher proportion of income on fuel.

*Scotland's Zero Waste Plan* employs a range of voluntary and market instruments, but also includes regulation of businesses.[8] However, it contains no acknowledgement of the socially unequal production of waste. The poorest tenth of the population are eight times more likely than the richest tenth to live next to polluting waste facilities.[9]

Development planning is where decisions are made which determine the location of polluting developments and, therefore, is key in the struggle for environmental justice. Robust planning control is essential to prevent polluting developments being located beside poor communities where land and labour are cheap. A major reform of planning in Scotland was initiated by the McConnell executive and continued under the Salmond government, with a view to delivering a 'more inclusive and efficient planning system, to support the Scottish government's central purpose of sustainable economic growth'.[10] This reform has attempted to address two, apparently contradictory, pressures: to improve consultation with those who would be affected by the development ('inclusive') and to speed up decisions on developments ('efficient'). The first of these could prevent dirty industries being dumped on poor communities, and citizens' groups are monitoring progress on this.[11] Although it is too early to assess the impact, there are concerns that, although developers are communicating their plans sooner, they are not addressing people's objections. Particularly problematic are 'national developments' (proposals regarded as having major national importance), so that decisions are made directly by the minister over the heads of local authorities and the communities most directly affected. To date, two national developments have been challenged: Hunterston coal-fired power station and Cockenzie gas-fired power station.

## Opportunities for environmental justice

It is essential to acknowledge the reality of environmental injustice in order to address the disproportionate impact of environmental damage on the poorest. Although Jack McConnell made steps towards this, his government failed adequately to connect social and environmental concerns with economic development, which remained oriented to market flexibility and minimal regulation. A structural transformation in the economy is needed to prevent environmental costs being shifted onto the poor.

There are many policy initiatives that could be taken up by any Scottish government. Investment in public transport and away from airports and roads would benefit the poor and the environment. As the price of energy inevitably escalates, improving efficiency rating in the social housing sector is a relatively cheap way to tackle fuel poverty and reduce carbon emissions. The *Green New Deal* proposes a range of initiatives led by public sector investment to tackle poverty and environment-related problems while generating jobs.[12] A sustainable conversion agency could bring together government, business, trade unions, community organisations and technical experts to identify 'just transition' arrangements to shift workers into alternative employment while closing down polluting industries, and stimulate a different kind of economic development based on social benefit.[13]

Regulation of polluters must be a key tool for environmental justice. The Scottish Environment Protection Agency should be more accountable to poor communities most at risk of pollution, and should explicitly report on progress against environmental inequalities. The Agency should also be tougher on polluters. SNP backbencher Bill Wilson's private member's Equity Fines Bill would be a significant step in bringing corporations to account.

Despite recent failings, the development planning process presents a means to work toward environmental justice in Scotland. In the short term, the obligation of developers to consult local communities needs to be strengthened. The right to appeal decisions, which developers enjoy, should be extended to objectors. The national development category should be revised to prevent local communities being sacrificed for a combination of political expediency and commercial benefit. However, a medium term aim should be to move away from the adversarial planning system, in which communities are pitted against well-resourced developers, towards multi-criteria analysis which can equalise power relationships between stakeholders in deciding what kind of development best meets their collective aspirations.

Pressure from campaign groups is necessary to resist environmental injustice. With the disappearance of environmental justice policies from the Salmond government, environmental non-governmental organisations have taken a less explicit approach to poverty issues. On the other hand, there has been some grassroots community action against environmental injustice, notably open-cast coal and incinerator developments,[14] and some promising connections between environmental protests and anti-poverty protests, and also with trade union hazards campaigns. Such alliances push against the economic logic of dumping on the poorest and increase pressure for policy on environmental justice.

## Notes

1   J Fairburn, G Walker and G Smith, *Investigating Environmental Justice in Scotland: links between measures of environmental quality and social deprivation*, SNIFFER report UE4(03)01, Scotland and Northern Ireland Forum for Environmental Research, 2005, p58

2   R D Bullard (ed), *The Quest for Environmental Justice: human rights and the politics of pollution*, Sierra Club Books, 2005

3   J Martinez-Alier, *Environmentalism of the Poor: a study of ecological conflicts and valuation*, Edward Elgar, 2002

4   Scottish Executive, 'First Minister's speech on environmental justice', 18 February, 200

5   See note I, pp14–15

6   See www.carbontradewatch.org

7   Transform Scotland, *Socially Just Transport*, Briefing, November 2005, available at http://transformscotland.org.uk

8   Scottish Government, *Scotland's Zero Waste Plan*, 2010, Annex B, p3, available at www.scotland.gov.uk/topics/environment/waste-and-pollution

9   See note 1, p56

10  Scottish Government, *A Brief Guide to the 2006 Scottish Planning Act*, 2007, available at www.scotland.gov.uk/publications/2007/03/07131521/1

11  For example, see www.planningdemocracy.org.uk

12  Green New Deal Group, *The Green New Deal*, New Economics Foundation, 2008, available at www.neweconomics.org

13  These and other policy proposals from civil society can be found in E Scandrett, *Scotlands of the Future: sustainability in a small nation*, Democratic Left Scotland/Luath, 2003

14  For example, Green Alternatives to Incineration in Scotland emerged from a 'Scottish No-Burn Action Day' at Scotland's parliament in October 2009. See www.gainscotland.org.uk/feature1.shtml

# Eighteen
# Rural poverty
*John H McKendrick*

## The best of times?

The installation of the Scottish National Party (SNP) as a minority Scottish government, following the third Scottish parliamentary elections on 3 May 2007, would have been welcomed in many parts of rural Scotland. Notwithstanding iconic electoral successes in urban Scotland, the core support for the SNP stretches across the rural heartland of Scotland in a large swathe of constituencies stretching from Argyll and Bute in the south west to Banff and Buchan in the north east. Surely, a government whose party support is rooted in rural Scotland would know how best to tackle the problem of poverty in rural Scotland?

## Rural poverty and deprivation in Scotland

One in seven people – 160,000 individuals – living in rural areas in Scotland is estimated to be living in income poverty.[1] Rural Scotland also contributes a significant share of overall poverty in Scotland: one in every six people experiencing poverty in Scotland lives in a rural area. Far too many and far too high a proportion of Scotland's rural population are living on an income that is insufficient to meet their needs. Although Scottish government data suggests that income poverty has fallen in rural Scotland in recent years (from 17 per cent in 2005/06 to 14 per cent in 2007/08) and that the level of poverty is lower in rural than in urban Scotland (18 per cent for urban Scotland in 2007/08), Scotland clearly has a substantial rural poverty problem that should be addressed.

Aggregate numbers alone do not convey the nature and depth of the problems of poverty and deprivation in rural Scotland. There are particularities of rural living, which may exacerbate the problems of living in rural Scotland. For example:

- **Higher cost of living**. Food and transport fuel, in particular, cost more in rural areas.[2]
- **Higher levels of consumption**. More money is required to heat the older and less energy efficient homes in rural areas and the greater distances to employment and services mean more money must be spent on transport.[3]
- **Fewer opportunities to earn an adequate income**. Although employment rates compare favourably with urban areas, low pay, seasonal employment and the historical low take-up of welfare benefits in rural areas each depress household income. To earn an adequate income is more likely to require multiple jobs.[4]
- **Dispersed 'invisible' deprivation**. Many rural communities appear affluent and thriving, yet deprivation exists beneath this veneer. Deprivation in rural areas is not clustered, but can be spread over considerable distances and can be found adjacent to affluence.[5]
- **Culture of independence and self-reliance**. Independence and self-sufficiency are more highly valued in rural areas, making it more likely that unmet need is unknown need to policy makers and service providers.[6]
- **Gender pay issues**. Research shows that part-time work is favoured by women in order to balance other commitments. In rural areas, part-time work tends to be low paid and below workers' skill levels and qualifications.[7]
- **Access**. Access issues compound and exacerbate need in rural areas.

## Words: rural focus by government in Scotland

Like its predecessors, this Scottish government has, at times, acknowledged the problem of rural poverty in Scotland. For example, there is explicit acknowledgement in *Achieving Our Potential*, the framework to tackle poverty and income inequality, of the importance of the rural dimension.[8] For example: 'Poverty is most visible in disadvantaged communities in urban Scotland, but it is no less real in rural areas.'[9] Data on rural poverty in Scotland is published more prominently than before.[10] Government has also been active in commissioning work to advance our understanding of rural poverty in Scotland, notably reports on: the possibility of developing rural performance indicators;[11] a desk-based review of research on living with poverty in rural Scotland;[12] and qualitative research to explore the experiences of poverty in rural Scotland. The latter reached strong conclusions on the nature of rural problems in Scotland:[13]

> A lack of opportunities for employment and training limits individuals' options for increasing their household income and moving out of poverty. With low-skill, low-pay jobs dominating the rural economy, the route out of poverty for vulnerable groups is, therefore, more challenging. (p67)

> The main conclusion of the study is that people in rural areas have to spend proportionately more on transport and goods and are less frequently provided with services than their urban counterparts. For people on low incomes, this has negative effects aggravating the experience of poverty and reducing available income significantly. (p69)

However, tackling poverty was less prominent when the Scottish government sought to engage rural stakeholders to canvass their thoughts on how rural Scotland can best contribute to the national purpose. To inform this consultation, a working group was brought together by the Rural Development Council to prepare a consultation document that would inform the rural economic development strategy. One of the briefings that the working group considered as part of the evidence was a report on the work of Highlands and Islands Enterprise in developing its Fragile Areas Index.[14] Although inclusion of such work in the thinking behind the resulting consultation document, *Speak Up for Rural Scotland*,[15] seems indicative of a will to address the broader problems of poverty, inequality and deprivation in rural Scotland, it is perhaps telling that none of these words are mentioned in the *Speak Up for Rural Scotland* report.

In its *Poverty in Scotland* report,[16] the Scottish Affairs Committee of the UK parliament identified three problems – one of which was rural poverty. The report focuses on the problems of 'income and employment' and 'service provision' in rural Scotland, and five of the 36 conclusions and recommendations make explicit reference to the problem of poverty in rural Scotland. Conclusion 24 summarises the challenge:

> We conclude that rural poverty presents its own challenges, which will not be solved by an approach tailored to the small pockets of deprivation characteristic of urban poverty. It is vital that the Government's anti-poverty poli-

cies are subject to 'rural proofing'... Greater investment in outreach is required to ensure that geographically dispersed communities have equal access to services.

Rural poverty in Scotland is not invisible to government.

## Action: rural action by local and Scottish government in Scotland

The Scottish government's anti-poverty interventions have impacted on rural areas. The Convention of Scottish Local Authorities' Tackling Poverty Rural Network acknowledge, this in its review of *Achieving Our Potential*, in particular valuing interventions such as those through the Fairer Scotland Fund and 'More Choices, More Chances' that emphasised supporting individuals in poverty. Although such interventions must still negotiate the structural and geographical barriers in rural Scotland that make the realisation of opportunity more problematic (eg, greater distances to travel at greater cost and, in general, fewer available opportunities), this desire to formulate policy in a manner that is closer to particular circumstances is welcomed as more appropriate to the challenges faced by rural Scotland. In this vein, according local government a central role in tackling local poverty (the concordat approach) should be welcomed too.

However, the rise of the local in tackling rural poverty in Scotland, together with the 'mainstreaming' of rural policy by the Scottish government have (perhaps inadvertently) conspired to create a rural silence on the national policy front. Many important policy documents make little or no reference to specifically rural issues. For example, *Equally Well* makes one reference to 'rural' in 83 pages – and none at all in the 2010 review.[18] Indeed, even the Tackling Poverty Board makes no reference to the particularities of rural poverty in its May 2010 monitoring review of *Achieving Our Potential* (other than to note that the Convention of Scottish Local Authorities had established the Tackling Poverty Rural Network).[19] The rural silence is perhaps understandable given the government approach. However, it is ominous when added to the dearth of attention to rural poverty in *Speak Up for Rural Scotland*.

## Key issues to address

Despite some welcome reductions in the level of poverty in rural Scotland and the awareness of the Scottish government to the problem of rural poverty, each of the five action points identified in the essay on rural poverty in the 2007 edition of *Poverty in Scotland* persist as issues outstanding. We still need to do the following.

- **Take rural anti-poverty activity more seriously in the fight against poverty in Scotland**. There is a need for a coherent, concerted strategy to tackle the particularities of rural poverty – in all of its guises – across Scotland.
- **Tackle low pay in rural Scotland**. For example, the median wage paid to men in rural Scotland is unacceptably lower than that paid to men in urban Scotland.
- **Articulate the role of the rural in Scottish anti-poverty strategies**. As we have noted, *Achieving Our Potential* is sensitive to the rural challenge. However, there is a need to 'rural proof' each specific anti-poverty intervention in order to ensure that the rural dimension is not being overlooked or marginalised.
- **Use sophistication in understanding poverty statistics**. We must continue to guard against crude interpretation of data leading to the erroneous conclusion that poverty is not a pressing problem in rural Scotland.
- **Introduce a measure of rural deprivation**. The Scottish Index of Multiple Deprivation is an excellent addition to the resources which aim to understand better the social inequities in Scotland. However, the focus on small area deprivation tends to undermine and underestimate the prevalence of *household multiple deprivation* in rural Scotland.

In conclusion, there appears to be the will to tackle rural poverty in Scotland. What is less clear is whether this will is being translated into effective government action. Who can say whether the interventions of the Scottish government – and of the concordat approach of the Scottish government and the Convention of Scottish Local Authorities – has made inroads into tackling rural poverty in Scotland in recent years? There is a need to 'rural proof' national policy and to seek more definitive answers to the question of whether poverty is being effectively tackled through national and local policy in rural Scotland.

## Notes

1 Scottish government analysis, based on data for 2007/08, using the HBAI dataset from the *Family Resources Survey*. See www.scotland.gov.uk/topics/ statistics/browse/social-welfare/incomepoverty/poverty-analysis/

2 Scottish Agricultural College Rural Policy Centre, *Special Study on Living in Poverty in Rural Areas*, Report to the Scottish Government Rural Research and Analysis Directorate, 2008, pp4–5

3 Economic and Social Development Consultancy, *The Experience of Rural Poverty in Scotland: qualitative research with organisations working with people experiencing poverty in rural areas*, Scottish Government Social Research, 2009, available at www.scotland.gov.uk/publications/2009/03/02144159/0

4 Commission for Rural Communities, *Rural Disadvantage: reviewing the evidence*, Commission for Rural Communities, 2006, p27

5 See note 3, p26

6 M Shucksmith, *Exclusive Countryside? Social inclusion and regeneration in rural areas*, Joseph Rowntree Foundation, 2000

7 EKOS, *Pay, Position and Occupational Options: women in the Highlands and Islands area*, 2004

8 *Achieving Our Potential: a framework to tackle poverty and income equality in Scotland*, The Scottish Government, 2008, available at www.scotland.gov.uk/ publications/2008/11/20103815/0

9 See note 8, p5

10 For example, www.scotland.gov.uk/topics/statistics/browse/social-welfare/ incomepoverty/coreanalysis#a2

11 Ecotec, *Developing Performance Indicators for Rural Scotland: a scoping study*, Scottish Government, 2010, available at www.scotland.gov.uk/publications/ 2010/03/18092820/0

12 L McSorley, *Special Study on Living in Poverty in Rural Areas*, Report to the Scottish Government Rural and Analysis Research and Analysis Directorate, Scottish Agricultural College, 2009, available at www.sac.ac.uk/mainrep/ pdfs/ruralpoverty.

13 See note 12

14 Scottish Government, *Socio-Economic Briefing on Rural Scotland: identifying fragile rural areas*, Paper 5: supporting evidence provided to the Rural Development Council Working Group, Office of the Chief Statistician, 2010

15 Scottish Government, *Speak Up for Rural Scotland*, 2010, available at www.scotland.gov.uk/publications/2010/07/22091602/2

16 House of Commons Scottish Affairs Committee, *Poverty in Scotland: second report of Session 2007–2008*, Vol I, The Stationery Office, 2007, available at www.publications.parliament.uk/pa/cm200708/cmselect/cmscotaf/128/128.pdf

17 The others were fuel poverty (which itself is a particular problem in rural Scotland) and debt.

18 Scottish Government, *Equally Well: report of the Ministerial Task Force on Health Inequalities,* Scottish Government, 2008, available at www.scotland. gov.uk.resource/doc/229649/0062206.pdf; Scottish Government *Ministerial Task Force on Implementing Equally Well*, the *Early Years Framework*, and *Achieving Our Potential*; Scottish Government, *Equally Well Review: report by the Scottish Government*, 2010, available at www.scotland/gov.uk/resource. doc/315880/0100454.pdf

19 See www.scotland.gov.uk/topics/people/tackling-poverty/initiatives/tackling povertyboard

# Nineteen
# Cultural participation
*Richard Holloway*

## Losing our way

The most dramatic characteristic of the human species is our brilliant rest-lessness, leading to revolution after revolution in the way we work and organise ourselves. Unfortunately, it is the vulnerable in any society who bear most of the cost of these changes. In Scotland, it is the death of heavy industry that has devastated people experiencing poverty. Heavy industry has been replaced by the knowledge economy, and we are only now try-ing to catch up with its consequential impact upon the less well educated.

As if that were not enough, social change has combined with this economic revolution to destroy the cultural cohesion of the most vulnera-ble sections of our society. When the cultural revolution of the sixties and seventies met the economic revolution of the eighties and nineties, a potent instrument of change was created that has transformed the social landscape of Scotland (and Britain), and its most devastating impact has been on young, uneducated, workless men. The institutions that once gave them a motive for responsible living, such as holding down a tough, demanding job with its own culture and honour, and presiding within a marriage and family that was the primary context for the nurture and socialisation of children, have largely disappeared, and with them, the main ways the human community traditionally disciplined and integrated children into the social contract.

## Counting the cost of cultural decline

This shattering of the structures that once gave people experiencing pov-erty significance and purpose has created a breeding ground for despair that prompts the kind of destructive behaviour that only reinforces their alienation. When most people were impoverished there was a camaraderie and cultural cohesion in belonging to the working class, giving them a strength and pride, fortifying them in the face of the structures that excluded them. But in a society where most people are prosperous, and the poor are a minority whose culture has disintegrated, the pain and anger they feel is heightened. The devastation these social and industrial revolutions have caused to traditional working-class communities has been heartbreaking.

Welfare dependency, and lack of work, is expensive not only on the lives it stunts, but on its impact on the public purse. A National Audit Office report on youth offending in 2004 estimated that it can cost up to £185,000 a year to keep a young person in secure accommodation.[1] This is a staggering sum. If we could find new and imaginative ways of keeping children out of custody, we could save them a lot of misery, and ourselves a lot of money. We know that more equal societies are happier and healthier for everyone, and that unequal societies are more dangerous and miserable for everyone.[2] Surely, if we willed it, we could find ways to turn those damaged and despairing communities around. It took generations to destroy the spiritual and cultural fabric of these communities, and it will take generations to restore them. Is there, somewhere, a process of slow, organic, revolutionary change that might overcome this damaging legacy and build new communities?

## Inspiration from afar

The Simón Bolivar National Youth Orchestra of Venezuela[3] has not only taken the world of classical music by storm, it has provoked interest among social reformers as a possible model for reaching out to young people who had been discarded and alienated by the social and industrial revolutions that had rushed like hurricanes through the fabric of British society. The music is miracle enough, but the greater miracle is the purpose that lies behind it, and the impact it has had on the half a million children who have gone through it and the quarter of a million children aged two to 25 who are currently in the programme, in a network of 125 youth orchestras, all in a country that did not get its first conservatoire until the 1920s. What began with 11 young people in a backstreet garage in Caracas as an attempt to make the glories of classical music available to ordinary Venezuelans soon metamorphosed into one of the most effective and revolutionary programmes of social transformation on our troubled and unequal planet.

## El Sistema comes to Raploch

The programme was driven by the *El Sistema* method. *El Sistema* gets children playing again, playing arduously. There are three aspects of the method that are instructive. In the classical European musical pedagogy, children learn to play a musical instrument in private tutorials. After years of solitary practice, if they are good enough, they will graduate to an orchestra. *El Sistema* turns this paradigm upside down, by placing children in orchestras from the very beginning. I have watched Venezuelan children aged two, dummies firmly in their mouths, solemnly bowing tiny violins with intense concentration. The other two aspects of this revolution are intensity and immersion. What we have to do here is find a more powerful and dominant social reality for the children than the one that is damaging them: the orchestra offers a complete alternative reality, day in and day out. It is this intense immersion in the orchestra and in the beauty of music that is the key to its revolutionary success in socialising children into disciplined, co-operative human beings, who discover pleasure in effort, and joy in the exultation of music.

After a visit to Venezuela in 2006 to study *El Sistema*, I came back to Scotland determined to see if it could work here. We formed a board and registered ourselves as a charity. We raised enough money to hire a gifted young woman as director of the project. In Raploch, we found a community in Scotland that was regenerating itself after a difficult history, and was keen to let us try the experiment with it.[4] But I did not want us just to be another youth music initiative inspired by *El Sistema*: I wanted us to be *El Sistema* in Scotland. We signed a covenant with Venezuela and sent our newly hired team of musicians to Venezuela, not only to gain some training in their approach, but to get the vibe, be evangelised, be motivated by what they saw.

After two years of intensive effort, we are already seeing significant changes not only in the lives of the children, but also in the pride the local community takes in its achievements. The Scottish government has paid for a research organisation to evaluate and report on the impact of the work on the children and the local community. However, though there have already been considerable improvements in measurable ways, we know it will take decades of patient and passionate work to make the kind of enduring change we expect to see in the lives of generations of children.

It is evident that the Venezuelan miracle is working in Scotland, a very different society with a very different culture. It works because children are children everywhere, and they know in their hearts how to play, creatively, redeemingly, if given half a chance: that is the chance we are giving them.

## Towards a beginning

Local authorities sincerely do what they can to patch up their fractured communities and respond to local needs. However, might they have got things the wrong way round? The scandal of our policy towards troubled children is that we only start cascading significant financial resources into their lives when problems emerge and they start offending. Then we can find fortunes to feed them through the human shredder that is the British penal system. If we are not to go on losing generations of children to alienation and criminality, we have to find another way. *El Sistema* in Scotland shows us that putting money into cultural solutions may be the answer we seek. We have at least made a beginning, and the children of Venezuela are teaching the children of Scotland how to play again.

This chapter is largely based on the Simón Bolivar Lecture, which I delivered on 9 June 2009.[4]

### Notes

1   National Audit Office, *Youth Offending: the delivery of community and custodial sentences*, 2004, available at www.nao.org.uk/

2   R Wilkinson and K Pickett, *The Spirit Level: why more equal societies almost always do better*, Penguin, 2009

3   For more information, see www.fesnojiv.gob.ve/en.html

4   For more information, see www.raploch.com

# Twenty

# Poverty and participation: progress in Scotland

*Peter Kelly*

> We urge the Government to ensure that policy on poverty is informed by the
> views of those living on low incomes.
>
> Scottish Affairs Committee, 2007, p15

Getting the voices of people with experience of poverty into the policy-
making process has become an increasingly important part of the activity
of many campaigners over the last ten years.[1] Across numerous policy
areas, there has also been a growing desire for 'participation', 'engagement' and 'community involvement' as a means to achieve better solutions to problems, and legitimacy for actions to tackle them. Both inside
and outside government, there is a broad and growing consensus that
'participation' matters.

## The right to be heard

'Participation' is hardly a new idea.[2] The election of New Labour to
government in 1997 saw a significant strengthening of the appeal to community, with many programmes, particularly in the areas of social inclusion
and urban regeneration, which regarded community involvement as a vital
element in their development and delivery.[3] There are many reasons for
promoting community participation: addressing the democratic deficit;
tackling the remoteness of local government from citizens; the desire
for better, more responsive local services; and the need to build 'social
capital'.[4]

Much of the thinking around direct, active participation is focused
on local policy making or the delivery of local services. In Scotland, for
example, participation and engagement in local policy making, through

community planning, is enshrined in legislation.[5] Rarely, however, do we consider how participation could be built into the development of national policy and strategy.

While there has been an increasing number of policy areas that have sought to increase 'participation', these have rarely focused specifically on the involvement of those in poverty. Despite this, many organisations have used the emphasis on community involvement from the late 1990s to demand that the voices of people in poverty are heard in the policy development process.[6] These demands were based on the belief that this involvement would not only bring about better policy making, but that it would also lead to the fulfilment of fundamental rights for those in poverty.

## Getting involved in Scotland

For some, the development of community planning partnerships from 2003 held out the possibility of community participation in local policy development and local resource allocation.[7] We have also seen the development of the National Standards for Community Engagement, which were launched in 2005 to promote and support better engagement between communities and public agencies. While welcome, it is not clear whether they have had the desired impact in terms of creating a 'culture' of participation within public agencies.[8]

The Scottish National Party (SNP) government sought to demonstrate its support for community participation, publishing a *Community Empowerment Action Plan* in March 2009. This sets out why community empowerment is important and gives examples of good practice. It also sets out some specific actions and pulls together the various funding streams that exist to support community engagement. However, the lack of ambition in the plan and its failure to create any real momentum for community empowerment have been disappointing.[10]

Most significantly, the Scottish government held out the promise of a new approach to involving people with experience of poverty in the development of national anti-poverty strategies when it published its discussion paper on tackling poverty. In the paper, it stated that one of the principles underpinning the new framework would be:[11]

> ... the adoption of policies and services that are founded upon user involvement, consultation with people experiencing poverty, and community

engagement and empowerment, so that policies and practice are informed by the real experience of those we are trying to help.

However, when the *Achieving Our Potential* framework was published, it contained little in the way of concrete proposals to ensure that people in poverty were involved in national policy development or monitoring. Apart from a reference to the (then) forthcoming publication of the *Community Empowerment Action Plan*, there was little thought given to how exactly people in poverty were to be involved in shaping policy.

## European drivers to Scottish solutions

The European Anti-Poverty Network has achieved some level of success by ensuring that the participation of people in poverty was included in the development of the national action plans on social inclusion, which all European member states had to produce in the period 2001 to 2008. It was this requirement that allowed for the development of a range of actions in the UK that sought to involve people with experience of poverty in the development of a national anti-poverty strategy. In the development of the 2006 national action plan, for example, the Get Heard project fed in the views of people living in poverty from across the UK, with a large amount of feedback from Scotland.[12] For the 2008–2010 national action plan, the Poverty Alliance organised the 'Bridging the Policy Gap' project, which brought together local and national policy makers with people experiencing poverty to discuss key anti-poverty policies.[13]

This experience encouraged the Poverty Alliance to develop the Evidence, Participation, Change (EPIC) project. This has been the most comprehensive approach attempted so far in Scotland to ensure that the voices of people in poverty are heard in policy development at a national level. It will operate between 2009 and 2013, and aims to ensure that people in poverty, and the organisations that represent them, have opportunities to influence policy and promote a culture of participation.

A key element of the project is training for the participants involved in the project. Training is being provided to people active in community organisations and to people with experience of poverty to help them identify how they can make change in their community, whether through local or national action, in relation to social justice issues. Alongside training, the project also has a rolling programme of community-based research training, and research projects which emphasise the importance of not just ensuring that policy draws directly from the experience of people in poverty, but that people experiencing poverty can also generate the evidence through community research.

But building the capacity of individuals is not enough, nor is gathering evidence about the experience of poverty. There must be clear structures and processes that allow people to engage in dialogue with policy makers in order to exert influence. EPIC has set up the two such processes. The Tackling Poverty Stakeholder Forum meets twice yearly to track developments in Scottish anti-poverty policy. The Forum has around 40 members drawn equally from communities, the voluntary sector and senior policy makers in Scottish local and national government. After only three meetings, this group has already produced evidence on the impact of *Achieving Our Potential*, created opportunities for communities to contribute directly to the review of *Equally Well* (see Chapter 11) and has created a range of materials which are being used to tackle the stigma associated with poverty.[14]

The other process which has been launched is the Scottish Assembly for Tackling Poverty. This will be an annual event, bringing together a wide range of participants, including politicians, people in poverty, faith groups, trade unions, policy makers and voluntary groups, to debate and discuss progress in anti-poverty policy. Together, these two processes will, it is hoped, provide the basis for ongoing engagement between people with experience of poverty, policy makers and civil society.

## Conclusions: meeting the participation challenge

What is required now is that 'participatory' activity must move out of the domain of worthy, but time-limited, projects. There is a need to be ambitious when it comes to the participation of people experiencing poverty in Scotland. There are a number of challenges that must first be met.

Participation must be adequately resourced. At the moment, there are virtually no resources available for the long-term, consistent engagement of people with direct experience of poverty in national policy development. The best efforts of faith groups, voluntary organisations and others will not be enough unless the state devotes resources to ensuring participation becomes a reality.

Ten years of developing more participatory processes has not always led to the desired policy goals, but what has been established is the principle of direct involvement of people in poverty in discussions about the policies that affect their lives. Establishing this principle allows for discussions to continue to take place on key areas of anti-poverty policy, even when there is disagreement between those inside and outside government. In times when so much policy seems to be directed against the interests of the poorest, having a seat at the policy-making table is perhaps more important than ever. The next Scottish government needs to build on the good practice that has taken place and ensure that well-resourced and transparent processes are created to ensure that there is real participation by people in poverty in policy development.

## Notes

1 Organisations such as Oxfam and Save the Children have been strong advocates for greater participation, alongside faith-based organisations such as Church Action on Poverty and Faith in Community (Scotland).

2 E Brodie, W Cowling, N Nissen, A E Paine, V Jocgum and D Warburton, *Understanding Participation: a literature review*, Involve, 2009

3 D Cook, 'Consultation, for a Change? Engaging users and communities in the policy process', *Social Policy and Administration*, Vol 36, No.5, 2002, pp516–31

4 See note 2

5 The Local Government (2005) Scotland Act places a duty on statutory agencies to set up mechanisms for participation and engagement with local communities.

6 See, for example, UK Coalition Against Poverty, *Listen Hear: report of the Commission on Poverty Participation and Power*, The Policy Press, 2000; L Horemans, 'Participation of People Experiencing Poverty and Social Exclusion', in F Farrell, M Moser and A Smeekes (eds), *The EU We Want*, European Anti-Poverty Network, 2005

7 S Sinclair, 'Dilemmas of Community Planning: lessons from Scotland', *Public Policy and Administration*, Vol 23.4, 2008, pp373-90

8 Scottish Community Development Centre, *Culture or Compliance: monitoring the use of the National Standards for Community Engagement*, available from www.scdc.org.uk/national-standards/support-materials

9 Scottish Government, *Community Empowerment Action Plan*, 2009

10 Local People Leading, *Empowerment Action Plan Lacks Momentum: a response to the Scottish Government's Community Empowerment Action Plan*, 2009, available at www.localpeopleleading.co.uk

11 Scottish Government, *Achieving Our Potential: a framework to tackle poverty*

*and inequality in Scotland*, The Scottish Government, 2008, at www.scotland.gov.uk/publications/2008/11/20103815/0, 2008

12 L Burnett, *Dignity Shouldn't Have to be Earned*, Poverty Alliance, 2008; C Cochrane, 'Involving People in the UK National Action on Social Inclusion 2006–2008', *Benefits: the journal of poverty and social justice*, Vol 12.2, 2008, pp147–49

13 S Mackenzie and P Kelly, *From the Local to the National: bridging the policy gap in social inclusion*, Poverty Alliance, 2008. For more information on both these projects, see www.povertyalliance.org/btpg

14 All documents and reports produced by the EPIC project are available from www.povertyalliance.org/projects.asp

# Twenty-one
# In-work poverty

*Kendra Strauss and Peter Kelly*

## Introduction

Low pay is back on the political agenda. One of the reasons that the target of ending child poverty by 2020 is not likely to be met is because the number of children experiencing 'in-work poverty' has risen sharply since 2003/04.[1] It is now clear that the preferred government tools to tackle low pay – using a combination of tax credits and the national minimum wage – are insufficient. There is now a need to go beyond the approaches that have been used over the last 10 years if we are to address low pay and eradicate the poverty that results.

## Understanding low pay in Scotland

### The scale of the problem

There are a number of ways of defining low pay. In this chapter we use the commonly used £7 an hour threshold. This should not be confused with the target amount of the living wage campaign in Scotland, which is £7.15 an hour for 2010/11.

Scotland has a lower proportion of low-paid workers than other parts of the UK.[2] Nevertheless, more than 20 per cent of women, and almost 15 per cent of men, earned less than £7 an hour in 2009. According to the *Labour Force Survey*, in 2009 the proportion of all workers in Scotland earning less than £7 an hour averaged around 24 per cent.[3] Indeed, many workers in Scotland earn well below the £7 per hour threshold: according to the Annual Survey of Hours and Earnings, in 2009 10 per cent of jobs paid £6.23 or less.

## The geography of low pay in Scotland

Rural areas feature prominently in the four local authorities in Scotland with the highest proportion of low-paid workers between 2007 and 2009 – Clackmannanshire, the Highlands and Islands, Dumfries and Galloway, and Moray. Dundee and Glasgow were the urban local authorities with the highest proportion of low-paid workers.

Looking at Clackmannanshire and Dundee in more detail, we see that:

- in Clackmannanshire in 2009, 25 per cent of jobs (approximately 3,000) paid £6.88 or less per hour;[4] 30 per cent of full-time female workers earned £6.81 or less per hour; and 60 per cent of part-time female workers earned less than £7 per hour;
- in Dundee in 2009, 20 per cent of all jobs (approximately 14,400) paid less than £7.13 an hour; 10 per cent of full-time male workers earned £6.75 or less per hour; and 40 per cent of part-time male workers and 30 per cent of part-time female workers earned less than £7 per hour.[5]

## Gender and low pay in Scotland

Women in Scotland are more likely to be in low-paid jobs than men. Indeed, they comprise two-thirds of low-paid workers in Scotland (67 per cent). This is largely because women are more likely to work part time: in 2009, 43 per cent of workers earning less than £7 an hour were women in part-time jobs (a further 24 per cent of low-paid workers are women in full-time jobs).

For women, low pay and part-time work (and, hence, the gender pay gap) are directly related to caring responsibilities. The lack of comprehensive public childcare in the UK (see Chapter 12), and the related high costs, is one reason why many women work part time or leave the labour market when they have children. The same issues affect men who are carers. For households headed by a lone parent, most of which are women, the risk of low income is thus twice as high: most part-time work is low paid, but full-time work is often incompatible with caring responsibilities. Moreover, those women who go to work in the care sector, looking after other people's children and relatives, are themselves at risk of low pay.

The gender patterns are not straightforward. Young men who work full time are more likely to be in low-paid jobs than young full-time women workers. This pattern is reversed as men and women age, a finding that supports the theory that the gender wage gap is influenced by women's childrearing and caring responsibilities.

## Low pay by industry and sector

Low pay in Scotland also varies by industrial sector.[6] Those with the lowest rates of pay in 2009 included:

- the food, beverage and accommodation service sector:
  - 70 per cent of jobs in food and beverage service activities paid less than £6.61 per hour;
  - in the accommodation and food services activities sector as a whole, 60 per cent of jobs paid £6.50 per hour or less;
  - more than 51,000 jobs in this sector paid a full-time annual wage (based on a 37.5-hour week) of less than £12,000;
- the retail sector:
  - 40 per cent of all jobs (approximately 82,000) (excluding motor vehicles) paid less than £6.28 per hour, and 60 per cent (123,000 jobs) less than £7.29 per hour.

Rates of low pay also vary between the public and private sectors. Although directly employed public sector workers are less at risk of low pay than those in the private sector, they nevertheless account for around one-fifth of all those in low pay. Nearly all of these are women, and just about all of them work in either education or health (including social work). These are workers directly employed. If contract workers in areas such as cleaning and care work are included, the numbers of low-wage workers employed by the public sector is likely to be higher. Moreover, cuts to public spending are likely to mean more low-paid work and more contracted-out services, unless commitments are made to protect those on low incomes.

## Conclusions

Low pay affects a significant number of individuals, families and households in Scotland.

There are two factors that increase the likelihood of low pay becoming more prevalent in Scotland. The first is the planned public sector cuts. Scotland has a high proportion of its workforce in the public sector, and it is likely that cuts will both reduce the number of jobs in the public sector and the levels of pay. The second is competition for jobs in the labour market. The imbalance between supply and demand in the labour market (with demand outstripping supply) suggests that wages will fall. There is 'room' for wages to fall, in that the median wage[7] (and, indeed, the low-pay threshold of £7 per hour) is well above the legal minimum of £5.90 per hour. These factors will conspire to exert a downward pressure on pay in both the public and private sector in Scotland.

The current context does not appear to be the best for addressing low pay. Some anti-poverty campaigners may even argue that it should not be the main priority at the moment. With wide-ranging reforms affecting the welfare benefits system over the next few years, including cuts to the level, and duration, of some key benefits, and unemployment levels unlikely to improve significantly in the near future, some might argue that a focus on low pay is misplaced. This would be a mistake. As the above figures show, low pay has become one of the key causes of poverty in Scotland and the UK. Any anti-poverty strategy that ignores the problem of low pay will only create problems in the future. It is arguable that one of the reasons why we have not made sufficient progress in tackling poverty has been the relative separation of concerns about in-work and out-of-work poverty. Future strategies must not make this same mistake. Moreover, during a period of scarce resources, we should be critical of policies that force people into low-paid, insecure work, while subsidising employers to pay below subsistence rates to their workers.

The development of living wage campaigns, most significantly in London and in Scotland, shows that there is the potential to take action and ensure that low pay remains an important policy concern even during the recession.[8] The campaign in Scotland has made real progress, with the main political parties now signed up to support the current living wage level of £7.15, advocated by the Scottish Living Wage Campaign. But however welcome, living wage commitments affecting only public sector workers will not be sufficient.

What is required is an approach to addressing low pay that becomes a mainstream part of anti-poverty and employment policy. The Scottish government's *Achieving Our Potential* framework recognised the importance of low pay, but the actions proposed to deal with the problem were insufficient. Whoever forms the next government in Scotland will need to redouble its efforts to address if we are to have a real impact on poverty.

## Notes

1  T MacInnes, P Kenway and A Parekh, *Monitoring Poverty and Social Exclusion 2009*, Joseph Rowntree Foundation/New Policy Institute, 2009

2  All figures are from www.poverty.org.uk unless otherwise stated.

3  Office for National Statistics, *Labour Force Survey Five-Quarter Longitudinal Dataset, October 2008 – December 2009*, UK Data Archive, 2010

4  All figures are for gross hourly pay excluding overtime. *ASHE, Hourly Pay – Excluding Overtime (£) – for all Employee Jobs: UK*, Office for National Statistics, 2009, Table 7.6a

5  There is no estimate of the number of part-time jobs filled by male workers in Dundee in 2009, but an estimated 16,000 part-time jobs were held by women in the city in 2009. Dundee also has the highest rates of part-time employment for any Scottish city (27 per cent of all those in employment worked part time in 2008, the latest year for which figures are available).

6  ASHE uses the UK Standard Industrial Classification of Economic Activities (SIC). See www.statistics.gov.uk/methods_quality/sic/default.asp. All figures are from *ASHE, Hourly Pay – Gross (£) – for all Employee Jobs: UK*, Office for National Statistics, 2009, Table 5.5a

7  The median hourly pay was £10.89 in 2009, *ASHE, Hourly Pay – Gross (£) – for all Employee Jobs: UK*, Office for National Statistics, 2009, Table 7.5a, available at www.statistics.gov.uk/statbase/product.asp?vlnk=13101

8  For more information about the Scottish Living Wage Campaign, see www.povertyalliance.org/slw-home.asp

# Twenty-two
# Housing

*Richard Grant and Zoe McGuire*

## Introduction

One of the primary objectives of housing policy should be to seek to ensure that satisfactory housing is available to all, not just those who can afford to provide it for themselves. In effect, housing policy instruments need to be able to counteract the wide variations in housing opportunities that result from the operation of the labour market and the distribution of wealth. Possible policy instruments include: subsidising the provision of housing for low-income or disadvantaged households; providing subsidies to allow low-income or disadvantaged households to compete effectively in the housing market; and indirect interventions such as regulating to set minimum standards and mechanisms for dealing with crisis situations such as homelessness or mortgage repossessions.

Poor-quality housing and neighbourhoods can also create disadvantage in other respects – children may be disadvantaged at school, some health problems such as asthma and mental illness can be exacerbated by poor housing, and bleak, remote housing estates with poor public transport can make it more difficult for residents to access jobs, or even good quality shops.

Despite the importance of tackling housing disadvantage, the information available for monitoring the housing situation of low-income households or particular groups of potentially vulnerable households in Scotland is limited. Since the creation of the Scottish parliament in 1999, responsibility for housing policy has been devolved to the Scottish government, and policies have increasingly diverged from those adopted 'south of the border'. But responsibility for welfare, including housing benefit, other inter-connected areas of policy, macro-economic policy and the regulation of financial institutions has remained with the UK government.

## Housing policy since 2007

Major initiatives in housing policy require considerable time to be developed and implemented, especially when this involves legislation. Housing policy since 2007 has often focused on the implementation of earlier legislation and programmes, and some of the new initiatives will only have an impact in the years to come. This chapter covers the main housing policy and programme issues, both inherited and new, which are likely to have an impact on poverty and disadvantage in Scotland.

For households with limited resources, social-rented housing and the cheaper properties in the privately rented sector offer the only viable housing options, and their condition and availability are crucial. In 1981, over 50 per cent of Scottish households lived in the social-rented sector, but this has fallen sharply in the last 40 years to around 24 per cent in 2009, largely as a result of the right to buy and demolitions.[1] Since 2007, new social-rented housing has increased somewhat from an annual average of 4,300 completions between 2000 and 2007 to over 4,800. One welcome initiative has been challenge funding, available for new local authority housing – with over 3,000 units approved. The future of this initiative, however, is unclear and there have been suggestions that, in future, new, possibly integrated, funding arrangements for social housing may be required.[2] Right-to-buy sales have fallen over this period – from 7,500 in 2007/08 to just under 2,200 in 2009/10, largely as a result of market conditions. The changes to the right to buy following the 2001 Housing (Scotland) Act have, so far, had a limited impact, and the further changes set out in the 2010 Housing (Scotland) Bill[3] may also result in only a modest further reduction. The net result of policy since 2007 is that the total social-rented housing stock has remained largely static. As a result, waiting lists have continued to grow, with an estimated 160,000 people on these lists in 2010. This compares with the 23,000 socially rented houses let to new tenants in 2009/10.

There has also been increasing pressure on the private-rented sector, especially from migrants from Eastern Europe and single people on low incomes who would generally be low priority for social housing. Increasingly, they have been competing with young professionals and families who can no longer afford to buy in the owner-occupied sector. Paradoxically, a significant amount of private-rented housing (estimated by the Scottish government at around 20 per cent of the total) is ex-social housing sold under the right-to-buy scheme and now let by private landlords, often at much higher rents.[4]

A substantial proportion of households in the rented sector need financial assistance through housing benefit to pay their rent. Average rents in the social-rented sector increased by about 15 per cent between 2006/07 and 2009/10, with an average weekly rent of £53 in the council sector and almost £60 in the housing association sector in 2009/10. Private-rented sector rents were much higher (at an average of £403 per month in 2008).[5] Some 380,700 tenants were in receipt of housing benefit in the social-rented sector in August 2010 (64 per cent of the total); 85,600 in the private-rented sector (34 per cent of the total).[6] The changes to the housing benefit scheme announced by the UK government in the 2010 emergency Budget and autumn Spending Review could impact severely on housing benefit claimants in the private-rented sector, as benefit will be capped at the 30th percentile of market rents rather than the median. This could force many tenants into poorer accommodation, or to give up their tenancies and become homeless.

For those who are fortunate enough to obtain housing in the social-rented sector, the quality of their housing and the neighbourhood in which they live is crucial in determining their standard of living. A Scottish Housing Quality Standard was set in 2005 and all social-rented houses are required to be brought up to this by 2015. Progress to date has been slow, but variable between different landlords. By 2008, some 67 per cent of all houses continued to fail the standard.[7]

At a neighbourhood level, the incoming administration in 2007 has continued the regeneration programmes linked to urban regeneration companies established by its predecessor, some of which are active in areas of predominantly social-rented housing, such as Craigmillar in Edinburgh and Raploch in Stirling. Over the past 40 years, there has been a succession of area-based regeneration schemes targeted at the most deprived and least popular council estates. Although this has undoubtedly resulted in many improvements at a local level, the *Scottish Index of Multiple Deprivation* for 2009 indicates that the areas identified as multiply deprived are very similar to those identified in 2006 and 2004. Indeed, the five most deprived areas are made up of predominantly social-rented housing that have been subject to various initiatives over the past 40 years.[8]

Data from the *Scottish House Condition Survey* indicates that conditions in the private-rented sector have improved in recent years, with the exception of energy efficiency standards, but there remains a 'bottom end' where both physical conditions and management standards are much more variable. A recent report suggests that this could account for 25 per cent or more of the sector as a whole and is much more likely to be lived in by low-income households.[9] Policy initiatives to improve standards at the bottom end of the private-rented sector (licensing of houses in multiple occupation and registration of private sector landlords), initiated by the previous administration, have had limited results[10] and there is currently a Bill[11] before Parliament which seeks to make some minor changes to improve the effectiveness of these measures.

Fuel poverty (defined as spending more than 10 per cent of income on fuel bills) is a particular problem for many households and this was recognised by the 2001 Act which set a statutory deadline for its abolition by 2016. Since 2007, the former Warm Deal and Central Heating programmes have been replaced by the Energy Assistance Package, providing advice and assistance to elderly and low-income households with insulation measures and new central heating boilers. Despite this initiative, the data from the *Scottish House Condition Survey* indicates that fuel poverty almost doubled between 2002 and 2008 (from 13.4 per cent to 26.5 per cent of all households), almost certainly as a result of increased fuel prices. At present, the prognosis for the achievement of the 2016 target is poor.

Fuel poverty is as high in the private sector as in the social-rented sector and this no doubt reflects the large number of elderly owner occupiers with low incomes and difficult-to-heat houses. There is a clear contradiction in the policy of the Scottish government towards elderly households in the private sector. On the one hand, grants for repairs and improvements have been substantially reduced (with the exception of disability adaptations). On the other, the government is actively promoting a policy to cope with the expected growth in the number of older people (known as the Reshaping Care Programme), which seeks to encourage them to stay in their own homes. The main housing response to this remains Care and Repair, but the financial viability of local teams is increasingly threatened by the abolition of ring-fenced funding from 2007/08. The Scottish government has recently announced a £70 million 'change fund', under the control of local NHS boards, to help develop new initiatives in line with the objectives of the Reshaping Care Programme. How this money will be allocated and the extent to which it will include housing initiatives, including Care and Repair, is still to be decided.

Homelessness is a severe form of housing disadvantage and there have been a number of legislative and other initiatives in this area stemming from the pioneering work of the Homelessness Task Force between 1999 and 2002. The current administration has reaffirmed its commitment to providing settled accommodation for all homeless people by 2012 –

rather than designated priority-need groups. But other recommendations have not been progressed, and the monitoring group set up to oversee implementation has been disbanded. The number of people applying as homeless has remained at approximately 57,000 a year since 2007/08, but this is a big increase from the 40,000 in 2000/01.[12] This increase is likely, in part, to reflect the fact that a wider range of households is now eligible for assistance in line with a progressive move towards the 2012 target. Overall, by 2009/10 councils should have been housing just over 90 per cent of all households assessed as unintentionally homeless, but they had only achieved a figure of 85 per cent. Progress is variable in different parts of Scotland, but there is clearly some catching up required if the 2012 target is to be achieved.

The Homelessness Task Force report also led to a greater emphasis on prevention and increased funding for support to homeless people provided through the Supporting People programme. Unfortunately, this ring-fenced budget has been abolished by the current administration in line with its concordat with the Convention of Scottish Local Authorities, and expenditure has fallen by about 25 per cent as a result. The Scottish parliament has, however, recently agreed an amendment to the Housing (Scotland) Bill 2010 which requires councils to assess the housing support needs of all homeless people and to provide support in line with this. To its credit, the Scottish government has introduced legislation which should give greater protection in the courts to owners and to social-rented sector tenants faced with repossession proceedings.[13]

## 2011: what is needed now?

Resources should be focused on improving both the quality and quantity of social-rented housing, ensuring the 2015 target for meeting the Scottish Housing Quality Standard is met and focusing new investment on affordable homes in diverse, socially mixed neighbourhoods. There is a strong case for reviewing the low-cost home ownership schemes, which, in recent years, have absorbed an increasing share of the resources from the affordable housing programme, with a view to ensuring that they are focused on increasing the stock of affordable housing for those in need, rather than helping purchasers buy existing houses.

The right to buy should be subject to continuing reform to ensure that sales only take place where these are socially beneficial. There also needs to be more careful consideration before existing social-rented houses are demolished.

A more radical review of the private-rented sector is required, with a view to achieving more targeted and less cumbersome regulation, new sources of investment and a tenancy regime which recognises that many households need better security than at present.

At a UK level, the structure of housing benefit should be reformed to improve work incentives, but not at the expense of putting at risk those households with few other options. At a local authority level, many councils need to review the efficiency of their housing benefit administration to ensure that benefit is provided swiftly and accurately.

And there needs to be continuing commitment to established targets, not only the 2015 target mentioned above, but also the 2012 homelessness target and the 2016 fuel poverty target. In all three cases, the policy goals are right, but there is a need to secure effective implementation.

Finally, there is a need to ensure effective prevention of homelessness by delivering on the 2010 legislative commitment on housing support.

## Notes

1   All housing data from Scottish Government, *Housing Statistics for Scotland*, available at www.scotland.gov.uk/Topics/Statistics/Browse/Housing-Regeneration/ HSfS, 2010 unless otherwise stated.

2   The Scottish government has recently published research which models the impact of different levels of subsidy on future housing output: G Bramley and others, *A Study into the Capacity of Registered Social Landlords and Local Authorities to Build Housing Across Scotland*, Scottish Government Research Findings No.53, 2010

3   The Housing (Scotland) Bill recently passed through the Scottish parliament and is due to come into force in 2011.

4   Scottish Executive, *The Right to Buy in Scotland: pulling together the evidence*, available at www.scotland.gov.uk/publications/2006/09/26114727/0

5   Scottish Government Social Research, *Review of the Private Rented Sector: views and experiences of tenants in the private rented sector in Scotland – Volume 2*, 2009, available at www.scotland.gov.uk/publications/2009/03/23153402/1

6   Based on figures from the Department for Work and Pensions, with 593,980 in the social-rented sector and 250,409 in the private-rented sector.

7   Scottish Government, *Scottish House Condition Survey: key findings 2008*, available at www.scotland.gov.uk/publications/2009/11/23090958/0

8   Scottish Government, *Scottish Index of Multiple Deprivation: 2009 general report*, 2009, available at www.scotland.gov.uk/publications/2009

9   Shelter Scotland, *Review of Research on Disadvantaged and Potentially Vulnerable Households in the Private Rented Sector,* Shelter Scotland, 2009

10  Shelter Scotland, *Landlord Registration in Scotland: three years on*, 2009, available at http://scotland.shelter.org.uk

11  Private Rented Housing (Scotland) Bill introduced on 4 October 2010, available at www.scottish.parliament.uk

12  Scottish Government, *Operation of the Homeless Persons Legislation in Scotland: 2009–10*, National Statistics, 2010, available at http://scotland.shelter.org.uk

13  The Home Owner and Debtor Protection (Scotland) Act 2010 and the Housing (Scotland) Bill recently passed through the Scottish parliament and are due to come into force in 2011.

# Section Six
## Conclusion

# Twenty-three

# Conclusion: towards a more equal Scotland?

*Gerry Mooney*

In October 2010, the Equality and Human Rights Commission published its first Triennial Review, *How Fair is Britain?*[1] Together with outlining some of the positive developments that have taken place in recent times (for instance, public attitudes towards diversity are more tolerant than in the past and there is less tolerance of discrimination), the overall picture it presents is of a Britain that is hugely divided, from birth through school and education more generally into the workplace and onto retirement. Progress towards equality for women seems to have halted, while class, ethnicity, age and disability continue to be major determining influences on the life chances of people. Focusing on Scotland, the Commission comments:[2]

> ... while the country has made significant progress in terms of tackling discrimination and changing attitudes over the past 30 years, there exists a huge new gap between aspiration and achievement. Old inequalities continue to hold us back while new social and economic fault-lines emerge as we get older and more diverse.

Scotland faces five challenges in the areas of: health and wellbeing, education and inclusion, work and wealth, safety and security, and in relation to autonomy and voice. While such challenges take us beyond the particular concern with poverty, they are directly related to the issue and question of poverty in Scotland and what should be done to address it. These challenges reflect some of the discussions and arguments presented throughout this book – and remind us that poverty does not stand alone, but is entangled with a series of other social issues, issues which lie at the heart of contemporary Scottish society, and which must be addressed if we are to start on the path towards a more equal Scotland.

The question and issue of what to do about poverty, disadvantage and inequality are, of course, long-standing ones. The discussion of poverty and how to tackle it is part of a wider issue around the condition of social welfare. It raises questions about how social justice and injustice are viewed and about the kind of society that we might wish to see. As might be expected, there are profound disagreements and ongoing debates as to what this might entail, and how poverty is to be best understood and addressed, though there is cross-party political support across the devolved UK for the 2010 Child Poverty Act that (in late 2010) locks government into a definition of poverty based primarily on relative low income. However, we can look back across the many contributions to this book in the knowledge that we have a shared view that poverty and disadvantage are part and parcel of larger questions around social injustice and social justice.[3] But as we reflect on the story of poverty and poverty policy in recent years, we find ourselves, once again, challenging ideas and narratives that work to discriminate against and marginalise those affected by poverty.

As we saw in Chapter 1 and in Chapter 9, the idea that the problem of poverty is 'really' the 'problem' of 'the poor' continues to resurface and circulate around discussions of social welfare in the contemporary UK – and that includes Scotland as much as it does other areas of the UK. All too often there is a tendency in Scotland to suggest that 'we' should pat ourselves on our collective Scottish backs that things are different up here and 'we' do not have an anti-poor ethos. Yet while there is general support for social welfare in Scotland and for some degree of redistribution of wealth and income in the fight against poverty, nonetheless, and as we have seen, we do not have to look too far (for instance, in sections of the media and among some politicians, or around the 1998 Glasgow East by-election) for demands for a much harsher and punitive welfare policy. However, there is something else which needs to be recognised here. Under both the previous Labour/Liberal Democrat Scottish administration, 2003–2007 and under the Scottish National Party (SNP) minority Scottish government from 2007 to 2011 there was, just as at UK level, a shared political and policy understanding that the best (and perhaps even only) route to tackling poverty is through work – work generated by strategies that emphasised economic growth, rather than job quality, as a priority. While there is some recognition of in-work poverty, this does not have the primacy of the work-first approach and tends to be more rhetoric than any meaningful commitment to policy in this area.

Let there be no mistake that, despite calls for fairness, solidarity and equality, a language of (workfare) welfare punitivism, increasing conditionality and of poor people as having multiple and diverse personal deficiencies is alive and well in contemporary Scotland. Even if now thankfully largely absent from official Scottish policy documents, such language still permeates policy discussions: the current proposed reforms of the welfare system by the UK coalition government draws in part on the old distinctions between a 'deserving' and 'undeserving' poor; the increasingly pervasive language of the last decade that talks of aspirational deficits, dysfunctional and deviant behaviours and an absence of social capital as being among the 'real' causes of poverty; and a seemingly expanding range of moral and behavioural problems which have some of the poorest sections of contemporary UK society trapped in a rediscovered culture of poverty. *The Scheme* documentary, discussed in Chapter 9, represents one, but not the only one, highly visible manifestation of such thinking.

Why do such ideas continue to circulate? At one level, there is a greater sense of fear and uncertainty in contemporary Scotland – an uncertainty that extends beyond those experiencing poverty, profound and significant that it is – to envelop larger sections of Scottish society. Such fears and insecurities around personal, family and community well-being are, of course, being exacerbated in the context of a deep-rooted economic recession that has seen poverty rise among some groups, along with increasing unemployment.[4] This has also seen inequality rise too – as the impact of the economic crisis of 2008/09 has not been evenly distributed across the population.[5] Far from it. Further, and as we have highlighted elsewhere in this book, the UK Conservative/Liberal Democrat coalition government has been determined to respond to such a crisis by further attacking social welfare and public services – as well as the several million workers who rely on public service employment. The 'age of austerity' promises little by way of challenging such fears, and it too will be hugely uneven in its economic, geographical and social impacts.[6]

Journalist Anna Minton has referred to the contemporary UK as a 'distrustful and fearful society'. This modern 'social evil', she argues, is the consequence of growing social and geographical inequalities, as well as of a media which has a vested commercial interest in promoting fear and insecurity. Minton is only one of a number of commentators who have highlighted the extent of inequality in contemporary Britain and how it is contributing to a heightened level of fear and distrust.[7] For the observers mentioned here, together with many others, such inequalities are increasingly visible, marked by sharp differences in the life chances of different sections of the population living in areas that are also sharply polarised.

This brings us back to the question of 'austerity' and to the measures announced by the UK Conservative/Liberal Democrat coalition government to reduce the UK's debt in autumn 2010. At the Conservative Party Conference in October 2010, the Chancellor George Osborne announced far-reaching changes to the welfare system, in particular the ending of universal child benefit (by 2013, people on 40 per cent and 50 per cent income tax rates will no longer be entitled). Widely criticised for taking this planned measure, nonetheless, there was some support from those who had long championed the cause of child poverty. One notable supporter of the government measures was the Chief Executive of Barnardo's, who claimed that universal child benefit is now 'impossible to justify' in a context of far-reaching cuts in other benefits and services.[8]

The ending of universal child benefit is being used by the coalition government to legitimate its claim that 'we are all in this together', that the well off are also being 'hit' by cuts. Further, it is also being claimed that such measures allow more targeting on people in 'real' need, that if the measure was not taken, poorer people would be even worse off in the longer term. There are, however, other far-reaching implications of this development: it effectively ends an upper-middle-class commitment to universal welfare, eroding one of the remaining ties that bound them to the welfare state. More significantly, perhaps, it also opens up the possibility for an even harsher and more punitive approach to welfare with the support of a middle class who feel that 'they have done their bit'.

As we noted in Chapter 1, the Comprehensive Spending Review announcement on 20 October 2010 outlined the far-reaching cuts in welfare and public spending, totalling some £81 billion, which the UK government believes will address Britain's budget deficit.[9] Among the most striking elements of the new cuts was a package of £7 billion of additional welfare cuts on top of the £11 billion already made in the June 2010 Budget. The Spending Review also announced major cuts in public sector budgets – and the expected loss of up to 490,000 public sector jobs.

Not surprisingly, these announcements provoked a furious debate and protests among trade unionists, service users, activists and community groups. With Chancellor George Osborne calling the cuts 'tough' but 'fair', the meaning of 'fairness' was thrown into centre stage. The UK's leading independent micro-economic research unit, the Institute for Fiscal Studies (IFS) estimated that the cuts were the deepest since the second world war, with benefits undergoing the most far-reaching squeeze since the 1970s. In sharp contrast to the views of Chancellor Osborne, the IFS argued that the tax and benefit changes announced in the Spending Review were regressive, hitting the less well off harder than the well off.[10]

It is difficult to see in the June 2010 Budget and the October 2010 Comprehensive Spending Review anything that supports the claim that the poorest and most disadvantaged sections of society will not be hardest hit by the government's policies. In addition, there is mounting evidence that these measures are also highly uneven across different sections of the population. The 500,000 job cuts announced for the public sector will have a highly disproportionate impact on women workers, for instance. With women accounting for over 65 per cent of all public sector workers and over 32 per cent of all women in employment working in the public sector, it is clear that women will be badly affected.

Women will be disproportionately affected in other ways too. Many families increasingly rely on women's earnings alongside benefit payments such as working tax credit, child tax credit and child benefit. The welfare 'reforms' and tax changes announced in June 2010 and in the October 2010 Spending Review make such families even more vulnerable to immediate poverty, especially child poverty. Many women will also be badly affected by the cuts in public services as they generally use such services more than men, especially in relation to caring tasks.

The gender dimension also overlaps with a geographical dimension. In Scotland, the public sector accounts for a higher proportion of employment than in the UK as a whole, with around 25 per cent of all workers in public sector employment, reaching around 32 per cent in some localities. Women are 67 per cent of the workforce in Scottish local authorities, where their employment – representing 41 per cent of all working women – is concentrated in low-paid areas such as catering, cleaning and care.

The further story is one of pay freezes (that is, pay cuts in real terms), increased pension contributions and other changes in services which will impact dramatically on all public sector workers. The consequence of all these combined changes is likely to be devastating on the many areas across Scotland already struggling in the midst of an economic downturn.

The question of 'fairness' is one that is likely to feature prominently in the Scottish parliamentary election campaigns in the early part of 2011 and beyond. The brief discussion that we can offer here, however, already challenges the political rhetoric of the coalition government, that we are 'all in this together'.

## Looking back on the Scottish government 2007–2011

It is important that we acknowledge that talk of fairness, solidarity and equality has taken us some way along the road from the dark days of the 1980s and 1990s, when the existence of poverty was rarely acknowledged at a political level (and equality not at all – beyond equality of opportunity that is). We have also come some way since earlier editions of *Poverty in Scotland* bemoaned a lack of data and analysis, especially in the Scottish context. In some respects, therefore, our ability to understand poverty and disadvantage, and their impacts, has developed greatly. But can we say that this has been reflected in a coherent anti-poverty strategy at a Scottish level?

Of course, immediately, this question provokes a response that much of the policy-making remit around poverty and social welfare is reserved to the UK parliament. However, the role of the Scottish government remains significant – in many different ways. Government is a significant employer across Scotland, as we have seen, with around one-quarter of the working population in public sector employment (higher in areas with large concentrations of poverty such as Dundee and West Central Scotland) – though in the context of far-reaching public spending cuts this is sure to fall with a corresponding knock-on effect on the private sector. Strategies adopted by public sector employers in relation to wages, income, conditions of employment and so on, have an enormous impact across the country.[11] The rhetorical approach of the Scottish government – that is, how it constructs and understands the 'poverty problem' (or more correctly the problem of inequality?) – is important in shaping the dominant ways in which poverty is understood in Scottish society.

Yet for all the rhetoric, evidence, repeated commitments to 'closing the opportunity gap' and 'achieving our potential' (the titles, of course, of the key devolved poverty policy documents of the last two Scottish administrations), it is difficult to say that we have in Scotland today a coherent national approach to poverty which ensures ambitious national commitments to reducing income inequality, tackling poverty and eradicating child poverty that translate into real changes on the ground in the way services, jobs and pay are delivered and distributed. There is a framework in place, *Achieving Our Potential* (sitting alongside health inequality (*Equally Well*) and an *Early Years Framework*), which sets out actions focusing on income inequality, income maximisation and adequacy as well as the 'reform' of welfare. While these have been important and useful developments, we have to ask whether the framework remains 'just' a framework, one that would be difficult to achieve in a climate of relative economic growth and prosperity, let alone in the context of an economic crisis. Further, to what extent is a 'framework approach' driving change at either the local or national level in Scotland? Despite the commitment that single-outcome agreements with local authorities would 'provide the vehicle for describing how poverty is being tackled at a local level', it is difficult to identify local strategic approaches or outcomes at local level from these single-outcome agreements, let alone evidence of an overall national impact.[12] As the authors of the *Monitoring Poverty and Social Exclusion in Scotland 2010* report highlight, between 2004/05 and 2008/09 the share of the total income going to the poorest 30 per cent of Scottish society actually fell by one-twelfth – in sharp contradiction to the government's 'solidarity purpose target',[13] albeit this important target was not set until 2007. And this is before the full impact of the 2008/09 recession and the resulting 'austerity measures'. Further, between 1998/99 and 2008/09, there was no change in the proportion of income going to the poorest three-tenths of the Scottish population.[14] By contrast, the share of total income going to the top three-tenths has increased dramatically over the decade. Scotland stands today as more unequal than in the late 1990s – a shocking statement of policy omission on the one hand, and of policy (and political) objective on the other, that has encouraged a trickle-down approach to inequality.

## Where do we go from here? Looking ahead to the next Scottish government

As we have seen, and a point that echoes across this collection, there is a massive gulf between rhetoric and aspiration on the one hand, and reality and outcome on the other.[15] Over the last decade, each new government in Edinburgh has, in coming into power, made promises to address poverty that have not been met, and which have often been in conflict with other economic and social policies which only serve to increase inequality. As we saw in a number of the chapters in Section 5, work-based approaches have proven incapable of effectively tackling poverty, not least because of other policies which pursue labour market flexibility and 'lean' (that is, low-cost) forms of employment. Further, incoming administrations often start with a new round of consultations (in place of more effective forms of participation?), but do these simply work to delay and even close down the adoption of radically alternative approaches? They are also, in part, a factor in the lack of coherence and continuity across Scottish parliaments, the commitment to economic growth aside.

As we head to the next Scottish elections in May 2011, and to the new parliament thereafter, the challenge for us all is to keep to the fore an alternative way of thinking of poverty – that sees it as part of the wider question of social justice and equality in contemporary Scotland. Reflecting the themes and conclusions of the chapters in the previous section, *towards a more equal Scotland*, therefore means a significant change in the dominant thinking around poverty, social exclusion and inequality. This entails:

- refocusing attention on the entire income distribution, considering the privileges and lifestyles of the affluent and rich, as much as those of the more disadvantaged;
- ensuring that equality means equality not only between different groups but also between different places;
- recognising that universal benefits continue to offer an important means by which public commitment to, and support for, social welfare is enabled, as well as meeting the needs of a sizeable proportion of the Scottish population without recourse to means testing;
- understanding that good quality and accessible public services are central to any anti-poverty strategy and that such services depend on a well-paid, well-respected and well-resourced workforce;
- adopting forms of participation that ensure that the knowledge of those experiencing poverty is taken into account in the development of anti-poverty strategies;
- acknowledging that while paid work has an important role to play in addressing poverty, pay levels and pay distribution, the quality of work and prospects for meaningful working lives are more important for a long-term approach to tackling poverty;
- accepting that income and wealth redistribution are central to any meaningful attempt to create a more equal Scotland;
- understanding that social welfare and the creation of a more equal Scotland brings benefits to all people living in Scotland.

## Notes

1   Equality and Human Rights Commission, *How Fair is Britain? The First Triennial Review: executive summary*, Equality and Human Rights Commission, 2010

2   Equality and Human Rights Commission Scotland, *Commission Launches Landmark Fairness Report: how does Scotland fare?* Equality and Human Rights Commission Scotland, 2010

3   G Mooney and G Scott (eds), *Social Justice and Social Policy in Scotland*, The Policy Press, 2011; G Scott and G Mooney, 'Poverty and Social Justice in the Devolved Scotland: neo-liberalism meets social democracy?' *Social Policy and Society*, Vol 3, issue 4, 2009, pp379–89; A Jarvis and P Gardner, *Poverty and Inequality in Scotland: report of expert seminars and stakeholder feedback on the relationship between equality and poverty*, Equality and Human Rights Commission, 2009

4   A Parekh, P Kenway and T MacInnes, *Monitoring Poverty and Social Exclusion in Scotland 2010*, Joseph Rowntree Foundation/New Policy Institute, 2010

5   D Dorling, *Injustice: why social inequality persists*, The Policy Press, 2010; A Parekh, P Kenway and T MacInnes, *Monitoring Poverty and Social Exclusion in Scotland 2010*, Joseph Rowntree Foundation/New Policy Institute, 2010; R Wilkinson and K Pickett, *The Spirit Level: why more equal societies almost always do better*, Penguin, 2010

6   Equality and Human Rights Commission Scotland, *Commission Launches Landmark Fairness Report: how does Scotland fare?* Equality and Human Rights Commission Scotland, 2010; Equality and Human Rights Commission, *How Fair is Britain? The First Triennial Review: executive summary*, Equality and Human Rights Commission, 2010; Institute for Fiscal Studies, *The Distributional Effect of Tax and Benefit Reforms to be Introduced Between June 2010 and April 2014: a revised assessment*, Briefing Note BN108, Institute for Fiscal Studies, 2010; Institute for Fiscal Studies, 'New IFS research challenges Chancellor's "progressive Budget" claim', Press Release, Institute for Fiscal Studies, August 2010

7   A Minton, *Why are Fear and Distrust Spiralling in Twenty-first Century Britain?* Joseph Rowntree Foundation, 2008; Joseph Rowntree Foundation, *Contemporary Social Evils*, The Policy Press, 2009

8   S Coates and R Bennett, 'Scrap child benefit but keep handouts for poor, says Barnardo's chief', the *Times*, 4 October 2010

9   HM Treasury, *Spending Review 2010*, Cm 7942, HM Treasury, 2010

10  Institute for Fiscal Studies, 'New IFS research challenges Chancellor's "progressive Budget" claim', Press Release, Institute for Fiscal Studies, August 2010

11  G Mooney, C Morelli and P Seaman, 'The Question of Economic Growth and Inequality in Contemporary Scotland', *Scottish Affairs*, 67, 2009, pp92–109; A Parekh, P Kenway and T MacInnes, *Monitoring Poverty and Social Exclusion in Scotland 2010*, Joseph Rowntree Foundation/New Policy Institute, 2010, p18

12  Campaign to End Child Poverty in Scotland, *Single Outcome Agreements: an*

*analysis by the Campaign to End Child Poverty in Scotland*, Campaign to End Child Poverty in Scotland, 2009, available from www.cpag.org.uk

13 See note 4, p3
14 See note 4, p11
15 S Maxwell, 'Tackling Scottish Poverty: principles and absences', *Scottish Affairs* 67, 2009, pp57–69

# Appendix
# Policy diary
*Peter Kelly*

| Date | Westminster/ Scotland | Legislation | Area of interest covered | Website |
|------|----------------------|-------------|--------------------------|---------|
| 2007 | Scotland | Adult Support and Protection (Scotland) Act | – Identify 'adults at risk' to provide support to them when they need it, and to provide the means to protect them from harm<br><br>– 'Public Guardian' for adults with incapacity | www.opsi.gov.uk/ legislation/scotland/ acts2007/asp_ 20070010_en_1 |
| 2007 | Scotland | Bankruptcy and Diligence etc. (Scotland) Act 2007 | – Personal bankruptcy and diligence, rights of creditors and debtors | www.opsi.gov.uk/ legislation/scotland/ acts2007/asp_ 20070003_en_1 |
| 2007 | Scotland | Schools (Health Promotion and Nutrition) (Scotland) Act | – Places health promotion at the heart of a schools' activities<br><br>– Ensures that food and drink served in schools meets nutritional requirements<br><br>– Gives local authorities the power to provide pupils with healthy snacks and drinks, either at a cost or free of charge | www.scotland.gov.uk/ Topics/Education/Schools/ HLivi/foodnutrition |

| 2007 | Westminster | Pensions Act | – Basic state pension, additional state pension, state pension age | www.legislation.gov.uk/ ukpga/2007/22/pdfs/ ukpga_20070022_en.pdf |
|------|-------------|--------------|----------------------|-----|
|      |             |              | – Personal Accounts Delivery Authority | |
| 2007 | Westminster | Welfare Reform Act | – Reform of incapacity benefits | www.legislation.gov.uk/ ukpga/2007/5/contents |
|      |             |              | – Changes to the administration of housing benefit | |
| 2008 | Westminster | Child Maintenance and Other Payments Act | – Child Maintenance and Enforcement Commission to do the job formerly done by the Child Support Agency | www.legislation.gov.uk/ ukpga/2008/6/introduction |
|      |             |              | – Debt management | |
|      |             |              | – Changes to system of maintenance collection and to the way maintenance payments are calculated | |
| 2008 | Westminster | Employment Act | – Enforcement of the national minimum wage | www.legislation.gov.uk/ ukpga/2008/24/contents |
|      |             |              | – Compensation for financial loss in cases of unlawful underpayment or non-payment | |
| 2008 | Westminster | Health and Social Care Act | – Health in pregnancy grant | www.legislation.gov.uk/ ukpga/2008/14/contents |
| 2008 | Westminster | Housing and Regeneration Act | – Amends the Housing (Scotland) Act 1987 to align the homelessness legislation for Scotland with the 1996 Act for England and Wales. | www.legislation.gov.uk/ ukpga/2008/17/contents? view=extent |

| | | | | |
|---|---|---|---|---|
| 2008 | Westminster | National Insurance Contributions Act | – State second pension: upper accrual point<br>– Aligning the income tax system with the national insurance system | www.legislation.gov.uk/ ukpga/2008/16/contents? view=extent |
| 2008 | Westminster | Pensions Act | – From 2012 all eligible workers, automatically enrolled into a qualifying workplace pension scheme<br><br>– National Employment Savings Trust aimed at employees on low to moderate incomes who currently have no access to a workplace pension scheme | www.legislation.gov.uk/ ukpga/2008/30/contents |
| 2009 | Westminster | Apprenticeships Skills, Children and Learning Act | – Assistance with employment and training<br><br>– Right to request time to train from the employer | www.legislation.gov.uk/ ukpga/2009/22/contents |
| 2009 | Westminster | Borders, Citizenship and Immigration Act | – Duty regarding the welfare of children who are in the UK | www.legislation.gov.uk/ ukpga/2009/11/contents |
| 2009 | Westminster | Welfare Reform Act | – Abolition of income support<br><br>– Opportunity to develop jobseekers' work skills through full-time work experience<br><br>– Paid national insurance con- tributions for at least 26 weeks in one of the last two tax years prior to the claim of | www.legislation.gov.uk/ ukpga/2009/24/pdfs/ ukpga_20090024_en.pdf |

|  |  |  |  |  |
|---|---|---|---|---|
|  |  |  | jobseeker's allowance and employment and support allowance |  |
|  |  |  | – Disabled people: right to control provision of services |  |
|  |  |  | – Child maintenance |  |
| 2010 | Scotland | Home Owner and Debtor Protection (Scotland) Act | – Greater protection to homeowners faced with repossession | www.opsi.gov.uk/ legislation/scotland/acts 2010/asp_20100006_en_1 |
| 2010 | Westminster | Child Poverty Act | – Establishes four separate child poverty targets to be met by 2020/21 | www.legislation.gov.uk/ ukpga/2010/9/pdfs/ ukpga_20100009_en.pdf |
|  |  |  | – Requires the UK government to publish a regular UK child poverty strategy, and Scottish and Northern Irish Ministers to publish child poverty strategies |  |
|  |  |  | – Establishes a Child Poverty Commission to provide advice |  |
|  |  |  | – Requires the UK government to publish annual progress reports |  |
| 2010 | Westminster | Equality Act | – Disabled and elderly carers' rights | www.legislation.gov.uk/ ukpga/2010/15/contents |
|  |  |  | – Harassment and victimisation |  |
|  |  |  | – Pay secrecy |  |